Enterprise Pharo
a Web Perspective

Damien Cassou
Stéphane Ducasse
Luc Fabresse
Johan Fabry
Sven Van Caekenberghe

May 30, 2016

release 1.0

Copyright 2015 by Damien Cassou, Stéphane Ducasse, Luc Fabresse, Johan Fabry, and Sven Van Caekenberghe.

The contents of this book are protected under the Creative Commons Attribution-ShareAlike 3.0 Unported license.

You are **free**:

- to **Share**: to copy, distribute and transmit the work,
- to **Remix**: to adapt the work,

Under the following conditions:

Attribution. You must attribute the work in the manner specified by the author or licensor (but not in any way that suggests that they endorse you or your use of the work).

Share Alike. If you alter, transform, or build upon this work, you may distribute the resulting work only under the same, similar or a compatible license.

For any reuse or distribution, you must make clear to others the license terms of this work. The best way to do this is with a link to this web page:
http://creativecommons.org/licenses/by-sa/3.0/

Any of the above conditions can be waived if you get permission from the copyright holder. Nothing in this license impairs or restricts the author's moral rights.

Your fair dealing and other rights are in no way affected by the above. This is a human-readable summary of the Legal Code (the full license):
http://creativecommons.org/licenses/by-sa/3.0/legalcode

[&] Published by Square Bracket Associates, Switzerland.
http://squarebracketassociates.org
ISBN 978-1-326-65097-1
First Edition, April 2016.

This book has been sponsored by ESUG.

Cover design by Liudmyla Dolia. Layout and typography based on the sbabook LaTeX class by Damien Pollet. The source code of the book itself lives at https://github.com/SquareBracketAssociates/EnterprisePharo

About this book

Enterprise Pharo is the third volume of the series, following *Pharo by Example* and *Deep into Pharo*. It covers enterprise libraries and frameworks, and in particular those useful for doing web development.

The book is structured in five parts.
The first part talks about simple web applications, starting with a minimal web application in chapter 1 on Teapot and then a tutorial on building a more complete web application in chapter 2.
Part two deals with HTTP support in Pharo, talking about character encoding in chapter 3, about using Pharo as an HTTP Client (chapter 4) and server (chapter 5), and about using WebSockets (chapter 6).
In the third part we discuss the handling of data for the application. Firstly we treat data that is in the form of comma-separated values (CSV) in chapter 7. Secondly and thirdly, we treat JSON (chapter 8) and its Smalltalk counterpart STON (chapter 9). Fourthly, serialization and deserialization of object graphs with Fuel is treated in chapter 10. Lastly, we discuss the Voyage persistence framework and persisting to MongoDB databases in chapter 11.
Part four deals with the presentation layer. Chapter 12 shows how to use Mustache templates in Pharo, and chapter 13 talks about programmatic generation of CSS files. The documentation of applications could be written in Pillar, which is presented in chapter 14. How to generate PDF files from the application with Artefact is shown in chapter 15.
The fifth part deals with deploying the web application. This is explained in chapter 16 that talks not only about how to build and run the application, but also other important topics like monitoring.

This book is a collective work The editors have curated and reformatted the chapters from blog posts and tutorials written by many people. Here is the complete list of contributors to the book, in alphabetical order:

Olivier Auverlot	Liudmyla Dolia	Guillaume Larchevêque
Sven Van Caekenberghe	Stéphane Ducasse	Max Leske
Damien Cassou	Luc Fabresse	Esteban Lorenzano
Gabriel Omar Cotelli	Johan Fabry	Attila Magyar
Christophe Demarey	Cyril Ferlicot Delbecque	Mariano Martinez-Peck
Martín Dias	Norbert Hartl	Damien Pollet

Contents

Illustrations — viii

I Simple Web applications

1 Teapot — 3
Attila Magyar with Johan Fabry
1.1 Getting Started 3
1.2 A REST Example, Showing some CRUD Operations 4
1.3 Route 5
1.4 Transforming Output from Actions 7
1.5 Before and After Filters 9
1.6 Error Handlers 10
1.7 Serving Static Files 10
1.8 Conclusion 10

2 Building and Deploying a Small Web application — 11
Sven Van Caekenberghe with Luc Fabresse and Johan Fabry
2.1 Saying Hello World 12
2.2 Serving an HTML Page With an Image 15
2.3 Allowing Users to Upload an Image 17
2.4 Live Debugging 19
2.5 Image Magic 21
2.6 Adding Tests 24
2.7 Saving Code to a Repository 27
2.8 Running a Real Cloud Server 32
2.9 Have Fun Extending this Web App 35
2.10 Conclusion 38

II HTTP

3 Character Encoding and Resource Meta Description — 41
Sven Van Caekenberghe with Luc Fabresse and Johan Fabry
3.1 Character Encoding 41
3.2 Mime-Types 50
3.3 URLs 53

4 Zinc HTTP: The Client Side — 57
Sven Van Caekenberghe with Luc Fabresse and Johan Fabry

- 4.1 HTTP and Zinc 57
- 4.2 Doing a Simple Request 58
- 4.3 HTTP Success ? 62
- 4.4 Dealing with Networking Reality 63
- 4.5 Building URL's 64
- 4.6 Submitting HTML Forms 65
- 4.7 Basic Authentication, Cookies and Sessions 67
- 4.8 PUT, POST, DELETE and other HTTP Methods 68
- 4.9 Reusing Network Connections, Redirect Following and Checking for Newer Data 70
- 4.10 Content-Types, Mime-Types and the Accept Header 71
- 4.11 Headers 72
- 4.12 Entities, Content Readers and Writers 73
- 4.13 Downloading, Uploading and Signalling Progress 75
- 4.14 Client Options, Policies and Proxies 76
- 4.15 Conclusion 77

5 Zinc HTTP: The Server Side — 79
Sven Van Caekenberghe with Luc Fabresse and Johan Fabry

- 5.1 Running a Simple HTTP Server 79
- 5.2 Server Delegate, Testing and Debugging 81
- 5.3 Server Authenticator 82
- 5.4 Logging 83
- 5.5 Server Variants and Life Cycle 84
- 5.6 Static File Server 85
- 5.7 Dispatching 87
- 5.8 Character Encoding 88
- 5.9 Resource Protection Limits, Content and Transfer Encoding 89
- 5.10 Seaside Adaptor 90
- 5.11 Scripting a REST Web Service with Zinc 90
- 5.12 Conclusion 95

6 WebSockets — 97
Sven Van Caekenberghe with Luc Fabresse

- 6.1 An Introduction to WebSockets 97
- 6.2 The WebSocket Protocol 98
- 6.3 Source Code 98
- 6.4 Using Client Side WebSockets 99
- 6.5 Using Server-Side WebSockets 100
- 6.6 Building a Pharo Statistics Web Page 102
- 6.7 Building a Web Chat 103
- 6.8 A Quick Tour of Zinc WebSocket Implementation 104
- 6.9 Live Demo 104
- 6.10 Conclusion 104

III Data

7 NeoCSV — 107
Sven Van Caekenberghe with Damien Cassou and Stéphane Ducasse

- 7.1 NeoCSV 107
- 7.2 Generic Mode 109
- 7.3 Customizing NeoCSVWriter 109
- 7.4 Customizing NeoCSVReader 111

8 NeoJSON — 113
Sven Van Caekenberghe with Damien Cassou and Stéphane Ducasse

- 8.1 An Introduction to JSON 113
- 8.2 NeoJSON 114
- 8.3 Primitives 114
- 8.4 Generic Mode 115
- 8.5 Schemas and Mappings 116
- 8.6 Emitting null Values 118
- 8.7 Conclusion 118

9 STON: a Smalltalk Object Notation — 119
Sven Van Caekenberghe with Stéphane Ducasse and Johan Fabry

- 9.1 Introduction 119
- 9.2 How Values are Encoded 123
- 9.3 Custom Representations of Objects 126
- 9.4 Usage 129
- 9.5 Handling CR, LF inside Strings 131
- 9.6 Conclusion 132
- 9.7 Appendix: BNF 132

10 Serializing Complex Objects with Fuel — 135
Martín Dias, Stéphane Ducasse, Mariano Martinez Peck and Max Leske with Johan Fabry

- 10.1 General Information 136
- 10.2 Getting Started 138
- 10.3 Managing Globals 140
- 10.4 Customizing the Graph 142
- 10.5 Errors 146
- 10.6 Object Migration 147
- 10.7 Fuel Format Migration 148
- 10.8 Built-in Header Support 149
- 10.9 Conclusion 150

11 Persisting Objects with Voyage — 151
Johan Fabry and Esteban Lorenzano with Damien Cassou and Norbert Hartl

- 11.1 Setup 152
- 11.2 Storing Objects 154
- 11.3 Enhancing Storage 158
- 11.4 Querying in Voyage 162

| 11.5 | Creating and Removing Indexes | 168 |
| 11.6 | Conclusion | 170 |

IV Presentation

12 Mustache Templates for Pharo — 173
Stéphane Ducasse and Norbert Hartl with Johan Fabry

12.1	Getting Started	173
12.2	Tags as Variables	174
12.3	Sections	175
12.4	Partial templates	179
12.5	Miscellaneous	181
12.6	Templates made Easy	181

13 Cascading Style Sheets with RenoirSt — 183
Gabriel Omar Cotelli with Damien Cassou

13.1	Getting Started	183
13.2	Defining the Rules	184
13.3	Defining the selectors	194
13.4	Important Rules	202
13.5	Media Queries	203
13.6	Vendor-Specific Extensions	205
13.7	Font Face Rules	205
13.8	Interaction with other Frameworks and Libraries	207

14 Documenting and Presenting with Pillar — 209
Damien Cassou and Cyril Ferlicot Delbecque

14.1	Introduction	209
14.2	5 Minutes Tutorial	211
14.3	Writing Pillar Documents	215
14.4	Configuring your Output	224
14.5	Templating	229
14.6	Command-Line Interface	229
14.7	Pillar from Pharo	230
14.8	Conclusion	232

15 Generate PDF Documents with Artefact — 233
Olivier Auverlot and Guillaume Larchevêque with Johan Fabry

15.1	Overview of Artefact	233
15.2	Getting Started in 10 Minutes	235
15.3	Document Definition	237
15.4	Pages, Formats and Models	240
15.5	Elements	241
15.6	Stylesheets for Newbies	248
15.7	Create your own PDF Composite Elements	252
15.8	Conclusion	255

V Deployment

16 Deploying a Pharo Web Application in Production — 259
Christophe Demarey with Johan Fabry

- 16.1 Where to Host your Application? 259
- 16.2 Which Operating System? 260
- 16.3 Build your Image 260
- 16.4 Run your Application 261
- 16.5 Dealing with Crashes 262
- 16.6 Put an HTTP server in front of your web application 265
- 16.7 Conclusion 266

Illustrations

1-1	The Teapot welcome at http://localhost:1701/welcome	4
1-2	Teapot producing plain text http://localhost:1701/sometext	9
2-1	A simple Web application	12
2-2	Defining a first version of the application	13
2-3	Your first hello world Web app in action	14
2-4	Using the debugger to navigate execution	15
2-5	Returning an HTML response	16
2-6	Serving the Pharo logo	18
2-7	Changing the displayed image	20
2-8	Debugging	21
2-9	Live change	22
2-10	Automatically create a test class	24
2-11	Running a test case	25
2-12	Opening Monticello on your package	27
2-13	The Monticello browser	28
2-14	Smalltalkhub project page	29
2-15	Adding a Smalltalkhub repository in Monticello for your project.	30
2-16	Multiple repositories for a project in Monticello	31
2-17	Our Web app, running in the cloud	35
4-1	Client/Server interacting via request/response	57
10-1	Example of changes to a class	147
14-1	An example Pillar output	210
14-2	This is the caption of the picture	220
14-3	My script	220
15-1	Page and Document Elements	242
15-2	Composite Elements	242

Part I

Simple Web applications

CHAPTER 1

Teapot

Attila Magyar with Johan Fabry

We begin the book in this first chapter by showing how basic web applications can be written using just a few lines of code. In the second chapter we will treat the construction of web applications more in depth, also touching on the fundamentals of web application building. But we start by keeping it simple, which is possible thanks to Teapot.

Teapot is a *micro* web framework on top of the Zinc HTTP web server described in Chapter Zinc Server. It focuses on simplicity and ease of use and is itself small: around 600 lines of code, not counting unit tests. Teapot is developed by Attila Magyar and this chapter is heavily inspired from the original documentation.

1.1 Getting Started

To get started, execute the following code snippet, it will load the latest stable version of Teapot.

```
Gofer it
    smalltalkhubUser: 'zeroflag' project: 'Teapot'; configuration;
    loadStable.
```

It is straightforward to launch Teapot and add a page:

```
Teapot on
    GET: '/welcome' -> 'Hello World!'; start.
```

Opening a browser on http://localhost:1701/welcome results in the following:

3

Figure 1-1 The Teapot welcome at http://localhost:1701/welcome

Differences between Teapot and other Web Frameworks

Teapot is not a singleton and doesn't hold any global state. You can run multiple Teapot servers inside the same image with their state being isolated from each other.

- There are no thread locals or dynamically scoped variables in Teapot. Everything is explicit.
- It doesn't rely on annotations or pragmas, the routes are defined programmatically.
- It doesn't instantiate objects (e.g. "web controllers") for you. You can hook http events to existing objects, and manage their dependencies as required.

1.2 A REST Example, Showing some CRUD Operations

Before getting into the details of Teapot. Here is a simple example for managing books. With the following code, we can list books, add a book and delete a book.

```
| books teapot |
books := Dictionary new.
teapot := Teapot configure: {
    #defaultOutput -> #json. #port -> 8080. #debugMode -> true }.
```

```
teapot
   GET: '/books' -> books;
   PUT: '/books/<id>' -> [ :req | | book |
      book := {'author' -> (req at: #author).
      'title' -> (req at: #title)} asDictionary.
      books at: (req at: #id) put: book ];
   DELETE: '/books/<id>' -> [ :req | books removeKey: (req at: #id)
     ];
   exception:
      KeyNotFound -> (TeaResponse notFound body: 'No such book');
   start.
```

Now you can create a book with ZNClient or your web client as follows:

```
ZnClient new
   url: 'http://localhost:8080/books/1';
   formAt: 'author' put: 'SquareBracketAssociates';
   formAt: 'title' put: 'Pharo For The Enterprise'; put
```

You can also list the contents using http://localhost:8080/books For a more complete example, study the Teapot-Library-Example package.

Now that you get the general feel of Teapot, let us see the key concepts.

1.3 Route

The most important concept of Teapot is the Route. The template for route definitions is as follows:

```
Method : '/url/*/pattern/<param>' -> Action
```

A route has three parts:

- an HTTP method (GET, POST, PUT, DELETE, HEAD, TRACE, CONNECT, OPTIONS, PATCH),
- an URL pattern (i.e. /hi, /users/<name>, /foo/*/bar/*, or a regular expression),
- an action (a block, message send or any object).

Here is another example:

```
Teapot on
   GET: '/hi' -> 'Bonjour!';
   GET: '/hi/<user>' -> [:req | 'Hello ', (req at: #user)];
   GET: '/say/hi/*' -> (Send message: #greet: to: greeter); start.
```

A wildcard character (*), as in the last route, matches to one URL path segment. A wildcard terminated pattern is a greedy match; '/foo/*' for example matches to '/foo/bar' and '/foo/bar/baz' too.

The second route shows that the action block optionally takes the HTTP request. The third route is an example of a message send, by using the Send class. The selector of the message can take maximum 2 arguments, which will be instances of a TeaRequest and TeaResponse.

It is also possible to use the Zinc client (see Chapter Zinc Client Side) to query the server. The example below illustrates the use of parameters, which we discuss next.

```
(ZnEasy get: 'http://localhost:1701/hi/user1') entity string.
   --> "Hello user1"
```

Parameters in URLs

The URL pattern may contain named parameters (e.g., <user> above), whose values are accessible via the request object. The request is an extension of ZnRequest with some extra methods.

Query parameters and Form parameters can be accessed the same way as path parameters (req at: #paramName). Teapot can perform conversions of parameters to a number, for example as follows:

```
Teapot on
   GET: '/user/<id:IsInteger>' -> [ :req |
      users findById: (req at: #id) ];
   output: #ston; start.
```

- IsInteger matches digits (negative or positive) only and converts the value to an Integer.
- IsNumber matches any integer or floating point number and converts the value to a Number.

See also the, IsInteger and IsNumber classes for information about introducing user defined conversions.

Using Regular Expressions

Instead of < and > surrounded named parameters, the regexp pattern may contain subexpressions between parentheses whose values are accessible via the request object.

The following example matches any /hi/user followed by two digits.

```
Teapot on
   GET: '/hi/([a-z]+\d\d)' asRegex -> [ :req | 'Hello ', (req at:
   1)];
   start.

(ZnEasy get: 'http://localhost:1701/hi/user01') entity string.
   --> "Hello user01"
```

```
ZnEasy get: 'http://localhost:1701/hi/user'
    --> not found
```

How are Routes Matched?

The routes are matched in the order in which they are defined.

The first route that matches the request method and the URL is invoked.

- If a route matches but it returns a 404 error, the search will continue.
- If no route matches, the error 404 is returned.
- If a route was invoked, its return value will be transformed to a HTTP response, e.g. if a string is returned it will be transformed to a response with the text/html content-type.
- If a route returns a ZnResponse, no transformation will be performed.
- If a route has a response transformer defined (see below), the specified transformation will be performed.

Aborting

An abort: message sent to the request object immediately stops a request (by signaling an exception) within a route. For example:

```
Teapot on
    GET: '/secure/*' -> [ :req | req abort: TeaResponse unauthorized];
    GET: '/unauthorized' -> [ :req | req abort: 'go away' ]; start.
```

1.4 Transforming Output from Actions

The default output for Teapot is HTML: the output of an action is interpreted as a string and the content-type of the HTML response is set to text/html. The output of an action may actually undergo any kind of transformations by a response transformer. Response Transformers heve the ultimate responsibility for constructing the outgoing HTTP response (an instance of the class ZnResponse). To clarify, HTTP requests take the following path through Teapot:

```
ZnRequest -> [Router] -> TeaRequest -> [Route] -> response ->
    [Resp.Transformer] -> ZnResponse
```

The response returned by the action can be:

- Any Object that will be transformed by the given response transformer (e.g., HTML, STON, JSON, Mustache, stream) to an HTTP response (instance of ZnResponse).

- A TeaResponse that allows additional parameters to be added (response code, headers).
- A ZnResponse that will be handled directly by the ZnServer without further transformation.

For example, the following three routes produce the same output.

```
GET: '/greet' -> [:req | 'Hello World!' ]
GET: '/greet' -> [:req | TeaResponse ok body: 'Hello World!' ]
GET: '/greet' -> [:req |
   ZnResponse new
      statusLine: ZnStatusLine ok;
      entity: (ZnEntity html: 'Hello World!'); yourself ]
```

Response Transformers

The responsibility of a response transformer is to convert the output of the action block to HTML and to set the content-type of the response. Some response transformers require external packages (e.g., NeoJSON, STON, Mustache). See the TeaOutput class for more information, for example the HTML transformer is TeaOutput html.

For example, with the following configuration:

```
Teapot on
   GET: '/jsonlist' -> #(1 2 3 4); output: #json;
   GET: '/sometext' -> 'this is text plain'; output: #text;
   GET: '/download' -> ['/tmp/afile' asFileReference readStream];
   output: #stream; start.
```

Figure 1-2 shows the result for the /sometext route.

If the NeoJSON package is loaded (See chapter NeoJSON.) the jsonlist transformer will return a JSON array:

```
(ZnEasy get: 'http://localhost:1701/jsonlist') entity string.
   --> '[1,2,3,4]'"
```

If you have a file located /tmp/afile you can access it

```
ZnEasy get: 'http://localhost:1701/download'
   --> a ZnResponse(200 OK application/octet-stream 35B)
```

If Mustache is installed (See chapter Mustache.) you can output templated information.

```
Teapot on
   GET: '/greet' -> {'phrase' -> 'Hello'. 'name' -> 'World'};
   output: (TeaOutput mustacheHtml: '<b>{{phrase}}</b>
      <i>{{name}}</i>!'); start.
```

1.5 Before and After Filters

Figure 1-2 Teapot producing plain text http://localhost:1701/sometext

1.5 Before and After Filters

Teapot also offers before and after filters. Before filters are evaluated before each request that matches the given URL pattern. Requests can also be aborted (by sending the abort: message) in before and after filters.

In the following example a before filter is used to enable authentication: if the session has no #user attribute, the browser is redirected to a login page.

```
Teapot on
    before: '/secure/*' -> [ :req |
        req session
            attributeAt: #user
            ifAbsent: [ req abort: (TeaResponse redirect location:
    '/loginpage')]];
    before: '*' -> (Send message: #logRequest: to: auditor);
    GET: '/secure' -> 'I am a protected string';
    start.
```

After filters are evaluated after each request and can read the request and modify the response.

```
Teapot on
    after: '/*' -> [ :req :resp |
        resp headers at: 'X-Foo' put: 'set by after filter'];
    start.
```

1.6 Error Handlers

Teapot also handles exceptions of a configured type(s) for all routes and before filters. The following example illustrates how the errors raised in actions can be captured by exception handlers.

```
Teapot on
    GET: '/divide/<a>/<b>' -> [ :req | (req at: #a) / (req at: #b)];
    GET: '/at/<key>' -> [ :req | dict at: (req at: #key)];
    exception: ZeroDivide -> [ :ex :req | TeaResponse badRequest ];
    exception: KeyNotFound -> {#result -> 'error'. #code -> 42};
    output: #json; start.
```

The request /div/6/3 succeeds and returns 2. The request /div/6/0 raises an error and it is caught and returns a bad request.

```
(ZnEasy get: 'http://localhost:1701/div/6/3') entity string.
    --> 2
(ZnEasy get: 'http://localhost:1701/div/6/0').
    --> "bad request"
```

You can use a comma-separated exception set to handle multiple exceptions.

```
exception: ZeroDivide, DomainError -> handler
```

The same rules apply for the return values of the exception handler as were used for the Routes.

1.7 Serving Static Files

Teapot can straightforwardly serve static files. The following example serves the files located on the file system at /var/www/htdocs at the /static URL.

```
Teapot on
    serveStatic: '/static' from: '/var/www/htdocs'; start.
```

1.8 Conclusion

Teapot is a powerful and simple web framework. It is based on the notion of routes and request transformations. It supports the definition of REST application.

Now an important point: Where does the name come from? *418 I'm a teapot (RFC 2324)* is an HTTP status code. It was defined in 1998 as one of the traditional IETF April Fools' jokes, in RFC 2324, Hyper Text Coffee Pot Control Protocol, and is not expected to be implemented by actual HTTP servers.

CHAPTER 2

Building and Deploying a Small Web application

Sven Van Caekenberghe with Luc Fabresse and Johan Fabry

This chapter details the whole development process of a Web application in Pharo through a detailed example. Of course, there are an infinite number of ways to make a Web application. Even in Pharo, there are multiple frameworks approaching this problem, most notably Seaside, AIDAweb and Iliad. However, the presented example is directly built on top of the foundational framework called Zinc HTTP Components. By doing so, we'll be touching the fundamentals of HTTP and Web applications and you will understand the actual basic mechanics of building and deploying a Web application.

You will also discover that using nice objects abstracting each concept in HTTP and related open standards makes the actual code easier than you might expect. The dynamic, interactive nature of Pharo combined with its rich IDE and library will allow us to do things that are nearly impossible using other technology stacks. By chronologically following the development process, you will see the app growing from something trivial to the final result. Finally, we will save our source code in a repository and deploy for real in the cloud.

The Web application that we are going to build, shown in Figure 2-1, will display a picture and allow users to change the picture by uploading a new one. Because we want to focus on the basic mechanics, the fundamentals as well as the build and deploy process, there are some simplifications. There will be one picture for all users, no login and we will store the picture in memory.

In our implementation, the route `/image` will serve an HTML page containing the image and a form. To serve the raw image itself, we'll add a parame-

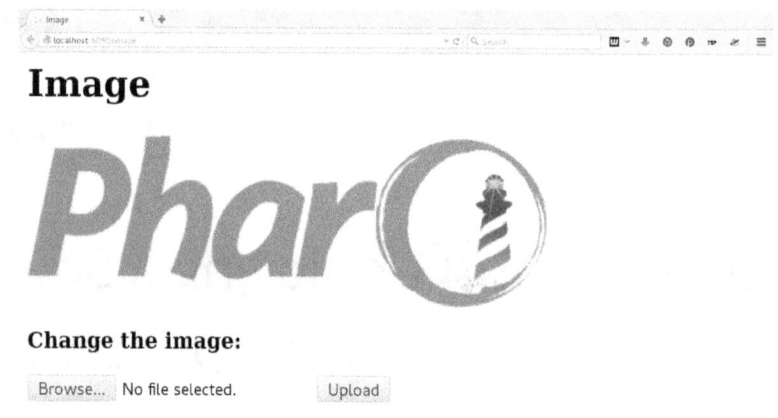

Figure 2-1 A simple Web application

ter, like /image?raw=true. These will be GET HTTP requests. The form will submit its data to /image as a POST request.

2.1 Saying Hello World

Let's lay the groundwork for our new Web application by making a version that only says 'Hello World!'. We'll be extending the Web app gradually until we reach our functional goal.

Open the Nautilus System Browser and create a new package (right click in the first column) called something like 'MyFirstWebApp'. Now create a new class (right click in the second column) with the same name, MyFirst-WebApp. You will be given a template: edit 'NameOfSubclass' and accept by clicking 'OK'. Your definition should now appear in the bottom pane.

```
Object subclass: #MyFirstWebApp
    instanceVariableNames: ''
    classVariableNames: ''
    poolDictionaries: ''
    category: 'MyFirstWebApp'
```

Any object can be a Web app, it only has to respond to the handleRequest: message to answer a response based on a request. Now add the following method:

```
MyFirstWebApp>>handleRequest: request
    request uri path = #image
        ifFalse: [ ^ ZnResponse notFound: request uri ].
```

2.1 Saying Hello World

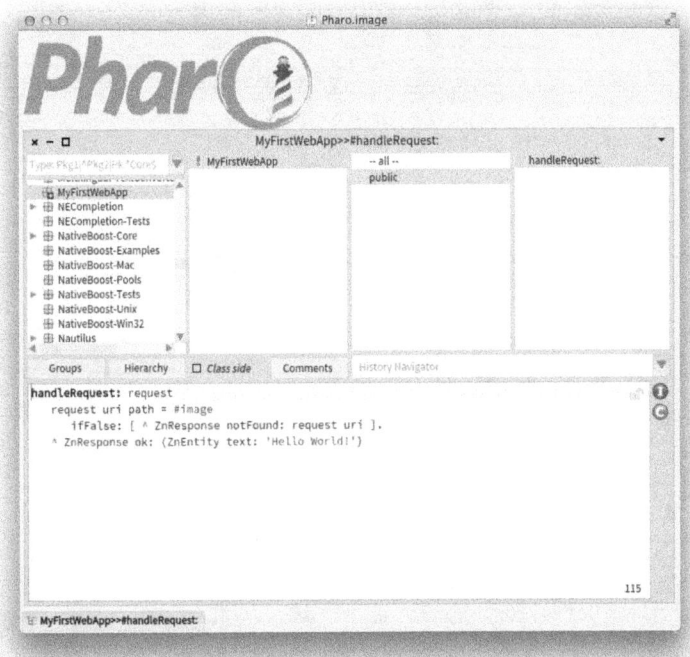

Figure 2-2 Defining a first version of the application

```
^ ZnResponse ok: (ZnEntity text: 'Hello World!')
```

Create a new protocol called public (by right-clicking in the third column). When the new protocol is selected, a new method template will appear in the bottom pane. Overwrite the whole template with the code above and accept it as shown Figure 2-2.

What we do here is to look at the incoming request to make sure the URI path is /image which will be the final name of our Web app. If not, we return a Not Found (code 404) response. If so, we create and return an OK response (code 200) with a simple text entity as body or payload.

Now we define the method value: to make it an alias of handleRequest: as follows:

```
MyFirstWebApp>>value: request
    ^ self handleRequest: request
```

This is needed so our Web app object can be used more flexibly. To test our Web app, we'll add it as one of the pages of the default server, like this:

Building and Deploying a Small Web application

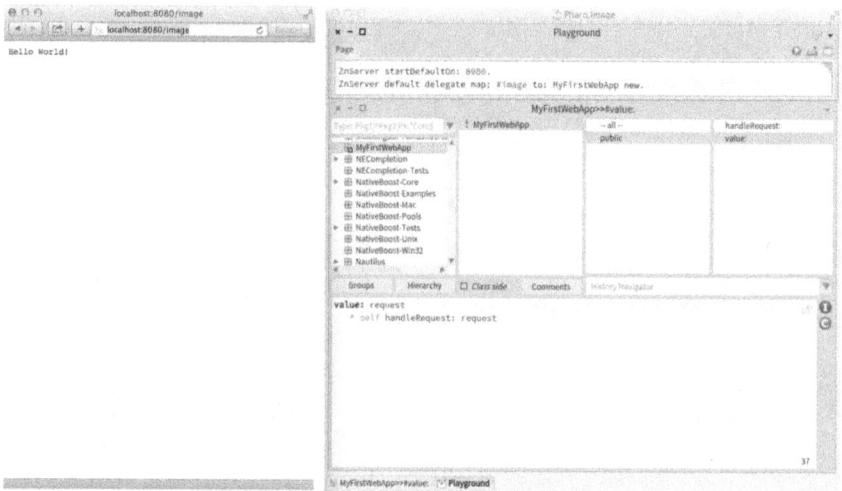

Figure 2-3 Your first hello world Web app in action

```
ZnServer startDefaultOn: 8080.
ZnServer default delegate map: #image to: MyFirstWebApp new.
```

The second expression adds a route from /image to an MyFirstWebApp instance. If all is well, http://localhost:8080/image should show a friendly message as shown in Figure 2-3. Note how we are not even serving HTML, just plain text.

Debugging our Web App

Try putting a breakpoint in MyFirstWebApp>>handleRequest: (by inserting self halt in the method source code). Then, if you refresh the page from the web browser, a debugger will open in Pharo allowing you to inspect things. You can just continue the execution by clicking on the proceed button. Or you can look into the actual request and response objects as shown in Figure 2-4.

Note how Pharo is a live environment: you can change the behavior of the application in the debugger window (such as changing the response's text) and the change is immediately used.

You can leave the server running. If you want you can enable logging, or switch to debug mode and inspect the server instance as explained in Chapter Zinc Server. Don't forget to remove any breakpoints you set before continuing.

2.2   Serving an HTML Page With an Image

Figure 2-4   Using the debugger to navigate execution

2.2 Serving an HTML Page With an Image

HTML generation can be done with some of existing high-level Pharo frameworks such as Mustache (see Chapter Mustache). In the following, we manually compose the HTML to focus on app building and deployment. Go ahead and add a new method named html.

```
MyFirstWebApp>>html
   ^ '<html><head><title>Image</title>
   <body>
   <h1>Image</h1>
   </body></html>'
```

Additionally, change the handleRequest: method to use the new method.

```
MyFirstWebApp>>handleRequest: request
   request uri path = #image
      ifFalse: [ ^ ZnResponse notFound: request uri ].
   ^ ZnResponse ok: (ZnEntity html: self html)
```

Refresh the page in your web browser. You should now see an HTML page as in Figure 2-5.

Building and Deploying a Small Web application

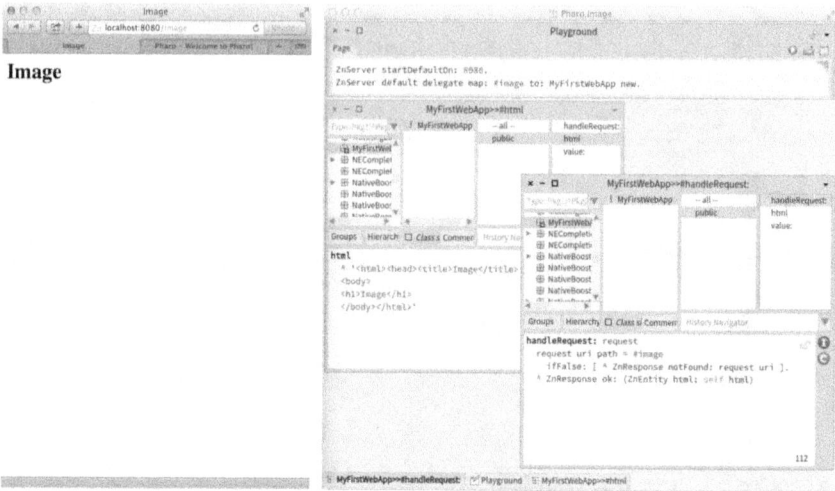

Figure 2-5 Returning an HTML response

You have probably noted the red exclamation mark icon in front of our class name in the browser. This is an indication that we have no class comment, which is not good: documentation is important. Click the Comments button and write some documentation. You can also use the class comment as a notepad for yourself, saving useful expressions that you can later execute in place such as the two expressions above to start the server.

Serving an Image

For the purpose of our Web app, images can be any of three types: GIF, JPEG and PNG. The application will store them in memory as an object wrapping the actual bytes together with a MIME type.

To simplify our app, we will arrange things so that we always start with a default image, then we always have something to show. Let's add a little helper: the downloadPharoLogo method:

```
MyFirstWebApp>>downloadPharoLogo
    ^ ZnClient new
        beOneShot;
        get: 'http://pharo.org/files/pharo.png';
        entity
```

Quickly test the code by selecting the method body (not including the name) and inspecting the result. You should get the bytes of an image back. Now add the accessor image defined as follow:

```
MyFirstWebApp>>image
    ^ image ifNil: [ image := self downloadPharoLogo ]
```

16

When you try to accept this method, you will get an error. The method is trying to use an unknown variable named image. Select the option to automatically declare a new instance variable.

Remember that we decided we were going to serve the raw image itself using a query variable, like /image?raw=true. Make the following modification to existing methods and add a new one as shown below.

```
MyFirstWebApp>>html
    ^ '<html><head><title>Image</title>
    <body>
    <h1>Image</h1>
    <img src="image?raw=true"/>
    </body></html>'

MyFirstWebApp>>handleRequest: request
    request uri path = #image
        ifFalse: [ ^ ZnResponse notFound: request uri ].
    ^ self handleGetRequest: request

MyFirstWebApp>>handleGetRequest: request
    ^ (request uri queryAt: #raw ifAbsent: [ nil ])
        ifNil: [ ZnResponse ok: (ZnEntity html: self html) ]
        ifNotNil: [ ZnResponse ok: self image ]
```

The HTML code now contains an img element. The handleRequest: method now delegates the response generation to a dedicated handleGetRequest: method. This method inspects the incoming URI. If the URI has a non-empty query variable raw, we serve the raw image directly. Otherwise, we serve the HTML page like before.

When you refresh the page in the web browser, you should now see an image as in Figure 2-6.

2.3 Allowing Users to Upload an Image

Interaction is what differentiates a Web site from a Web application. We will now add the ability for users to upload a new image to change the one on the server. To add this ability we need to use an HTML form. Let's change our HTML one last time.

```
MyFirstWebApp>>html
    ^ '<html><head><title>Image</title>
    <body>
    <h1>Image</h1>
    <img src="image?raw=true"/>
    <br/>
    <form enctype="multipart/form-data" action="image" method="POST">
        <h3>Change the image:</h3>
        <input type="file" name="file"/>
```

Building and Deploying a Small Web application

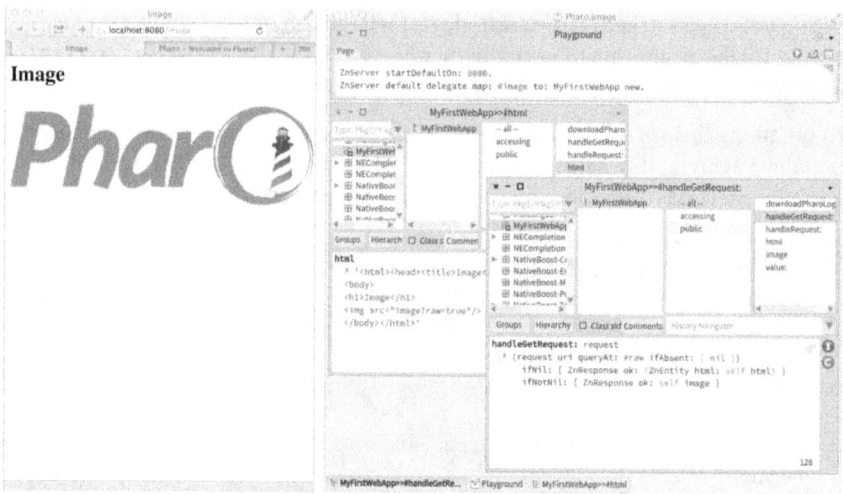

Figure 2-6 Serving the Pharo logo

```
    <input type="submit" value= "Upload"/>
</form> </body> </html>'
```

The user will be able to select a file on the local disk for upload. When he clicks on the Upload submit button, the web browser will send an HTTP POST request to the action URL, /image, encoding the form contents using a technique called multi-part form-data. With the above change, you will see the form but nothing will happen if you click the submit button: this is because the server does not know how to process the incoming form data.

In our request handling, we have to distinguish between GET and POST requests. Change handleRequest: one last time:

```
MyFirstWebApp>>handleRequest: request
    request uri path = #image ifTrue: [
        request method = #GET ifTrue: [
            ^ self handleGetRequest: request ].
        request method = #POST ifTrue: [
            ^ self handlePostRequest: request ] ].
    ^ ZnResponse notFound: request uri
```

Now we have to add an implementation of handlePostRequest: to accept the uploaded image and change the current one.

```
MyFirstWebApp>>handlePostRequest: request
    | part |
    part := request entity partNamed: #file.
    image := part entity.
    ^ ZnResponse redirect: #image
```

We start with a simple version without error handling. The entity of the incoming request is a multi-part form-data object containing named parts. Each part, such as the file part, contains another sub-entity: in our case, the uploaded image. Note how the response to the POST is a redirect to the main page. You should now have a fully functional web application.

Nevertheless, we have taken a bit of a shortcut in the code above. It is pretty dangerous to just accept what is coming in from the internet without doing any checking. Here is an improved version.

```
MyFirstWebApp>>handlePostRequest: request
    | part newImage badRequest |
    badRequest := [ ^ ZnResponse badRequest: request ].
    request hasEntity ifFalse: badRequest.
    (request contentType matches: ZnMimeType multiPartFormData)
        ifFalse: badRequest.
    part := request entity
        partNamed: #file
        ifNone: badRequest.
    newImage := part entity.
    (newImage notNil
        and: [ newImage contentType matches: 'image/*' asZnMimeType ])
        ifFalse: badRequest.
    image := newImage.
    ^ ZnResponse redirect: #image
```

Our standard response when something is wrong will be to return a Bad Request (code 400). We define this behavior in a temporary variable so that we can reuse it multiple times over. The first test makes sure the current POST request actually contains an entity and that it is of the correct type. Next, the code checks that there is no file part. Finally, the code makes sure the file part is actually an image by matching with the wildcard image/* MIME type. The user can now upload a new image through the application as can be seen in Figure 2-7. This image is saved in memory and displayed for all visitors until the application is restarted.

If you are curious, set a breakpoint in the handlePostRequest: method and inspect the request object of an actual request. You will learn a lot from inspecting and manipulating live objects.

2.4 Live Debugging

Let's make a deliberate error in our code. Change handlePostRequest: so that the last line reads like:

```
[ ^ ZnResponse redirectTo: #image
```

The compiler will already complain, ignore the warning and accept the code anyway. If you try to upload a new image, your browser window will display

Building and Deploying a Small Web application

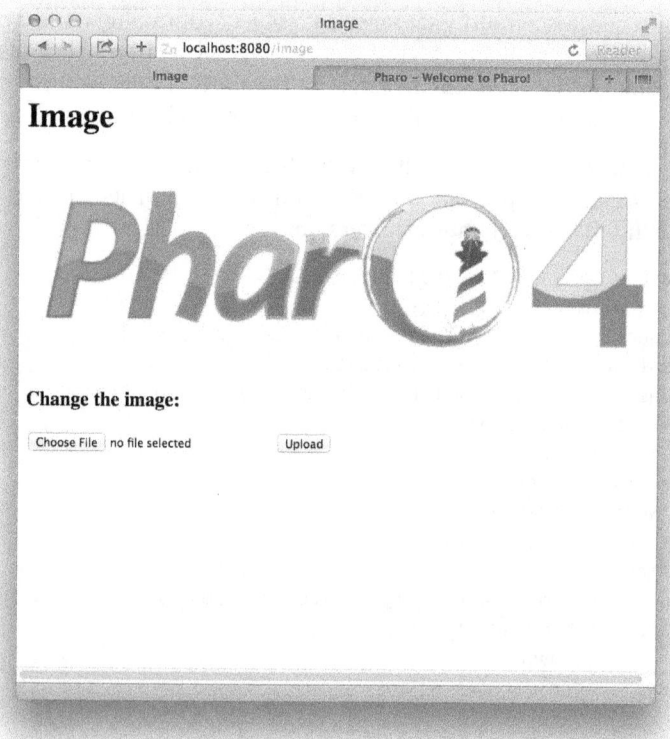

Figure 2-7 Changing the displayed image

a following text which corresponds to a Pharo error:

```
MessageNotUnderstood: ZnResponse class>>redirectTo:
```

But, we can do better and activate the debug mode of the server. Let's stop and restart our Web app using:

```
ZnServer stopDefault.
(ZnServer startDefaultOn: 8080) debugMode: true.
ZnServer default delegate map: #image to: MyFirstWebApp new.
```

If you now try to upload an image through the Web browser, the debugger will pop up in Pharo telling you that ZnResponse does not understand redirectTo: and show you the offending code. You could fix the code and try uploading again to see if it works as shown in Figure 2-8.

But we can do even better! Just fix the code directly within the debugger window and accept it. Now you can restart and proceed the execution. The same request is still active and the server will now do the correct thing. Have

2.5 Image Magic

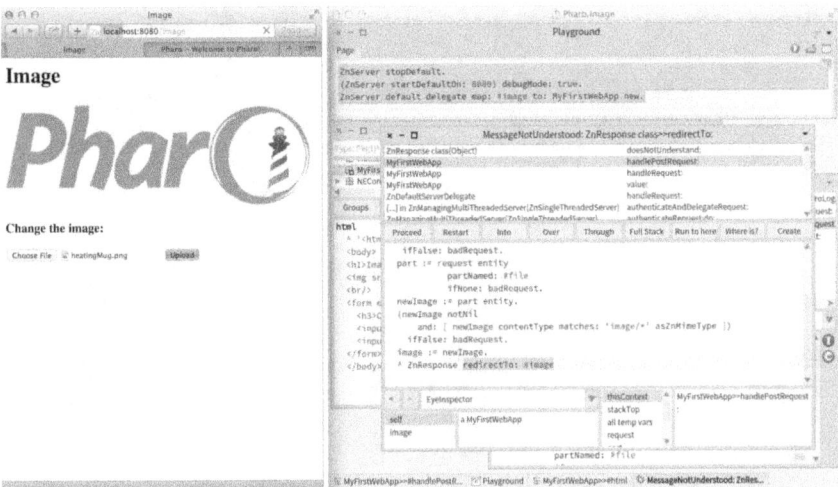

Figure 2-8 Debugging

a look at your Web browser: you will see that your initial action, the upload, that first initially hung, has now succeeded.

Up to now, the suggestion was that you can use the debugger and inspector tools to look at requests and responses. But you can actually change them while they are happening! Prepare for our experiment by making sure that you change the image to be different from the default one. Now set a breakpoint in `handleGetRequest:` and reload the main page. There will be two requests coming in: the first request for `/image` and the second request for `/image?raw=true`. Proceed the first one.

Now, with the execution being stopped for the second request, click on the image instance variable in the bottom left pane (see Figure 2-9). The pane next to it will show some image entity. Select the whole contents and replace it with `self downloadPharoLogo` and accept the change. Now proceed the execution. Your previously uploaded image is gone, replaced again by the default Pharo logo. We just changed an object in the middle of the execution. Imagine doing all your development like that, having a real conversation with your application, while you are developing it. Be warned though: once you get used to this, it will be hard to go back.

2.5 Image Magic

The abilities to look at the requests and responses coming in and going out of the server, to set breakpoints, to debug live request without redoing the user interaction or to modify data structure live are already great and quite unique. But there is more. Pharo is not just a platform for server applica-

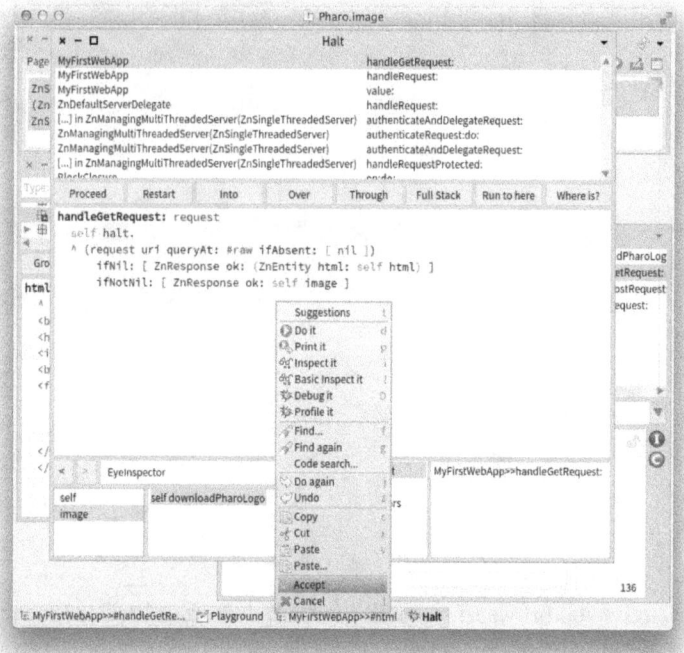

Figure 2-9 Live change

tions, it can be used to build regular applications with normal graphics as well. In fact, it is very good at it. That is why it has built-in support to work with JPEG, GIF or PNG.

Would it not be cool to be able to actually parse the image that we were manipulating as an opaque collection of bytes up till now? To make sure it is real. To look at it while debugging. Turns out this is quite easy. Are you ready for some image magick, pun intended?

The Pharo object that represents images is called a form. There are objects called GIFReadWriter, PNGReadWriter and JPEGReadWriter that can parse bytes into forms. Add two helper methods, formForImageEntity: and form.

```
MyFirstWebApp>>formForImageEntity: imageEntity
  | imageType parserClassName parserClass parser |
  imageType := imageEntity contentType sub.
  parserClassName := imageType asUppercase, #ReadWriter.
  parserClass := Smalltalk globals at: parserClassName asSymbol.
  parser := parserClass on: imageEntity readStream.
  ^ parser nextImage
```

2.5 Image Magic

```
MyFirstWebApp>>form
    ^ self formForImageEntity: self image
```

What we do is use the sub type of the mime type, like "png" in image/png, to find the parser class. Then we instantiate a new parser on a read stream on the actual bytes and invoke the parser with sending `nextImage`, which will return a form. The `form` method makes it easy to invoke all this logic on our current image.

Now we can have a look at, for example, the default image like this:

```
MyFirstWebApp new form asMorph openInWindow.
```

Obviously you can do this while debugging too. We can also use the image parsing logic to improve our error checking even further. Here is the final version of `handlePostRequest`:

```
MyFirstWebApp>>handlePostRequest: request
    | part newImage badRequest |
    badRequest := [ ^ ZnResponse badRequest: request ].
    (request hasEntity
        and: [ request contentType matches: ZnMimeType
        multiPartFormData ])
        ifFalse: badRequest.
    part := request entity
                partNamed: #file
                ifNone: badRequest.
    newImage := part entity.
    (newImage notNil
        and: [ newImage contentType matches: 'image/*' asZnMimeType ])
        ifFalse: badRequest.
    [ self formForImageEntity: newImage ]
    on: Error
    do: badRequest.
    image := newImage.
    ^ ZnResponse redirect: #image
```

Before making the actual assignment of the new image to our instance variable we added an extra expression. We try parsing the image. We are not interested in the result, but we do want to reply with a bad request when the parsing has failed.

Once we have a form object, the possibilities are almost endless. You can query a form for its size, depth and other elements. You can manipulate the form in various ways: scaling, resizing, rotating, flipping, cropping, compositing. And you can do all this in an interactive and dynamic environment.

Building and Deploying a Small Web application

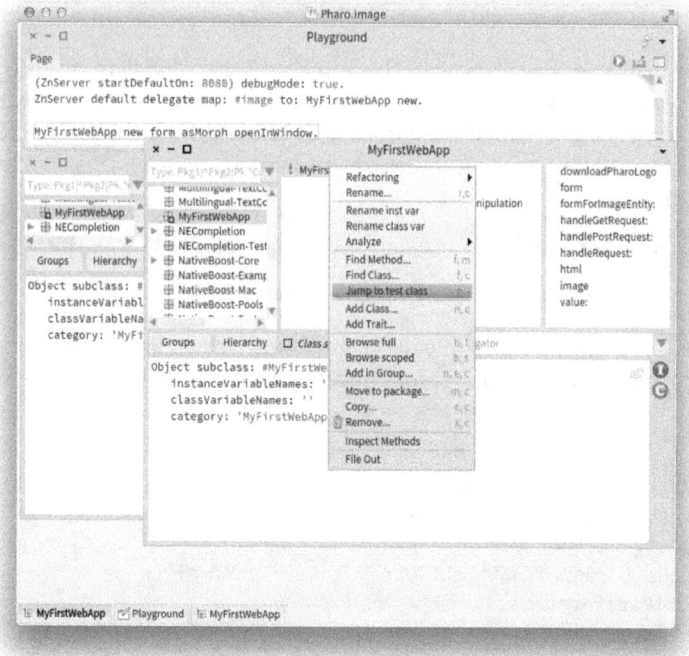

Figure 2-10 Automatically create a test class

2.6 Adding Tests

We all know that testing is good, but how do we actually test a Web app? Writing some basic tests is actually not difficult, since Zinc HTTP Components covers both the client and the server side with the same objects.

Writing tests is creating objects, letting them interact and asserting some conditions. Start by creating a new subclass MyFirstWebAppTest of TestCase. The Pharo browser helps you here using the "Jump to test class" item in the contextual menu on MyFirstWebApp (see Figure 2-10).

Add now the following helper method on MyFirstWebAppTest:

```
MyFirstWebAppTest>>withServerDo: block
    | server |
    server := ZnServer on: 1700 + 10 atRandom.
    [
    server start.
    self assert: server isRunning & server isListening.
    server delegate: MyFirstWebApp new.
    block cull: server
```

2.6 Adding Tests

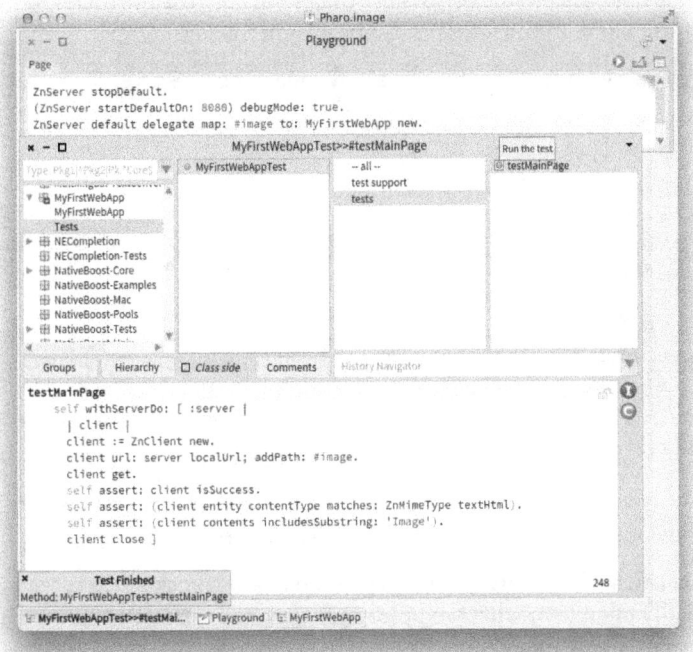

Figure 2-11 Running a test case

```
] ensure: [ server stop ]
```

Since we will need a configured server instance with our Web app as delegate for each of our tests, we move that logic into #withServerDo: and make sure the server is OK and properly stopped afterwards. Now we are ready for our first test.

```
MyFirstWebAppTest>>testMainPage
   self withServerDo: [ :server |
      | client |
      client := ZnClient new.
      client url: server localUrl; addPath: #image.
      client get.
      self assert: client isSuccess.
      self assert: (client entity contentType matches: ZnMimeType textHtml).
      self assert: (client contents includesSubstring: 'Image').
      client close ]
```

In testMainPage we do a request for the main page, /image, and assert that the request is successful and contains HTML. Make sure the test is green by

25

running it from the system browser by clicking on the round icon in front of the method name in the fourth pane (see Figure 2-11).

Let's try to write a test for the actual raw image being served.

```
MyFirstWebAppTest>>testDefaultImage
    self withServerDo: [ :server |
      | client |
      client := ZnClient new.
      client url: server localUrl; addPath: #image; queryAt: #raw
    put: #true.
      client get.
      self assert: client isSuccess.
      self assert: (client entity contentType matches: 'image/*'
    asZnMimeType).
      self assert: client entity equals: server delegate image.
      client close ]
```

Note how we can actually test for equality between the served image and the one inside our app object (the delegate). Run the test.

Our final test will actually do an image upload and check if the served image did actually change to what we uploaded. Here we define the method image that returns a new image.

```
MyFirstWebAppTest>>image
    ^ ZnClient new
      beOneShot;
      get: 'http://zn.stfx.eu/zn/Hot-Air-Balloon.gif';
      entity

MyFirstWebAppTest>>testUpload
    self withServerDo: [ :server |
      | image client |
      image := self image.
      client := ZnClient new.
      client url: server localUrl; addPath: #image.
      client addPart: (ZnMimePart fieldName: #file entity: image).
      client post.
      self assert: client isSuccess.
      client resetEntity; queryAt: #raw put: #true.
      client get.
      self assert: client isSuccess.
      self assert: client entity equals: image.
      client close ]
```

The HTTP client object is pretty powerful. It can do a correct multi-part form-data POST, just like a browser. Furthermore, once configured, it can be reused, like for the second GET request.

2.7 Saving Code to a Repository

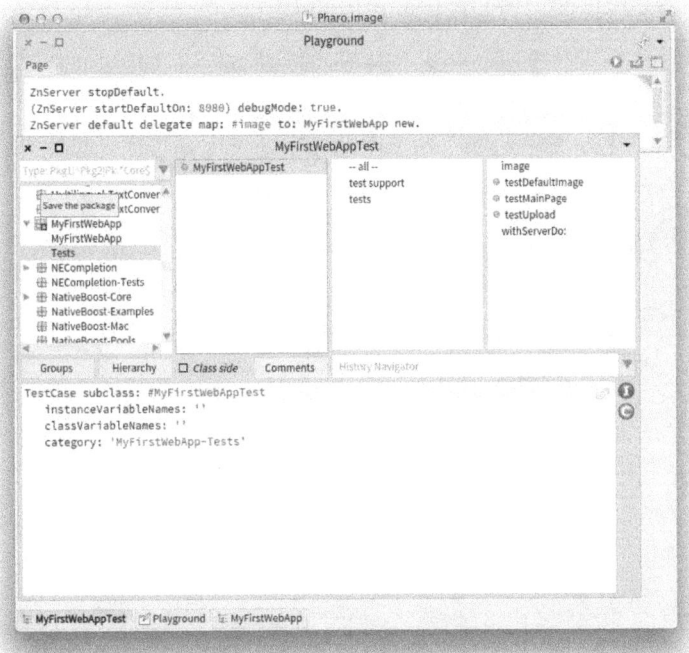

Figure 2-12 Opening Monticello on your package

2.7 Saving Code to a Repository

If all is well, you now have a package called MyFirstWebApp containing two classes, MyFirstWebApp and MyFirstWebAppTest. The first one should have 9 methods, the second 5. If you are unsure about your code, you can double check with the full listing at the end of this document. Our Web app should now work as expected, and we have some tests to prove it.

But our code currently only lives in our development image. Let's change that and move our code to a source code repository.

The Monticello Browser

For this we first have to use the Monticello Browser tool. In the first pane of the Nautilus Browser, click on the icon in front of your package named MyFirstWebApp as shown in Figure 2-12.

Once opened, Monticello shows on it left pane the list of loaded packages. The currently selected one should be yours as depicted in Figure 2-13.

27

Building and Deploying a Small Web application

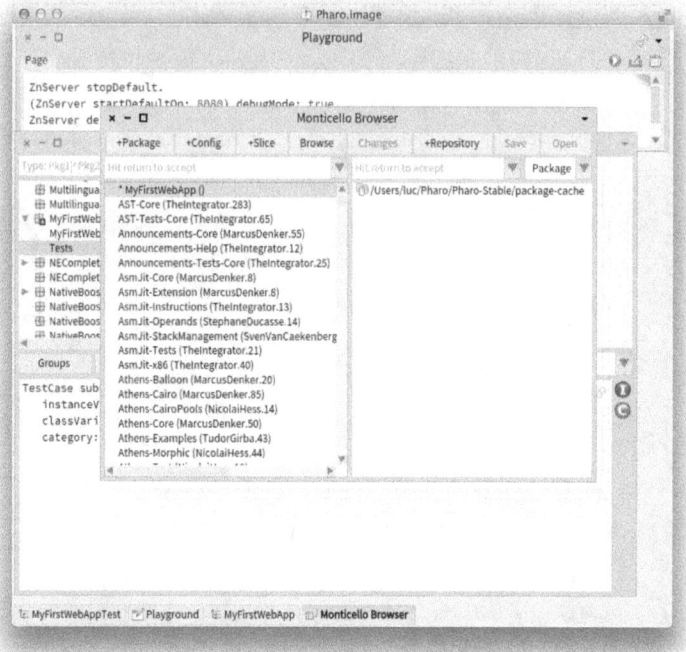

Figure 2-13 The Monticello browser

The left pane of Monticello shows the list of repositories in which the currently selected package can be saved. Indeed, Pharo uses distributed source code management. Your code can live on your local file system, or it can live on a server. As shown in Figure 2-13, by default, your `MyFirstWebApp` package can only be saved locally in a directory. We can easily add a remote repository. The main place for storing Pharo code is SmalltalkHub http://www.smalltalkhub.com. Go over there and create yourself a new account. Once you have an account, create a `'MyFirstWebApp'` project. You can leave the public option checked, it means that you and others can download the code without having to enter any credentials. Your project's page should look like the one on Figure 2-14.

On this page, select and copy the Monticello registration template (make sure to copy the whole contents, including the username and password parts). Now, go back to Pharo and in Monticello, click on the **+Repository** button (be sure that your package is selected in the left pane).

Select Smalltalkhub.com as repository type and overwrite the presented template with the one you just copied. It should look similar to Figure 2-15. Before accepting, fill in your user(name) and password (between the single

2.7 Saving Code to a Repository

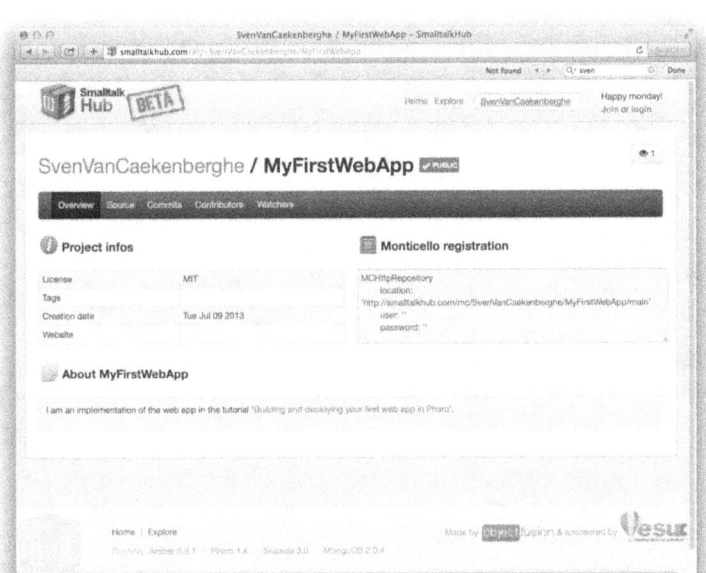

Figure 2-14 Smalltalkhub project page

quotes), the ones you gave during registration on SmalltalkHub.

Now, Monticello Browser shows you to select repositories to save your package as shown in Figure 2-16.

You may have noticed that there is an asterisk (*) in front of your package name, indicating the package is dirty: i.e., it has uncommitted changes. By clicking on the 'Changes' button, Monticello will list everything that has changed or will tell you nothing has changed (this happens sometimes when Monticello gets out of sync). If Monticello finds actual changes, you will get a browser showing all the changes you made. Since this is the first version, all your changes are additions.

Committing to SmalltalkHub

Go back to the Monticello Browser and click the 'Save' button (with your package and repository selected). Leave the version name, something like MyFirstWebApp-SvenVanCaekenberghe.1 alone, write a nice commit message in the second pane and press Accept to save your code to SmalltalkHub. When all goes well, you will see an upload progress bar and finally a version window that confirms the commit. You can close it later on.

If something goes wrong, you probably made a typo in your repository spec-

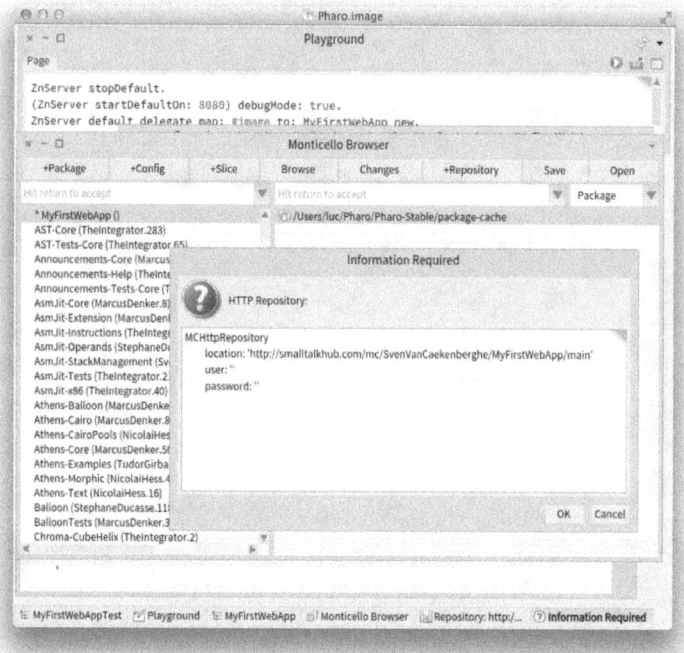

Figure 2-15 Adding a Smalltalkhub repository in Monticello for your project.

ification. You can edit it by right-clicking on it in the Monticello Browser and selecting 'Edit repository info'. If a save fails, you will get a Version Window after some error message. Don't close the Version Window. Your code now lives in your local package cache. Click the 'Copy' button and select your SmalltalkHub repository to try saving again.

You can now browse back to Smalltalkhub.com to confirm that your code arrived there.

After a successful commit, it is a good idea to save your image. In any case, your package should now no longer be dirty, and there should be no more differences between the local version and the one on SmalltalkHub.

Defining a Project Configuration

Real software consists of several packages and will depend on extra external libraries and frameworks. In practice, software configuration management, including the management of dependencies and versions, is thus a necessity. To solve this problem, Pharo is using Metacello (the book Deep into Pharo http://deepintopharo.com contains a full chapter on it). And although

2.7 Saving Code to a Repository

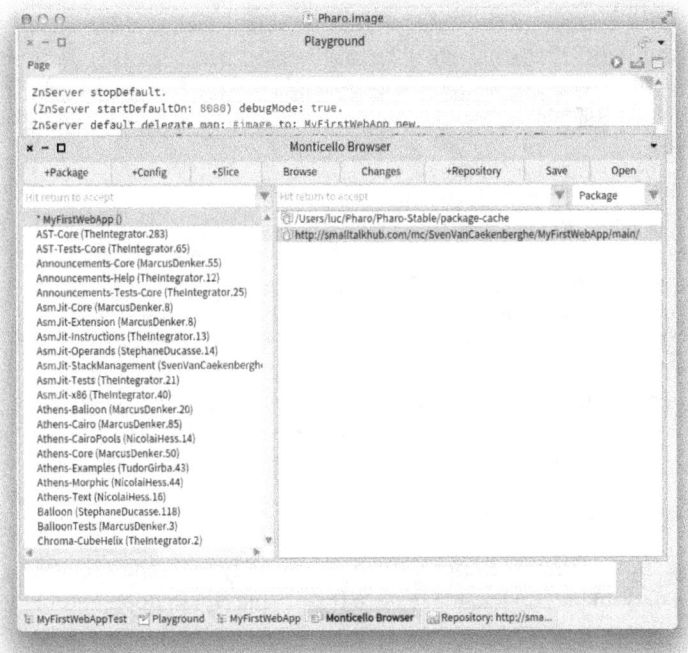

Figure 2-16 Multiple repositories for a project in Monticello

we don't really need it for our small example, we are going to use it anyway. Of course, we will not go into details as this is a complex subject.

To create a Metacello configuration, you define an object, what else did you expect? But we must respect some name conventions so Monticello can help us to generate part of this Metacello configuration. Open Monticello and click on the +Config button to add the ConfigurationOfMyFirstWebApp configuration. With a right click on it, you can "Browse configuration" which open a Nautilus browser on this newly created class. We are now going to define three methods: one defining a baseline for our configuration, one defining concrete package versions for that baseline, and one declaring that version as the stable released version. Here is the code:

```
ConfigurationOfMyFirstWebApp>>baseline1: spec
    <version: '1-baseline'>
    spec for: #common do:[
        spec
            blessing: #baseline;
            repository:

    'http://smalltalkhub.com/mc/SvenVanCaekenberghe/MyFirstWebApp/main';
```

31

Building and Deploying a Small Web application

```
            package: 'MyFirstWebApp' ]
ConfigurationOfMyFirstWebApp>>version1: spec
    <version: '1' imports: #('1-baseline')>
    spec for: #common do: [
        spec
            blessing: #release;
            package: 'MyFirstWebApp'
            with: 'MyFirstWebApp-SvenVanCaekenberghe.1' ]
ConfigurationOfMyFirstWebApp>>stable: spec
    <symbolicVersion: #'stable'>
    spec for: #common version: '1'
```

Once you committed the project (that consists in both the Metacello configuration and the Monticello package `'MyFirstWebApp'`), you can test your configuration by trying to load it.

```
ConfigurationOfMyFirstWebApp load.
```

Of course, not much will happen since you already have the specified version loaded. For some feedback, make sure the Transcript is open and inspect the above expression.

Now add your SmalltalkHub repository to the `ConfigurationOfMyFirstWebApp` Monticello package. Double-check the changes in the Monticello Browser, remember we copied a whole class. Now commit by saving to your SmalltalkHub repository. Use the Web interface to verify that all went well.

2.8 Running a Real Cloud Server

So we created our first Web app and tested it locally. We stored our source code in the SmalltalkHub repository and created a Metacello configuration for it. Now we need a real cloud server to run our Web app.

It used to be hard and expensive to get access to a real server permanently connected to the internet. Not anymore: prices have comes down and operating cloud servers has become a much easier to use service. If you just want to test the deployment of this Pharo Web app, you can use cloud9 (http://c9.io). It freely provides some testing environments after creating an account. Note that cloud9 is for testing purpose only and that a real hosting solution such as Digital Ocean (http://www.digitalocean.com) is better.

For this guide, we will be using Digital Ocean. The entry level server there, which is more than powerful enough for our experiment, costs just $5 a month. If you stop and remove the server after a couple of days, you will only pay cents. Go ahead and make yourself an account and register a credit card.

2.8 Running a Real Cloud Server

Create a Droplet

A server instance is called a Droplet. Click the 'Create Droplet' button and fill in the form. Pick a hostname, select the smallest size, pick a region close to you. As operating system image, we'll be using a 32-bit Ubuntu Linux, version 13.04 x32. You can optionally use an SSH key pair to log in - it is a good idea, see How to Use SSH Keys with DigitalOcean Droplets - just skip this option for now if you are uncomfortable with it, it is not necessary for this tutorial. Finally click the 'Create Droplet' button.

In less than a minute, your new server instance will be ready. Your root password will be emailed to you. If you look at your droplets, you should see your new server in the list. Click on it to see its details.

The important step now is to get SSH access to your new server, preferably through a terminal. With the IP address from the control panel and the root password emailed to you, try to log in.

```
$ ssh root@82.196.12.54
```

Your server is freshly installed and includes only the most essential core packages. Now we have to install Pharo on it. One easy way to do this is using the functionality offered by http://get.pharo.org. The following command will install a fresh Pharo 2.0 image together with all other files needed.

```
# curl get.pharo.org/40+vm | bash
```

Make sure the VM+image combination works by asking for the image version.

```
# ./pharo Pharo.image printVersion
[version] 4.0 #40614
```

Let's quickly test the stock HTTP server that comes with Pharo, like we did in the third section of this guide.

```
# ./pharo Pharo.image eval --no-quit 'ZnServer startDefaultOn: 8080'
```

This command will block. Now access your new HTTP server. You should see the Zinc HTTP Components welcome page. If this works, you can press ctrl-C in the terminal to end our test.

Deploy for Production

We now have a running server. It can run Pharo too, but it is currently using a generic image. How do we get our code deployed? To do this we use the Metacello configuration. But first, we are going to make a copy of the stock Pharo.image that we downloaded. We want to keep the original clean while we make changes to the copy.

```
# ./pharo Pharo.image save myfirstwebapp
```

We now have a new image (and changes) file called myfirstwebapp.image
(and myfirstwebapp.changes). Through the config command line option
we can load our Metacello configuration. Before actually loading anything,
we will ask for all available versions to verify that we can access the repository.

```
# ./pharo myfirstwebapp.image config \
   http://smalltalkhub.com/mc/SvenVanCaekenberghe/MyFirstWebApp/main
     \
   ConfigurationOfMyFirstWebApp
'Available versions for ConfigurationOfMyFirstWebApp'
1
1-baseline
bleedingEdge
last
stable
```

You should have only one version, all the above are equivalent references to
the same version. Now we will load and install the stable version.

```
# ./pharo myfirstwebapp.image config \
   http://smalltalkhub.com/mc/SvenVanCaekenberghe/MyFirstWebApp/main
     \
   ConfigurationOfMyFirstWebApp --install=stable
'Installing ConfigurationOfMyFirstWebApp stable'

Loading 1 of ConfigurationOfMyFirstWebApp...
...
```

After loading all necessary code, the config option will also save our image so
that it now permanently includes our code. Although we could try to write
a (long) one line expression to start our Web app in a server and pass it to
the eval option, it is better to write a small script. Create a file called 'run.st'
with the following contents:

```
ZnServer defaultOn: 8080.
ZnServer default logToTranscript.
ZnServer default delegate
    map: 'image' to: MyFirstWebApp new;
    map: 'redirect-to-image' to: [ :request | ZnResponse redirect:
      'image' ];
    map: '/' to: 'redirect-to-image'.
ZnServer default start.
```

We added a little twist here: we changed the default root (/) handler to redirect to our new /image Web app. Test the startup script like this:

```
# ./pharo myfirstwebapp.image run.st

2015-06-15 15:59:56 001 778091 Server Socket Bound 0.0.0.0:8080
2015-06-15 15:59:56 002 013495 Started ZnManagingMultiThreadedServer
```

2.9   Have Fun Extending this Web App

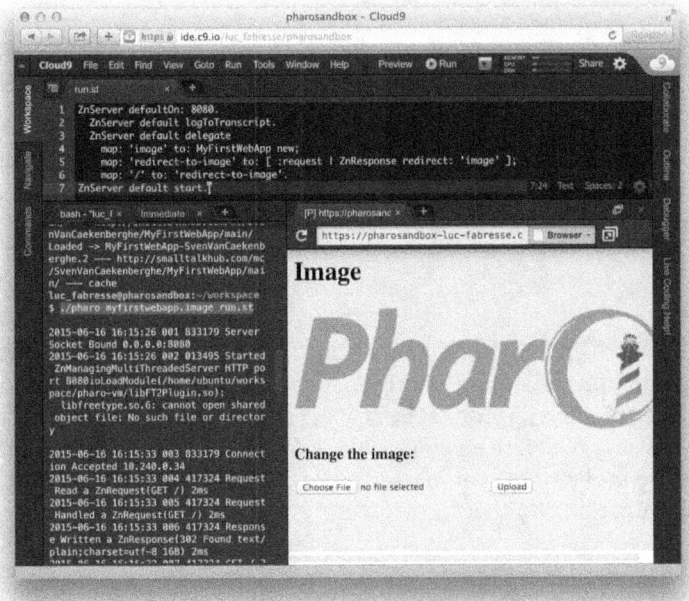

Figure 2-17   Our Web app, running in the cloud

```
    HTTP port 8080
...
```

You can surf to the correct IP address and port to test you application. Note that /welcome, /help and /image are still available too. Type ctrl-c to kill the server again. You can then put the server in background, running for real.

```
# nohup ./pharo myfirstwebapp.image run.st &
```

Figure 2-17 shows how the deployment looks like on cloud9.

2.9   Have Fun Extending this Web App

Did you like the example so far? Would you like to take one more step? Here is a little extension left as an exercise. Add an extra section at the bottom of the main page that shows a miniature version of the previous image. Initially, you can show an empty image. Here are a couple of hints. Read only as far as you need, try to figure it out by yourself.

Hint 1

You can scale a form object into another one using just one message taking a single argument. You can use the same classes that we used for parsing as a tool to generate PNG, JPEG or GIF images given a form.

When you are done, save your code as a new version. Then update your configuration with a new, stable version. Finally, go to the server, update your image based on the configuration and restart the running vm+image.

Hint 2

Change the html method referring to a new variant, /image?previous=true, for the second image. Adjust handleGetRequest: to look for that attribute. Add a helper method pngImageEntityForForm: and a previousImage accessor. It is easy to create an empty, blank form as default. Call a updatePreviousImage at the right spot in handlePostRequest: and implement the necessary functionality there.

Hint 3

If you found it difficult to find the right methods, have a look at the following ones:

- Form>>scaledIntoFormOfSize:
- Form class>>extent:depth:
- PNGReadWriter>>nextPutImage:
- ByteArray class>>streamContents:
- ZnByteArrayEntity class>>with:type:

Solution, Part 1, New Methods

Here are 3 new methods that are part of the solution.

```
pngImageEntityForForm: form
    ^ ZnByteArrayEntity
        with: (ByteArray streamContents: [ :out |
                (PNGReadWriter on: out) nextPutImage: form ])
        type: ZnMimeType imagePng

previousImage
    ^ previousImage ifNil: [
        | emptyForm |
        emptyForm:= Form extent: 128 @ 128 depth: 8.
        previousImage := self pngImageEntityForForm: emptyForm ]

updatePreviousImage
```

2.9 Have Fun Extending this Web App

```
    | form scaled |
    form := self form.
    scaled := form scaledIntoFormOfSize: 128.
    previousImage := self pngImageEntityForForm: scaled
```

Solution, Part 2, Changed Methods

Here are the changes to 3 existing methods for the complete solution.

```
html
    ^ '<html><head><title>Image</title>
    <body>
       <h1>Image</h1>
       <img src="image?raw=true"/>
       <br/>
       <form enctype="multipart/form-data" action="image"
     method="POST">
          <h3>Change the image:</h3>
          <input type="file" name="file"/>
          <input type="submit" value= "Upload"/>
       </form>
       <h3>Previous Image</h3>
       <img src="image?previous=true"/>
    </body></html>'

handleGetRequest: request
    (request uri queryAt: #raw ifAbsent: [ nil ])
       ifNotNil: [ ^ ZnResponse ok: self image ].
    (request uri queryAt: #previous ifAbsent: [ nil ])
       ifNotNil: [ ^ ZnResponse ok: self previousImage ].
    ^ ZnResponse ok: (ZnEntity html: self html)

handlePostRequest: request
    | part newImage badRequest |
    badRequest := [ ^ ZnResponse badRequest: request ].
    (request hasEntity
       and: [ request contentType matches: ZnMimeType
      multiPartFormData ])
         ifFalse: badRequest.
    part := request entity
                partNamed: #file
                ifNone: badRequest.
    newImage := part entity.
    (newImage notNil
       and: [ newImage contentType matches: 'image/*' asZnMimeType ])
         ifFalse: badRequest.
    [ self formForImageEntity: newImage ]
       on: Error
       do: badRequest.
```

```
self updatePreviousImage.
image := newImage.
^ ZnResponse redirect: #image
```

Solution, Part 3, Updated Configuration

To update our configuration, add 1 method and change 1 method.

```
version2: spec
    <version: '2' imports: #('1-baseline')>
    spec for: #common do: [
        spec
            blessing: #release;
            package: 'MyFirstWebApp' with:
        'MyFirstWebApp-SvenVanCaekenberghe.2' ]

stable: spec
    <symbolicVersion: #'stable'>
    spec for: #common version: '2'
```

Of course, you will have to substitute your name for the concrete version.

2.10 Conclusion

Congratulations: you have now built and deployed your first Web app with Pharo. Hopefully you are interested in learning more. From the Pharo website you should be able to find all the information you need. Don't forget about the Pharo by Example book and the mailing lists. This guide was an introduction to writing Web applications using Pharo, touching on the fundamentals of HTTP. Like we mentioned in the introduction, there are a couple of high level frameworks that offer more extensive support for writing Web applications. The three most important ones are Seaside, AIDAweb and Iliad.

The code of the Web app, including tests and the Metacello configuration, is on SmalltalkHub[1]. A similar example is also included in the Zinc HTTP Components project itself, under the name ZnImageExampleDelegate[Tests].

---

[1] http://smalltalkhub.com/#!/~SvenVanCaekenberghe/MyFirstWebApp

Part II

HTTP

CHAPTER 3

Character Encoding and Resource Meta Description

Sven Van Caekenberghe with Luc Fabresse and Johan Fabry

The rise of the Internet and of Open Standards resulted in the adoption of a number of fundamental mechanisms to enable communication and collaboration between different systems.

One such mechanism is the ability to encode strings or characters to bytes or to decode strings or characters from bytes. Different encoding standards have been developed over the years and Pharo supports many current and legacy encodings.

Another important aspect of collaboration is the ability to describe resources such as files. Both Mime-Type and URLs or URIs are basic building blocks for creating meta descriptions of resources and Pharo also has objects that implement these fundamental aspects.

In this chapter we discuss Character encoding, MIME types and URL/URIs. They are essential for the correct implementation of HTTP, but they are independent from it, as they are used for many other purposes.

3.1 Character Encoding

We will first show how to get Unicode from characters and strings within Pharo. We will then show how to decode and encode characters and strings from and to bytes.

Characters and Strings use Unicode Internally

Proper character encoding and decoding is crucial in today's international world. Internally, Pharo stores characters and strings using Unicode. Unicode[1] is a very large internationally standardized collection of code points (integer numbers) representing all of the world languages' characters.

We can obtain the code point (Unicode value) of a character by sending it the codePoint message, for example:

```
$H codePoint
   --> 72
```

Here are some example strings in multiple languages with their Unicode code points:

```
'Hello' collect: #codePoint as: Array.
   --> #(72 101 108 108 111)

'Les élèves français' collect: #codePoint as: Array.
   --> #(76 101 115 32 233 108 232 118 101 115
         32 102 114 97 110 231 97 105 115)

'Ελλάδα' collect: #codePoint as: Array.
   --> #(917 955 955 940 948 945)
```

For a simple language like English, all characters have code points below 128 (which fits in 7 bits, for historical reasons). These characters are part of ASCII[2]. The very first part of the so called Basic Multilingual Plane of Unicode (the first 128 code points of it) are identical to ASCII.

```
$a codePoint
   --> 97
```

Next come a number of European languages, like French, which have code points below 256 (fitting in 8 bits or one byte). These characters are part of Latin-1 (ISO-8859-1)[3], whose first 256 code points are identical in Unicode.

```
$é codePoint
   --> 233
```

And finally, there are hundreds of other languages, like Chinese, Japanese, Cyrillic, Arabic or Greek. You can see from the example above: Greece written in Greek, that those code points are higher than 256 (and thus no longer fit in one byte).

```
λ
$ codePoint
   --> 955
```

---

[1] http://en.wikipedia.org/wiki/Unicode
[2] http://en.wikipedia.org/wiki/ASCII
[3] http://en.wikipedia.org/wiki/ISO/IEC_8859-1

Unicode code points are often written using a specific hexadecimal notation. For example, the previous character, the Greek lowercase lambda, is written as U+03BB. The Pharo inspector also shows this value next to the codepoint.

The good thing is, we can work with text in any language in Pharo. However, to display everything correctly a font must be used that is capable of showing all the characters (or glyphs) needed, for example Arial Unicode MS.

Encoding and Decoding

For communication with the world outside Pharo, the operating system, files, the internet, et cetera, we have to represent our strings as a collection of bytes. Yet code points are different to bytes, as will be shown below. Therefore we need a way to transform our internal strings into external collection of bytes and vice versa.

Character encoding is the standard way of converting a native Pharo string, i.e. a collection of Unicode code points, to a series of bytes. Character decoding is the reverse process: interpreting a series of bytes as a collection of Unicode code points, to create a Pharo string.

To implement character encoding or decoding, a concrete subclass of the class ZnCharacterEncoder is used, e.g. ZnUTF8Encoder. Character encoders do the following:

- encode a character (message nextPut:toStream:) or string (message next:putAll:startingAt:toStream:) onto a binary stream
- convert a string (encodeString:) to a byte array
- decode a binary stream to a character (nextFromStream:) or string (readInto:startingAt:count:fromStream:)
- convert a byte array to string (decodeBytes:)
- compute the number of bytes that are needed to encode a character (encodedByteCountFor:) or string (encodedByteCountForString:)
- move a binary stream backwards one character (backOnStream:)

Character encoders do proper error handling, throwing an error of the class ZnCharacterEncodingError when something goes wrong. The strict/lenient setting controls some behavior in this respect, and this will be discussed later in this chapter.

The recommended encoding is the primary internet encoding: UTF-8[4]. It is a variable length encoding that is optimized somewhat for ASCII and to a lesser degree for Latin1 and some other common European encodings.

---

[4] http://en.wikipedia.org/wiki/UTF-8

Converting Strings and ByteArrays

The first use of encoders is to convert Strings to ByteArrays and vice-versa. We however deal only indirectly with character encoders. The `ByteArray` and `String` classes have some convenience methods to do encoding and decoding:

```
'Hello' utf8Encoded.
   --> #[72 101 108 108 111]

'Hello' encodeWith: #latin1.
   --> #[72 101 108 108 111]
```

Our ASCII string, `'Hello'` encodes identically using either UTF-8 or Latin-1.

```
'Les élèves français' utf8Encoded.
   --> #[76 101 115 32 195 169 108 195 168 118 101 115
         32 102 114 97 110 195 167 97 105 115]

'Les élèves français' encodeWith: #latin1.
   --> #[76 101 115 32 233 108 232 118 101 115
         32 102 114 97 110 231 97 105 115]
```

Our French string, `'Les élèves français'`, encodes differently though. The reason is that UTF-8 uses two bytes for the accented letters like é, è and ç. Note how for Latin-1, and **only** for Latin-1 and ASCII, the Unicode code points are equal to the encoded byte values.

```
'éèç' utf8Encoded.
   --> #[195 169 195 168 195 167]

'éèç' encodeWith: #latin1.
   --> #[233 232 231]

'éèç' collect: #codePoint as: ByteArray
   --> #[233 232 231]
```

```
'Ελλάδα' utf8Encoded.
   --> #[206 149 206 187 206 187 206 172 206 180 206 177]

'Ελλάδα' encodeWith: #latin1.
   --> ZnCharacterEncodingError: 'Character Unicode code point
      outside encoder range'
```

Our greek string, `'Ελλάδα'`, gives an error when we try to encode it using Latin-1. The reason is that the Greek letters are outside of the alphabet of Latin-1. Still, UTF-8 manages to encode them using just two bytes.

The reverse process, decoding, is equally simple:

```
#[72 101 108 108 111] utf8Decoded.
   --> 'Hello'
```

3.1 Character Encoding

```
#[72 101 108 108 111] decodeWith: #latin1.
   --> 'Hello'

#[76 101 115 32 195 169 108 195 168 118 101 115
  32 102 114 97 110 195 167 97 105 115] utf8Decoded.
   --> 'Les élèves français'

#[76 101 115 32 195 169 108 195 168 118 101 115
  32 102 114 97 110 195 167 97 105 115] decodeWith: #latin1.
   --> 'Les Ã©lÃ¨ves franÃ§ais'

#[76 101 115 32 233 108 232 118 101 115
  32 102 114 97 110 231 97 105 115] utf8Decoded.
   --> ZnInvalidUTF8: 'Illegal continuation byte for utf-8 encoding'

#[76 101 115 32 233 108 232 118 101 115
  32 102 114 97 110 231 97 105 115] decodeWith: #latin1.
   --> 'Les élèves français'

#[206 149 206 187 206 187 206 172 206 180 206 177] utf8Decoded.
   --> 'Ελλάδα'

#[206 149 206 187 206 187 206 172 206 180 206 177] decodeWith:
    #latin1.
   --> ZnCharacterEncodingError: 'Character Unicode code point
    outside encoder range'
```

Our English 'Hello', being pure ASCII, can be decoded using either UTF-8 or Latin-1. Our French 'Les élèves français' is another story: using the wrong encoding gives either gibberish or ZnInvalidUTF8 error. The same is true for our Greek 'Ελλάδα'.

You might wonder why in the first case the latin1 encoder produced gibberish, while in the second case it gave an error. This is because in the second case, there was a byte with value 149, which is outside its alphabet. So called byte encoders, like Latin-1, take a subset of Unicode characters and compress them in 256 possible byte values. This can be seen by inspecting the character or byte domains of a ZnByteEncoder, as follows:

```
(ZnByteEncoder newForEncoding: 'iso-8859-1') byteDomain.
(ZnByteEncoder newForEncoding: 'ISO_8859_7') characterDomain.
```

Note that identifiers for encodings are interpreted flexibly (case and punctuation do not matter).

There exists a special ZnNullEncoder that basically does nothing: it treats bytes are characters and vice versa. This is actually mostly equivalent to Latin-1 or ISO-8859-1. (And yes, that is a bit confusing.)

Converting Streams

The second primary use of encoders is when dealing with streams. More specifically, when interpreting a binary read or write stream as a character stream. Note that at their lowest level, all streams to and from the operating system or network are binary and thus need the use of an encoder when treating them as character streams.

To treat a binary write stream as a character write stream, wrap it with a ZnCharacterWriteStream. Similary, ZnCharacterReadStream should be used to treat a binary read stream as a character stream. Here is an example:

```
'encoding-test.txt' asFileReference writeStreamDo: [ :out |
   (ZnCharacterWriteStream on: out binary encoding: #utf8)
      nextPutAll: 'Hello'; space; nextPutAll: 'Ελλάδα'; crlf;
      nextPutAll: 'Les élèves français'; crlf ].

'encoding-test.txt' asFileReference readStreamDo: [ :in |
   (ZnCharacterReadStream on: in binary encoding: #utf8)
      upToEnd ]
   --> 'Hello Ελλάδα
Les élèves français
'
```

We used the message on:encoding: here, but there is also a plain message on: instance creation message that defaults to the UTF-8 encoding. Internally, the character streams will use an encoder instance to do the actual work.

ByteStrings and WideStrings are Concrete Subclasses of String

Up until now we spoke about Strings as being a collection of Characters, each of which is represented as a Unicode code point. And this is conceptually totally how they should be thought about. However, in reality, the class String is an abstract class with two concrete subclasses. This will show up when inspecting String instances, so it is important to understand what is going on. Consider the following example strings:

```
'Hello' class.
   --> ByteString

'Les élèves français' class.
   --> ByteString

'Ελλάδα' class.
   --> WideString
```

Simple ASCII strings are ByteStrings. Strings using special characters may be WideStrings or may still be ByteStrings. The explanation of the use of the

3.1 Character Encoding

`WideString` or `ByteString` class is very simple when considering the Unicode code points used for each character.

In the first case, for ASCII, the code points are always less than 128. Hence they fit in one byte. The second string is using Latin-1 characters, whose code points are less than 256. These still fit in a byte. A `ByteString` is a `String` that only stores Unicode code points that fit in a byte, in an implementation that is very efficient. Note that `ByteString` is a variable byte subclass of `String`.

Our last example has code points that no longer fit in a byte. To be able to store these, `WideString` allocates 32-bit (4 byte) slots for each character. This implementation is necessarily less efficient. Note that `WideString` is a variable word subclass of `String`.

In practice, the difference between `ByteString` and `WideString` should not matter. Conversions are done automatically when needed.

```
'abc' copy at: 1 put: α$; class.
   --> WideString
```

As the above example shows, in a `ByteString` `'abc'` putting the Unicode character $α, converts it to a `WideString`. (This is actually done using a `becomeForward:` message.) When benchmarking, this conversion might show up as taking significant time. If you know upfront that you will need WideStrings, it can be better to start with the right type.

ByteString and ByteArray Equivalence is an Implementation Detail

There is another implementation detail worth mentioning: for the Pharo virtual machine, more specifically, for a number of primitives, `ByteString` and `ByteArray` instances are equivalent. Given what we now know, that makes sense. Consider the following code:

```
'abcdef' asByteArray.
   --> #[97 98 99 100 101 102]

'ABC' asByteArray.
   --> #[65 66 67]

'abcdef' copy replaceFrom: 1 to: 3 with: #[65 66 67].
   --> 'ABCdef'

#[97 98 99 100 101 102] copy replaceFrom: 1 to: 3 with: 'ABC'.
   --> #[65 66 67 100 101 102]
```

In the third expression, we send the message `replaceFrom:to:with:` on a `ByteString`, but give a `ByteArray` as third argument. So we are replacing part of a `ByteString` with a `ByteArray`. And it works!

The last example goes the other way around: we replace part of a `ByteArray` with a `ByteString`, which works as well.

What about doing the same mix up with elements ?

```
'abc' copy at: 1 put: 65; yourself.
   --> Error: improper store into indexable object

#[97 98 99] copy at: 1 put: $A; yourself.
   --> Error: improper store into indexable object
```

This is more what we expect: we're not allowed to do this. We are mixing two types that are not equivalent, like `Character` and `Integer`.

So although it is true that there is some equivalence between ByteString and ByteArray, you should not mix up the two. It is an implementation detail that you should not rely upon.

Beware of Bogus Conversions

Given a string, it is tempting to send it the message `asByteArray` to convert it to bytes. Similarly, it is tempting to convert a byte array by sending it the message `asString`. These are however bogus conversions that should not be used as for some strings they will work, but for others not. Success depends on the code points of the characters in the string. Basically the conversion is possible for strings for which the following property holds:

```
'Hello' allSatisfy: [ :each | each codePoint < 256 ].
   --> true

'Les élèves français' allSatisfy: [ :each | each codePoint < 256 ].
   --> true

'Ελλάδα' allSatisfy: [ :each | each codePoint < 256 ].
   --> false
```

Now, even though the first two can be converted, they will not be using the same encoding. Here is a way to explicitly express this idea:

```
#(null ascii latin1 utf8) allSatisfy: [ :each |
   ('Hello' encodeWith: each) = 'Hello' asByteArray ].
   --> true.

('Les élèves français' encodeWith: #latin1) = 'Les élèves français'
      asByteArray.
   --> true.

('Les élèves français' encodeWith: #null) = 'Les élèves français'
      asByteArray.
   --> true.
```

3.1 Character Encoding

```
'Les élèves français' utf8Encoded = 'Les élèves français'
    asByteArray.
  --> false.
```

For pure ASCII strings, with all code points below 128, no encoding (null encoding), ASCII, Latin-1 and UTF-8 are all the same. For other `ByteString` instances, like `'Les élèves français'`, only Latin-1 works. In that case it is also equivalent of doing no encoding.

The lazy conversion for proper Unicode WideStrings will give unexpected results:

```
'Ελλάδα' asByteArray.
  --> #[0 0 3 149 0 0 3 187 0 0 3 187 0 0 3 172 0 0 3 180 0 0 3 177]
```

This 'conversion' does not correspond to any known encoding. It is the result of writing 4-byte Unicode code points as Integers.

> **Note** Using this is a bug no matter how you look at it. In this century you will look silly for not implementing proper support for all languages. When converting between strings and bytes, use a proper, explicit encoding.

Strict and Lenient Encoding

No encoding (or the null encoder) and Latin-1 encoding are in fact not completely the same. This is because there are 'holes' in the table: some byte values are undefined, which a strict encoder won't allow, and the default encoder is strict.

For example, the Unicode code point 150 is strictly speaking not in Latin-1:

```
ZnByteEncoder latin1 encodeString: 150 asCharacter asString.
  --> ZnCharacterEncodingError: 'Character Unicode code point
     outside encoder range'

ZnByteEncoder latin1 decodeBytes: #[ 150 ].
  --> ZnCharacterEncodingError: 'Character Unicode code point
     outside encoder range'
```

The encoder can however be instructed to beLenient, which will produce a silent conversion (if that is possible). In this case, Unicode character 150 (U+0096) is an unprintable control character meaning 'Start of Protected Area' (SPA) and is strictly speaking not part of Latin-1.

```
ZnByteEncoder latin1 beLenient encodeString: 150 asCharacter
    asString.
  --> #[ 150 ]

ZnByteEncoder latin1 beLenient decodeBytes: #[ 150 ].
  --> ''
```

You can explicity access both the allowed byte or character values, i.e. the domain of encoder or decoder:

```
ZnByteEncoder latin1 characterDomain includes: 150 asCharacter.
   --> false

ZnByteEncoder latin1 byteDomain includes: 150.
   --> false
```

Note that the lower half of a byte encoding, the ASCII part between 0 and 127, is always treated as a one to one mapping.

Available Encoders

Pharo comes with support for the most important encodings currently used, as well as with support for some important legacy encodings. Seen as the classes implementing them, the following encoders are available:

- ZnUTF8Encoder
- ZnUTF16Encoder
- ZnByteEncoder
- ZnNullEncoder

Where ZnByteEncoder groups a large number of encodings. This list is available as ZnByteEncoder knownEncodingIdentifiers. Here is a list of all recognized, canonical names: arabic, cp1250, cp1251, cp1252, cp1253, cp1254, cp1255, cp1256, cp1257, cp1258, cp850, cp866, cp874, cyrillic, dos874, doslatin1, greek, hebrew, ibm819, ibm850, ibm866, iso885910, iso885911, iso885913, iso885914, iso885915, iso885916, iso88592, iso88593, iso88594, iso88595, iso88596, iso88597, iso88598, iso88599, koi8, koi8r, koi8u, latin2, latin3, latin4, latin5, latin6, mac, maccyrillic, macintosh, macroman, oem850, windows1250, windows1251, windows1252, windows1253, windows1254, windows1255, windows1256, windows1257, windows1258, windows874, xcp1250, xcp1251, xcp1252, xcp1253, xcp1254, xcp1255, xcp1256, xcp1257, xcp1258, xmaccyrillic and xmacroman.

3.2 Mime-Types

A mime-type is a standard, cross-platform definition of a file or document type or format. The official term is an Internet media type[5].

Mime-types are modeled using ZnMimeType objects, which have 3 components:

1. a main type, for example text or image,

---

[5] http://en.wikipedia.org/wiki/Internet_media_type

3.2 Mime-Types

2. a sub type, for example `plain` or `html`, or `jpeg`, `png` or `gif`, and
3. a number of attributes, for example `charset=utf-8`.

The mime-type syntax is as follows:

`<main>/<sub> [;<param1>=<value1>[,<param2>=<value2>]*].`

Creating Mime-Types

Instances of `ZnMimeType` are created by explicitly specifying its components, through parsing a string or by accessing predefined values. In any case, a new instance is always created.

The class side of `ZnMimeType` has some convenience methods (in the protocol convenience) for accessing well known mime-types, which is the recommended way for obtaining these mime-types:

```
ZnMimeType textHtml.
    --> text/plain;charset=utf-8

ZnMimeType imagePng
    --> image/png
```

Here is an example of how to create a mime-type by explicitly specifying its components:

```
ZnMimeType main: 'image' sub: 'png'.
    --> image/png
```

The main parsing interface of `ZnMimeType` is the class side `fromString:` message.

```
ZnMimeType fromString: 'image/png'.
    --> image/png
```

To make it easier to write code that accepts both instances and strings, the `asZnMimeType` message can be used:

```
'image/png' asZnMimeType
    --> image/png

ZnMimeType imagePng asZnMimeType = 'image/png' asZnMimeType
    --> true
```

Finally, `ZnMimeType` also knows how to convert file name extensions to mime-types using the `forFilenameExtension:` message. This mapping is based on the Debian/Ubuntu /etc/mime.types file, which is encoded into the method `mimeTypeFilenameExtensionsSpec`.

```
ZnMimeType forFilenameExtension: 'html'.
    --> text/html;charset=utf-8
```

In most applications, the concept of a default mime-type exists. It basically means: we don't know what these bytes represent.

```
ZnMimeType default
    --> application/octet-stream
```

Working with Mime-Types

Once you have a ZnMimeType instance, you can access its components using the `main`, `sub` and `parameters` messages.

An important aspect of mime-types is whether the type is textual or binary, which is testable with the `isBinary` message. Typically, text, XML or JSON are considered textual, while images are binary.

For textual (non-binary) types, the encoding (or charset parameter) defaults to UTF-8, the prevalent internet standard. With the convencience messages `charSet:`, `setCharSetUTF8` and `clearCharSet` you can manipulate the charset parameter.

Comparing mime-types using the standard = message takes all components into account, including the parameters. Different parameters lead to different mime-types. As a result, when charsets are involved it is often better to compare using the `matches:` message, as follows:

```
'text/plain' asZnMimeType = ZnMimeType textPlain.
    --> false

ZnMimeType textPlain = 'text/plain' asZnMimeType.
    --> false

'text/plain' asZnMimeType matches: ZnMimeType textPlain.
    --> true

ZnMimeType textPlain matches: 'text/plain' asZnMimeType.
    --> true
```

The charset=UTF-8 that is part of what `ZnMimeType textPlain` returns is not taken into account in the second set of comparisons.

The main or sub types can be a wildcard, indicated by a *. This allows for matching. Obviously, everything matches */* (`ZnMimeType any`). Otherwise, when the sub type is *, the main types must be equal. Here is an example.

```
ZnMimeType text.
    --> text/*

ZnMimeType textHtml matches: ZnMimeType text.
    --> true

ZnMimeType textPlain matches: ZnMimeType text.
```

```
    --> true

ZnMimeType applicationXml matches: ZnMimeType text.
    --> false
```

3.3 URLs

URLs (or URIs) are a way to name or identify an entity. Often, they also contain information of where the entity they name or identify can be accessed.

We will be using the terms URL (Uniform Resource Locator[6]) and URI (Uniform Resource Identifier[7]) interchangeably, as is most commonly done in practice. A URI is just a name or identification, while a URL also contains information on how to find or access a resource. Consider the following example: the URI /documents/cv.html identifies and names a document, while the URL http://john-doe.com/documents/cv.html also specifies that we can use HTTP to access this resource on a specific server.

By considering most parts of an URL as optional, we can use one abstraction to implement both URI and URL using one class. The class ZnUrl models URLs (or URIs) and has the following components:

1. scheme - like #http, #https , #ws, #wws, #file or nil
2. host - hostname string or nil
3. port - port integer or nil
4. segments - collection of path segments, ends with #/ for directories
5. query - query dictionary or nil
6. fragment - fragment string or nil
7. username - username string or nil
8. password - password string or nil

The syntax of the external representation of a ZnUrl informally looks like this: scheme://username:password@host:port/segments?query#fragment

Creating URLs

ZnUrls are most often created by parsing an external representation using either the fromString: class message or by sending the asUrl or asZnUrl convenience message to a string.

---

[6] http://en.wikipedia.org/wiki/Uniform_resource_locator
[7] http://en.wikipedia.org/wiki/Uniform_resource_identifier

```
ZnUrl fromString: 'http://www.google.com/search?q=Smalltalk'.
'http://www.google.com/search?q=Smalltalk' asUrl.
```

The same instance can also be constructed programmatically:

```
ZnUrl new
    scheme: #http;
    host: 'www.google.com';
    addPathSegment: 'search';
    queryAt: 'q' put: 'Smalltalk';
    yourself.
```

ZnUrl components can be manipulated destructively. Here is an example:

```
'http://www.google.com/?one=1&two=2' asZnUrl
    queryAt: 'three' put: '3';
    queryRemoveKey: 'one';
    yourself.
    --> http://www.google.com/?two=2&three=3
```

External and Internal Representation of URLs

Some characters of parts of a URL are considered as illegal because including them would interfere with the syntax and further processing. They thus have to be encoded. The methods of ZnUrl in the accessing protocols do not do any encoding, while those in parsing and printing do. Here is an example:

```
'http://www.google.com'
    addPathSegment: 'an encoding';
    queryAt: 'and more' put: 'here, too';
    yourself
    --> http://www.google.com/an%20encoding?and%20more=here,%20too
```

The ZnUrl parser is somewhat forgiving and accepts some unencoded URLs as well, like most browsers would.

```
'http://www.example.com:8888/a path?q=a, b, c' asZnUrl.
    --> http://www.example.com:8888/a%20path?q=a,%20b,%20c
```

Relative URLs

ZnUrl can parse in the context of a default scheme, like a browser would do.

```
ZnUrl fromString: 'www.example.com' defaultScheme: #http
    --> http://www.example.com/
```

Given a known scheme, ZnUrl knows its default port, and this is accessed by portOrDefault.

A path defaults to what is commonly referred to as slash, which is testable with isSlash. Paths are most often (but don't have to be) interpreted as

3.3 URLs

filesystem paths. To support this, the `isFilePath` and `isDirectoryPath` tests and `file` and `directory` accessors are provided.

ZnUrl has some support to handle one URL in the context of another one, this is also known as a relative URL in the context of an absolute URL. This is implemented using the `isAbsolute`, `isRelative` and `inContextOf:` methods. For example:

```
'/folder/file.txt' asZnUrl inContextOf:
    'http://fileserver.example.net:4400' asZnUrl.
  --> http://fileserver.example.net:4400/folder/file.txt
```

Operations on URLs

To add operations to URLs you could add an extension method to the ZnUrl class. In many cases though, it will not work on all kinds of URLs but only on a subset. In other words, you need to dispatch, not just on the scheme but maybe even on other URL elements. That is where `ZnUrlOperation` comes in.

The first step for its use is defining a name for the operation. For example, the symbol `#retrieveContents`. Second, one or more subclasses of `ZnUrlOperation` need to be defined, each defining the class side message operation to return the name, `#retrieveContents` in the example. Then all subclasses with the same operation form the group of applicable implementations. Third, these handler subclasses overwrite `performOperation` to do the actual work.

Given a ZnUrl instance, sending the message `performOperation:` or `performOperation:with:` will send the message `performOperation:with:on:` to `ZnUrlOperation`. In turn, it will look for an applicable handler subclass, instanciate and invoke it.

Each subclass will be sent `handlesOperation:with:on:` to test if it can handle the named operation with an optional argument on a specific URL. The default implementation already covers the most common case: the operation name has to match and the scheme of the URL has to be part of the collection returned by `schemes`.

For our example, the message `retrieveContents` on ZnUrl is implemented as an operation named `#retrieveContents`. The handler class is either the class `ZnHttpRetrieveContents` for the schemes `http` and `https` or the class `ZnFileRetrieveContents` for the scheme `file`.

This dispatching mechanism is more powerful than scheme specific `ZnUrl` subclasses because other elements can be taken into account. It also addresses another issue with scheme specific `ZnUrl` subclasses, which is that there are an infinite number of schemes which no hierarchy could cover.

Odds and Ends

Sometimes, the combination of a host and port are referred to as authority, and this is accessable with the `authority` message.

There are convenience methods to download the resource a ZnUrl points to: `retrieveContents` and `saveContentsToFile`. The first retrieves the contents and returns it directly, while the expression saves the contents directly to a file.

```
'http://zn.stfx.eu/zn/numbers.txt' asZnUrl retrieveContents.
'http://zn.stfx.eu/zn/numbers.txt' asZnUrl saveContentsToFile:
    'numbers.txt'.
```

ZnUrl can be used to handle file URLs. Use `isFile` to test for this scheme.

Given a file URL, it can be converted to a regular `FileReference` using the `asFileReference` message. In the other direction, you can get a file URL from a `FileReference` using the `asUrl` or `asZnUrl` messages. Do keep in mind that there is no such thing as a relative file URL, only absolute file URLs exist.

CHAPTER 4

Zinc HTTP: The Client Side

Sven Van Caekenberghe with Luc Fabresse and Johan Fabry

HTTP is arguably the most important application level network protocol for what we consider to be the Internet. It is the protocol that allows web browsers and web servers to communicate. It is also becoming the most popular protocol for implementing web services.

With Zinc, Pharo has out of the box support for HTTP. Zinc is a robust, fast and elegant HTTP client and server library written and maintained by Sven van Caekenberghe.

4.1 HTTP and Zinc

HTTP, short for Hypertext Transfer Protocol, functions as a request-response protocol in the client-server computing model. As an application level protocol it is layered on top of a reliable transport such as a TCP socket stream. The most important standard specification document describing HTTP version 1.1 is RFC 2616[1]. As usual, a good starting point for learning about HTTP is its Wikipedia article[2].

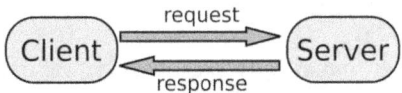

Figure 4-1 Client/Server interacting via request/response

---

[1] http://tools.ietf.org/html/rfc2616
[2] http://en.wikipedia.org/wiki/Http

A client, often called user-agent, submits an HTTP request to a server which will respond with an HTTP response (see Fig. 4-1). The initiative of the communication lies with the client. In HTTP parlance, the client requests a resource. A resource, sometimes also called an entity, is the combination of a collection of bytes and a mime-type. A simple text resource will consist of bytes encoding the string in some encoding, for example UTF-8, and the mime-type text/plain;charset=utf-8, in contrast, an HTML resource will have a mime-type like text/html;charset=utf-8.

To specify which resource you want, a URL (Uniform Resource Locator) is used. Web addresses are the most common form of URL. Consider for example http://pharo.org/files/pharo-logo-small.png : it is a URL that refers to a PNG image resource on a specific server.

The reliable transport connection between an HTTP client and server is used bidirectionally: both to send the request as well as to receive the response. It can be used for just one request/response cycle, as was the case for HTTP version 1.0, or it can be reused for multiple request/response cycles, as is the default for HTTP version 1.1.

Zinc, the short form for Zinc HTTP[3] Components, is an open-source Smalltalk framework to deal with HTTP. It models most concepts of HTTP and its related standards and offers both client and server functionality. One of its key goals is to offer understandability (Smalltalk's design principle number one). Anyone with a basic understanding of Smalltalk and the HTTP principles should be able to understand what is going on and learn, by looking at the implementation. Zinc, or Zn, after its namespace prefix, is an integral part of Pharo Smalltalk since version 1.3. It has been ported to other Smalltalk implementations such as Gemstone.

The reference Zn implementation lives in several places:

- http://www.squeaksource.com/ZincHTTPComponents
- http://mc.stfx.eu/ZincHTTPComponents
- https://www.github.com/svenvc/zinc

Installation or updating instructions can be found on its web site[4].

4.2 Doing a Simple Request

The key object to programmatically execute HTTP requests is called ZnClient. You instantiate it, use its rich API to configure and execute an HTTP request and access the response. ZnClient is a stateful object that acts as a builder.

---

[3] http://zn.stfx.eu/
[4] http://zn.stfx.eu/

4.2 Doing a Simple Request

Basic Usage

Let's get started with the simplest possible usage.

```
ZnClient new get: 'http://zn.stfx.eu/zn/small.html'.
```

Select the expression and print its result. You should get a String back containing a very small HTML document. The get: method belongs to the convenience API. Let's use a more general API to be a bit more explicit about what happened.

```
ZnClient new
    url: 'http://zn.stfx.eu/zn/small.html';
    get;
    response.
```

Here we explicitly set the url of the resource to access using url:, then we execute an HTTP GET using get and we finally ask for the response object using response. The above returns a ZnResponse object. Of course you can inspect it. It consists of 3 elements:

1. a ZnStatusLine object,
2. a ZnHeaders object and
3. an optional ZnEntity object.

The status line says HTTP/1.1 200 OK, which means the request was successful. This can be tested by sending isSuccess to either the response object or the client itself. The headers contain meta data related to the response, including:

- the content-type (a mime-type), accessible with the contentType message
- the content-length (a byte count), accessible with the contentLength message
- the date the response was generated
- the server that generated the response

The entity is the actual resource: the bytes that should be interpreted in the context of the content-type mime-type. Zn automatically converts non-binary mime-types into Strings using the correct encoding. In our example, the entity is an instance of ZnStringEntity, a concrete subclass of ZnEntity.

Like any Smalltalk object, you can inspect or explore the ZnResponse object. You might be wondering how this response was actually transferred over the network. That is easy with Zinc, as the key HTTP objects all implement writeOn: that displays the raw format of the response i.e. what has been transmitted through the network.

```
| response |
response := (ZnClient new)
    url: 'http://zn.stfx.eu/zn/small.html';
    get;
    response.
response writeOn: Transcript.
Transcript flush.
```

If you have the Transcript open, you should see something like the following:

```
HTTP/1.1 200 OK
Date: Thu, 26 Mar 2015 23:26:49 GMT
Modification-Date: Thu, 10 Feb 2011 08:32:30 GMT
Content-Length: 113
Server: Zinc HTTP Components 1.0
Vary: Accept-Encoding
Content-Type: text/html;charset=utf-8

<html>
<head><title>Small</title></head>
<body><h1>Small</h1><p>This is a small HTML document</p></body>
</html>
```

The first CRLF terminated line is the status line. Next are the headers, each on a line with a key and a value. An empty line ends the headers. Finally, the entity bytes follows, either up to the content length or up to the end of the stream.

You might wonder what the request looked like when it went over the network? You can find it out using the same technique.

```
| request |
request := (ZnClient new)
    url: 'http://zn.stfx.eu/zn/small.html';
    get;
    request.
request writeOn: Transcript.
Transcript flush.
```

In an opened Transcript you will now see:

```
GET /zn/small.html HTTP/1.1
Accept: */*
User-Agent: Zinc HTTP Components 1.0
Host: zn.stfx.eu
```

A ZnRequest object consists of 3 elements:

1. a ZnRequestLine object,
2. a ZnHeaders object and
3. an optional ZnEntity object.

4.2 Doing a Simple Request

The request line contains the HTTP method (sometimes called verb), URL and the HTTP protocol version. Next come the request headers, similar to the response headers, meta data including:

- the host we want to talk to,
- the kind of mime-types that we accept or prefer, and
- the user-agent that we are.

If you look carefully at the Transcript you will see the empty line terminating the headers. For most kinds of requests, like for a GET, there is no entity.

For debugging and for learning, it can be helpful to enable logging on the client. Try the following.

```
ZnClient new
   logToTranscript;
   get: 'http://zn.stfx.eu/zn/small.html'.
```

This will print out some information on the Transcript, as shown below.

```
2015-03-26 20:32:30 001 Connection Established zn.stfx.eu:80
    46.137.113.215 223ms
2015-03-26 20:32:30 002 Request Written a ZnRequest(GET
    /zn/small.html) 0ms
2015-03-26 20:32:30 003 Response Read a ZnResponse(200 OK
    text/html;charset=utf-8 113B) 223ms
2015-03-26 20:32:30 004 GET /zn/small.html 200 113B 223ms
```

In a later subsection about server logging, which uses the same mechanism, you will learn how to interpret and customize logging.

Simplified HTTP Requests

Although `ZnClient` is absolutely the preferred object to deal with all the intricacies of HTTP, you sometimes wish you could to a quick HTTP request with an absolute minimum amount of typing, especially during debugging. For these occasions there is `ZnEasy`, a class side only API for quick HTTP requests.

```
ZnEasy get: 'http://zn.stfx.eu/zn/numbers.txt'.
```

The result is always a `ZnResponse` object. Apart from basic authentication, there are no other options. A nice feature here, more as an example, is some direct ways to ask for image resources as ready to use Forms.

```
ZnEasy getGif:
   'http://esug.org/data/Logos+Graphics/ESUG-Logo/2006/gif/',
   'esug-Logo-Version3.3.-13092006.gif'.
ZnEasy getJpeg: 'http://caretaker.wolf359.be/sun-fire-x2100.jpg'.
ZnEasy getPng: 'http://pharo.org/files/pharo.png'.
```

```
(ZnEasy getPng: 'http://chart.googleapis.com/chart?cht=tx&chl=',
   'a^2+b^2=c^2') asMorph openInHand.
```

When you explore the implementation, you will notice that ZnEasy uses a ZnClient object internally.

4.3 HTTP Success?

A simple view of HTTP is: you request a resource and get a response back containing the resource. But even if the mechanics of HTTP did work, and even that is not guaranteed (see the next section), the response could not be what you expected.

HTTP defines a whole set of so called status codes to define various situations. These codes turn up as part of the status line of a response. The dictionary mapping numeric codes to their textual reason string is predefined.

```
ZnConstants httpStatusCodes.
```

A good overview can be found in the Wikipedia article List of HTTP status codes[5]. The most common code, the one that indicates success is numeric code 200 with reason 'OK'. Have a look at the testing protocol of ZnResponse for how to interpret some of them.

So if you do an HTTP request and get something back, you cannot just assume that all is well. You first have to make sure that the call itself (more specifically the response) was successful. As mentioned before, this is done by sending isSuccess to the response or the client.

```
| client |
client := ZnClient new.
client get: 'http://zn.stfx.eu/zn/numbers.txt'.
client isSuccess
   ifTrue: [ client contents lines collect: [ :each | each asNumber 
      ] ]
   ifFalse: [ self inform: 'Something went wrong' ]
```

To make it easier to write better HTTP client code, ZnClient offers some useful status handling methods in its API. You can ask the client to consider non-successful HTTP responses as errors with the enforceHTTPSuccess option. The client will then automatically throw a ZnHTTPUnsuccesful exception. This is generally useful when the application code that uses Zinc handles errors.

Additionally, to install a local failure handler, there is the ifFail: option. This will invoke a block, optionally passing an exception, whenever something goes wrong. Together, this allows the above code to be rewritten as follows.

---

[5]http://en.wikipedia.org/wiki/List_of_HTTP_status_codes

```
ZnClient new
    enforceHttpSuccess: true;
    ifFail: [ :ex | self inform: 'Cannot get numbers: ', ex
      printString ];
    get: 'http://zn.stfx.eu/zn/numbers.txt'.
```

Maybe it doesn't look like a big difference, but combined with some other options and features of ZnClient that we'll see later on, the code does become more elegant and more reliable at the same time.

4.4 Dealing with Networking Reality

As a network protocol, HTTP is much more complicated than an ordinary message send. The famous Fallacies of Distributed Computing[6] paper by Deutsch et. al. eloquently lists the issues involved:

- The network is reliable.
- Latency is zero.
- Bandwidth is infinite.
- The network is secure.
- Topology doesn't change.
- There is one administrator.
- Transport cost is zero.
- The network is homogeneous.

Zn will signal various exceptions when things go wrong, at different levels. ZnClient and the underlying framework have constants, settings and options to deal with various aspects related to these issues.

Doing an HTTP request-response cycle can take an unpredictable amount of time. Client code has to specify a timeout: the maximum amount of time to wait for a response, and be prepared for when that timeout is exceeded. When there is no answer within a specified timeout can mean that some networking component is extremely slow, but it could also mean that the server simply refuses to answer.

Setting the timeout directly on a ZnClient is the easiest.

```
ZnClient new
    timeout: 1;
    get: 'http://zn.stfx.eu/zn/small.html'.
```

The timeout counts for each socket level connect, read and write operation, separately. You can dynamically redefine the timeout using the ZnConnectionTimeout class, which is a DynamicVariable subclass.

---

[6]http://en.wikipedia.org/wiki/Fallacies_of_Distributed_Computing

```
ZnConnectionTimeout
    value: 5
    during: [ ^ ZnClient new get: 'http://zn.stfx.eu/zn/small.html' ].
```

Zn defines its global default timeout in seconds as a setting.

```
ZnNetworkingUtils defaultSocketStreamTimeout.
ZnNetworkingUtils defaultSocketStreamTimeout: 60.
```

This setting affects most framework level operations, if nothing else is specified.

During the execution of HTTP, various network exceptions, as subclasses of NetworkError, might be thrown. These will all be caught by the ifFail: block when installed.

To deal with temporary or intermittent network or server problems, ZnClient offers a retry protocol. You can set how many times a request should be retried and how many seconds to wait between retries.

```
ZnClient new
    numberOfRetries: 3;
    retryDelay: 2;
    get: 'http://zn.stfx.eu/zn/small.html'.
```

In the above example, the request will be tried up to 3 times, with a 2 second delay between attempts. Note that the definition of failure/success is broad: it includes for example the option to enforce HTTP success.

4.5 Building URL's

Zn uses ZnUrl objects to deal with URLs. ZnClient also contains an API to build URLs. Let us revisit our initial example, using explicit URL construction with the ZnClient API.

```
ZnClient new
    http;
    host: 'zn.stfx.eu';
    addPath: 'zn';
    addPath: 'small.html';
    get.
```

Instead of giving a string argument to be parsed into a ZnUrl, we now provide the necessary elements to construct the URL manually, by sending messages to our ZnClient object. With http we set what is called the scheme. Then we set the hostname. Since we don't specify a port, the default port for HTTP will be used, port 80. Next we add path elements, extending the path one by one.

A URL can also contain query parameters. Let's do a Google search as an example:

```
ZnClient new
    http;
    host: 'www.google.com';
    addPath: 'search';
    queryAt: 'q' put: 'Pharo Smalltalk';
    get.
```

Query parameters have a name and a value. Certain special characters have to be encoded. You can build the same URL with the ZnUrl object, in several ways.

```
ZnUrl new
    scheme: #http;
    host: 'www.google.com';
    port: 80;
    addPathSegment: 'search';
    queryAt: 'q' put: 'Pharo Smalltalk';
    yourself.
```

If you print the above expression, it gives you the printable representation of the URL.

```
http://www.google.com/search?q=Pharo%20Smalltalk
```

This string version can easily be parsed again into a ZnUrl object

```
'http://www.google.com/search?q=Pharo%20Smalltalk' asZnUrl.
'http://www.google.com:80/search?q=Pharo Smalltalk' asZnUrl.
```

Note how the ZnUrl parser is forgiving with respect to the space, like most browsers would do. When producing an external representation, proper encoding will take place. Please consult the class comment of ZnUrl for a more detailed look at the capabilities of ZnUrl as a standalone object.

4.6 Submitting HTML Forms

In many web applications HTML forms are used. Examples are forms to enter a search string, a form with a username and password to log in or complex registration forms. In the classic and most common way, this is implemented by sending the data entered in the fields of a form to the server when a submit button is clicked. It is possible to implement the same behavior programmatically using ZnClient.

First you have to find out how the form is implemented by looking at the HTML code. Here is an example.

```
<form action="search-handler" method="POST"
    enctype="application/x-www-form-urlencoded">
  Search for: <input type="text" name="search-field"/>
  <input type="submit" value="Go!"/>
</form>
```

This form shows one text input field, preceded by a 'Search for:' label and
followed by a submit button with 'Go!' as label. Assuming this appears on a
page with URL http://www.search-engine.com/, we can implement the
behavior of the browser when the user clicks the button, submitting or sending the form data to the server.

```
ZnClient new
   url: 'http://www.search-engine.com/search-handler';
   formAt: 'search-field' put: 'Pharo Smalltalk';
   post.
```

The URL is composed by combining the URL of the page that contains the
form with the action specified. There is no need to set the encoding of the
request here because the form uses the default encoding application/x-
www-form-urlencoded. By using the formAt:put: method to set the value
of a field, an entity of type ZnApplicationFormUrlEncodedEntity will be
created if needed, and the field name/value association will be stored in it.
When finally post is invoked, the HTTP request sent to the server will include a properly encoded entity. As far as the server is concerned, it will
seem as if a real user submitted the form. Consequently, the response should
be the same as when you submit the form manually using a browser. Be care-
ful to include all relevant fields, even the hidden ones.

There is a second type of form encoding called multipart/form-data. Here,
instead of adding fields, you add ZnMimePart instances.

```
<form action="search-handler" method="POST"
    enctype="multipart/form-data">
  Search for: <input type="text" name="search-field"/>
  <input type="submit" value="Go!"/>
</form>
```

The code to submit this form would then be as follows.

```
ZnClient new
   url: 'http://www.search-engine.com/search-handler';
   addPart: (ZnMimePart
               fieldName: 'search-field'
               value: 'Pharo Smalltalk');
   post.
```

In this case, an entity of type ZnMultiPartFormDataEntity is created and
used. This type is often used in forms that upload files. Here is an example.

```
<form action="upload-handler" method="POST"
    enctype="multipart/form-data">
  Photo file: <input type="file" name="photo-file"/>
  <input type="submit" value="Upload!"/>
</form>
```

This would be the way to do the upload programmatically.

```
ZnClient new
    url: 'http://www.search-engine.com/upload-handler';
    addPart: (ZnMimePart
                fieldName: 'photo-file'
                fileNamed: '/Pictures/cat.jpg');
    post.
```

Sometimes, the form's submit method is GET instead of POST, just send `get` instead of `post` to the client. Note that this technique of sending form data to a server is different than what happens with raw POST or PUT requests using a REST API. In a later subsection we will come back to this.

4.7 Basic Authentication, Cookies and Sessions

There are various techniques to add authentication, a mechanism to control who accesses which resources, to HTTP. This is orthogonal to HTTP itself. The simplest and most common form of authentication is called 'Basic Authentication'.

```
ZnClient new
    username: 'john@hacker.com' password: 'trustno1';
    get: 'http://www.example.com/secret.txt'.
```

That is all there is to it. If you want to understand how this works, look at how `ZnRequest>>#setBasicAuthenticationUsername:password:` is implemented.

Basic authentication over plain HTTP is insecure because it transfers the username/password combination obfuscated by encoding it using the trivial Base64 encoding. When used over HTTPS, basic authentication is secure though. Note that when sending multiple requests while reusing the same client, authentication is reset for each request, to prevent the accidental transfer of sensitive data.

Basic authentication is not the same as a web application where you have to log in using a form. In such web applications, e.g an online store that has a login part and a shopping cart per user, state is needed. During the interaction with the web application, the server needs to know that your requests/responses are part of your session: you log in, you add items to your shopping cart and you finally check out and pay. It would be problematic if the server mixed the requests/responses of different users. However, HTTP is by design a stateless protocol: each request/response cycle is independent. This principle is crucial to the scalability of the internet.

The most commonly used technique to overcome this issue, enabling the tracking of state across different request/response cycles is the use of so called cookies. Cookies are basically key/value pairs connected to a specific server domain. Using a special header, the server asks the client to remember or update the value of a cookie for a domain. On subsequent requests to the same domain, the client will use a special header to present the cookie and its value back to the server. Semantically, the server manages a key/value pair on the client.

As we saw before, a `ZnClient` instance is essentially stateful. It not only tries to reuse a network connection but it also maintains a `ZnUserAgentSession` object, which represents the session. One of the main functions of this session object is to manage cookies, just like your browser does. `ZnCookie` objects are held in a `ZnCookieJar` object inside the session object.

Cookie handling will happen automatically. This is a hypothetical example of how this might work, assuming a site where you have to log in before you are able to access a specific file.

```
ZnClient new
    url: 'http://cloud-storage.com/login';
    formAt: 'username' put: 'john.doe@acme.com';
    formAt: 'password' put: 'trustno1';
    post;
    get: 'http://cloud-storage.com/my-file'.
```

After the `post`, the server will presumably set a cookie to acknowledge a successful login. When a specific file is next requested from the same domain, the client presents the cookie to prove the login. The server knows it can send back the file because it recognizes the cookie as valid. By sending `session` to the client object, you can access the session object and then the remembered cookies.

4.8 PUT, POST, DELETE and other HTTP Methods

A regular request for a resource is done using a GET request. A GET request does not send an entity to the server. The only way for a GET request to transfer information to the server is by encoding it in the URL, either in the path or in query variables. (To be 100% correct we should add that data can be sent as custom headers as well.)

PUT and POST Methods

HTTP provides for two methods (or verbs) to send information to a server. These are called PUT and POST. They both send an entity to the server in order to transfer data.

In the subsection about submitting HTML forms we already saw how POST is used to send either a `ZnApplicationFormUrlEncodedEntity` or to send a `ZnMultiPartFormDataEntity` containing structured data to a server.

Apart from that, it is also possible to send a raw entity to a server. Of course, the server needs to be prepared to handle this kind of entity coming in. Here are a couple of examples of doing a raw PUT and POST request.

4.8 PUT, POST, DELETE and other HTTP Methods

```
ZnClient new
    put: 'http://zn.stfx.eu/echo' contents:'Hello there!'.

ZnClient new
    post: 'http://zn.stfx.eu/echo' contents: #[0 1 2 3 4 5 6 7 8 9].

ZnClient new
    entity: (ZnEntity
                with: '<xml><object><id>42</id></object></xml>'
                type: ZnMimeType applicationXml);
    post.
```

In the last example we explicitly set the entity to be XML and do a POST. In the first two examples, the convenience contents system is used to automatically create a ZnStringEntity of the type ZnMimeType textPlain, respectively a ZnByteArrayEntity of the type ZnMimeType applicationOctect-Stream.

The difference between PUT and POST is semantic. POST is generally used to create a new resource inside an existing collection or container, or to initiate some action or process. For this reason, the normal response to a POST request is to return the URL (or URI) of the newly created resource. Conventionally, the reponse contains this URL both in the Location header accessible via the message location and in the entity part.

When a POST successfully created the resource, its HTTP response will be 201 Created. PUT is generally used to update an existing resource of which you know the exact URL (or URI). When a PUT is successful, its HTTP response will be just 200 OK and nothing else will be returned. When we will discuss REST Web Service APIs, we will come back to this.

DELETE and other Methods

The fourth member of the common set of HTTP methods is DELETE. It is very similar to both GET and PUT: you just specify an URL of the resource that you want to delete or remove. When successful, the server will just reply with a 200 OK. That is all there is to it.

Certain HTTP based protocols, like WebDAV, use even more HTTP methods. These can be queried explicitly using the method: setter and the execute operation.

```
ZnClient new
    url: 'http://www.apache.org';
    method: #OPTIONS;
    execute;
    response.
```

An OPTIONS request does not return an entity, but only meta data that are included in the header of the response. In this example, the response header contains an extra meta data named `Allow` which specifies the list of HTTP methods that may be used on the resource.

4.9 Reusing Network Connections, Redirect Following and Checking for Newer Data

ZnClient Lifecycle

HTTP 1.1 defaults to keeping the client connection to a server open, and the server will do the same. This is useful and faster if you need to issue more than one request. `ZnClient` implements this behavior by default.

```
Array streamContents: [ :stream | | client |
    client := ZnClient new url: 'http://zn.stfx.eu'.
    (1 to: 10) collect: [ :each | | url |
      url := '/random/', each asString.
      stream nextPut: (client path: url; get) ].
    client close ].
```

The above example sets up a client to connect to a specific host. Then it collects the results of 10 different requests, asking for random strings of a specific size. All requests will go over the same network connection.

Neither party is required to keep the connection open for a long time, as this consumes resources. Both parties should be prepared to deal with connections closing, this is not an error. `ZnClient` will try to reuse an existing connection and reconnect once if this reuse fails. The option `connectionReuseTimeout` limits the maximum age for a connection to be reused.

Note how we also close the client using the message `close`. A network connection is an external resource, like a file, that should be properly closed after use. If you don't do that, they will get cleaned up eventually by the system, but it is more efficient to do it yourself.

In many situations, you only want to do one single request. HTTP 1.1 has provisions for this situation. The beOneShot option of `ZnClient` will do just that.

```
ZnClient new
    beOneShot;
    get: 'http://zn.stfx.eu/numbers.txt'.
```

With the beOneShot option, the client notifies the server that it will do just one request and both parties will consequently close the connection after use, automatically. In this case, an explicit close of the `ZnClient` object is no longer needed.

Redirects

Sometimes when requesting a URL, an HTTP server will not answer immediately but redirect you to another location. For example, Seaside actually does this on each request. This is done with a 301 or 302 response code. You can ask a ZnResponse whether it's a redirect with isRedirect. In case of a redirect response, the Location header will contain the location the server redirects you to. You can access that URL using location.

By default, ZnClient will follow redirects automatically for up to 3 redirects. You won't even notice unless you activate logging. If for some reason you want to disable this feature, send a followRedirects: false to your client. To modify the maximum number of redirects that could be followed, use maxNumberOfRedirects:.

Following redirects can be tricky when PUT or POST are involved. Zn implements the common behavior of changing a redirected PUT or POST into a GET while dropping the body entity. Cookies will be resubmitted. Zn also handles relative redirect URLs, although these are not strictly part of the standard.

If-Modified-Since

A client that already requested a resource in the past can also ask a server if that resource has been modified, i.e. is newer, since he last requested it. If so, the server will give a quick 304 Not Modified response without sending the resource over again. This is done by setting the If-Modified-Since header using ifModifiedSince:. This works both for regular requests as well as for downloads.

```
ZnClient new
    url: 'http://zn.stfx.eu/zn/numbers.txt';
    setIfModifiedSince: (Date year: 2011 month: 1 day: 1);
    downloadTo: FileLocator imageDirectory.

ZnClient new
    url: 'http://zn.stfx.eu/zn/numbers.txt';
    setIfModifiedSince: (Date year: 2012 month: 1 day: 1);
    get;
    response.
```

For this to work, the server has to honor this particular protocol interaction, of course.

4.10 Content-Types, Mime-Types and the Accept Header

Asking for a resource with a certain mime-type does not mean that the server will return something of this type. The extension at the end of a URL has no real significance, and the server might have been reconfigured since last you asked for this resource. For example, asking for http://example.com/foo, http://example.com/foo.txt or http://example.com/foo.text could all be the same or all be different, and this may change over time. This is why HTTP resources (entities) are accompanied by a content-type: a mime-type that is an official, cross-platform definition of a file or document type or format. Again, see the Wikipedia article Internet media type[7] for more details.

Zn models mime-types using its ZnMimeType object which has 3 components:

- a main type, for example text or image,
- a sub type, for example plain or html, or jpeg, png or gif, and
- a number of attributes, for example charset=utf-8.

The class side of ZnMimeType has some convenience methods for accessing well known mime-types, for example:

```
ZnMimeType textHtml.
```

Note that for textual (non-binary) types, the encoding defaults to UTF-8, the prevalent internet standard. Creating a ZnMimeType object is also as easy as sending asZnMimeType to a String.

```
'text/html;charset=utf-8' asZnMimeType.
```

The subtype can be a wildcard, indicated by a *. This allows for matching.

```
ZnMimeType textHtml matches: ZnMimeType text.
```

With ZnClient you can set the accept request header to indicate what you as a client expect, and optionally enforce that the server returns the type you asked for.

```
ZnClient new
    enforceAcceptContentType: true;
    accept: ZnMimeType textPlain;
    get: 'http://zn.stfx.eu/zn/numbers.txt'.
```

The above code indicates to the server that we want a text/plain type resource by means of the Accept header. When the response comes back and it is not of that type, the client will raise a ZnUnexpectedContentType exception. Again, this will be handled by the ifFail: block, when specified.

4.11 Headers

HTTP meta data, both for requests and for responses, is specified using headers. These are key/value pairs, both strings. A large number of predefined

---

[7] http://en.wikipedia.org/wiki/Mime-type

headers exists, see this List of HTTP header fields[8]. The exact semantics of each header, especially their value, can be very complicated. Also, although headers are key/value pairs, they are more than a regular dictionary. There can be more values for the same key and keys are often written using a canonical capitalization, like Content-Type.

HTTP provides for a way to do a request, just like a regular GET but with a response that contains only the meta data, the status line and headers, but not the actual resource or entity. This is called a HEAD request.

```
ZnClient new
    head: 'http://zn.stfx.eu/zn/small.html';
    response.
```

Since there is no content, we have to look at the headers of the response object. Note that the content-type and content-length headers will be set, as if there was an entity, although none is transferred.

ZnClient allows you to easily specify custom headers for which there is not yet a predefined accessor, which is most of them. At the framework level, ZnResponse and ZnRequest offer some more predefined accessors, as well as a way to set and query any custom header by accessing their headers sub object. The following are all equivalent:

```
ZnClient new accept: 'text/*'.
ZnClient new request setAccept: 'text/*'.
ZnClient new request headers at: 'Accept' put: 'text/*'.
ZnClient new request headers at: 'ACCEPT' put: 'text/*'.
ZnClient new request headers at: 'accept' put: 'text/*'.
```

Once a request is executed, you can query the response headers like this:

```
client response isConnectionClose.
(client response headers at: 'Connection' ifAbsent: [ '' ])
    sameAs: 'close'.
```

4.12 Entities, Content Readers and Writers

As mentioned before, ZnMessages (ZnRequests and ZnResponses) can hold an optional ZnEntity as body. By now we used almost all concrete subclasses of ZnEntity:

- ZnStringEntity
- ZnByteArrayEntity
- ZnApplicationFormUrlEncodedEntity
- ZnMultiPartFormDataEntity

---

[8] http://en.wikipedia.org/wiki/HTTP_header

- ZnStreamingEntity

Like all other fundamental Zn domain model objects, these can and are used both by clients and servers. All ZnEntities have a content type (a mime-type) and a content length (in bytes). Their basic behavior is that they can be written to or read from a binary stream. All but the last one are classic, in-memory objects.

ZnStreamingEntity is special: it contains a read or write stream to be used once in one direction only. If you want to transfer a 10 Mb file, using a normal entity, this would result in the 10 Mb being taken into memory. With a streaming entity, a file stream is opened to the file, and the data is then copied using a buffer of a couple of tens of Kb. This is obviously more efficient. The limitation is that this only works if the exact size is known up-front.

Knowing that a ZnStringEntity has a content type of XML or JSON is however not enough to interpret the data correctly. You might need a parser to convert the representation to Smalltalk or a writer to convert Smalltalk into the proper representation. That is where the ZnClient options contentReader and contentWriter are useful.

If the content reader is nil (the default), contents will return the contents of the response object, usually a String or ByteArray.

To customize the content reader, you specify a block that will be given the incoming entity and that is then supposed to parse the incoming representation, for example as below:

```
ZnClient new
   systemPolicy;
   url: 'http://zn.stfx.eu/zn/numbers.txt';
   accept: ZnMimeType textPlain;
   contentReader: [ :entity |
      entity contents lines
         collect: [ :each | each asInteger ] ];
   get.
```

In this example, get (which returns the same as contents) will no longer return a String but a collection of numbers. Note also that by using systemPolicy in combination with an accept: we handle most error cases before the content reader start doing its work, so it does no longer have to check for good incoming data. In any case, when the contentReader throws an exception, it can be caught by the ifFail: block.

If the content writer is nil (the default), contents: will take a Smalltalk object and pass it to ZnEntity class' with: instance creation method. This will create either a text/plain String entity or an application/octect-stream ByteArray entity.

You could further customize the entity by sending `contentType:` with another mime type. Or you could completely skip the `contents:` mechanism and supply your own entity to `entity:`.

To customize the content writer, you need to pass a one-argument block to the `contentWriter:` message. The block should create and return an entity. A theoretical example is given next.

```
ZnClient new
   url: 'http://internet-calculator.com/sum';
   contentWriter: [ :numberCollection |
      ZnEntity text:
         (Character space join:
            (numberCollection collect: [ :each | each asString ])) ];
   contentReader: [ :entity | entity contents asNumber ];
   post.
```

Assuming there is a web service at `http://internet-calculator.com` where you can send numbers to, we send a whitespace separated list of numbers to its sum URI and expect a number back. Exceptions occuring in the content writer can be caught with the `ifFail:` block.

4.13 Downloading, Uploading and Signalling Progress

Often, you want to download a resource from some internet server and store its contents in a file. The well known curl and wget Unix utilities are often used to do this in scripts. There is a handy convenience method in `ZnClient` to do just that.

```
ZnClient new
   url: 'http://zn.stfx.eu/zn/numbers.txt';
   downloadTo: FileLocator imageDirectory.
```

The example will download the URL and save it in a file named `numbers.txt` next to your image. The argument to `downloadTo:` can be a `FileReference` or a path string, designating either a file or a directory. When it is a directory, the last component of the URL will be used to create a new file in that directory. When it is a file, that file will be used as given. Additionally, the `downloadTo:` operation will use streaming so that a large file will not be taken into memory all at once, but will be copied in a loop using a buffer.

The inverse, uploading the raw contents of file, is just as easy thanks to the convenience method `uploadEntityFrom:`. Given a file reference or a path string, it will set the current request entity to a `ZnStreamingEntity` reading bytes from the named file. The content type will be guessed based on the file name extension. If needed you can next override that mime type using `contentType:`. Here is a hypothetical example uploading the contents of the file `numbers.txt` using a POST to the URL specified, again using an efficient streaming copy.

```
ZnClient new
    url: 'http://cloudstorage.com/myfiles/';
    username: 'john@foo.co.uk' password: 'asecret';
    uploadEntityFrom: FileLocator imageDirectory / 'numbers.txt';
    post.
```

Some HTTP operations, particularly those involving large resources, might take some time, especially when slower networks or servers are involved. During interactive use, Pharo Smalltalk often indicates progress during operations that take a bit longer. ZnClient can do that too using the signal-Progress option. By default this is off. Here is an example.

```
UIManager default informUserDuring: [ :bar |
    bar label: 'Downloading latest Pharo image...'.
    [ ^ ZnClient new
        signalProgress: true;
        url: 'http://files.pharo.org/image/stable/latest.zip';
        downloadTo: FileLocator imageDirectory ]
    on: HTTPProgress
    do: [ :progress |
        bar label: progress printString.
        progress isEmpty ifFalse: [ bar current: progress
    percentage ].
        progress resume ] ]
```

4.14 Client Options, Policies and Proxies

To handle its large set of options, ZnClient implements a uniform, generic option mechanism using the optionAt:put: and optionAt:ifAbsent: methods (this last one always defines an explicit default), storing them lazily in a dictionary. The method category options includes all accessors to actual settings.

Options are generally named after their accessor, a notable exception is beOneShot. For example, the timeout option has a getter named timeout and setter named timeout: whose implementation defines its default

```
^ self
    optionAt: #timeout
    ifAbsent: [ ZnNetworkingUtils defaultSocketStreamTimeout ]
```

The set of all option defaults defines the default policy of ZnClient. For certain scenarios, there are policy methods that set several options at once. The most useful one is called systemPolicy. It specifies good practice behavior for when system level code does an HTTP call:

```
ZnClient>>systemPolicy
    self
        enforceHttpSuccess: true;
```

```
        enforceAcceptContentType: true;
        numberOfRetries: 2
```

Also, in some networks you do not talk to internet web servers directly, but indirectly via a proxy. Such a proxy controls and regulates traffic. A proxy can improve performance by caching often used resources, but only if there is a sufficiently high hit rate.

Zn client functionality will automatically use the proxy settings defined in your Pharo image. The UI to set a proxy host, port, username or password can be found in the Settings browser under the Network category. Accessing localhost will bypass the proxy. To find out more about Zn's usage of the proxy settings, start by browsing the `proxy` method category of `ZnNetworkingUtils`.

4.15 Conclusion

Zinc is a solid and very flexible HTTP library. This chapter only presented the client-side of Zinc i.e. how to use it to send HTTP requests and receive responses back. Through several code examples, we demonstrated some of the possibilities of Zinc and also its simplicity. Zinc relies on a very good object-centric decomposition of the HTTP concepts. It results in an easy to understand and extensible library.

CHAPTER 5

Zinc HTTP: The Server Side

Sven Van Caekenberghe with Luc Fabresse and Johan Fabry

Zinc is both a client and server HTTP library written and maintained by Sven van Caekenberghe. HTTP clients and servers are each others' mirror: An HTTP client sends a request and receives a response. An HTTP server receives a request and sends a response. Hence the fundamental Zn framework objects are used to implement both clients and servers.

This chapter focuses on the server-side features of Zinc and demonstrates through small, elegant and robust examples some possibilities of this powerful library. The client side is described in Chapter Zinc Client side

5.1 Running a Simple HTTP Server

Getting an independent HTTP server up and running inside a Pharo image is surprisingly easy.

```
ZnServer startDefaultOn: 1701.
```

Don't try this just yet. To be able to see what is going on, it is better to enable logging, as follows:

```
(ZnServer defaultOn: 1701)
   logToTranscript;
   start.
```

This starts the default HTTP server, listening on port 1701. We use 1701 in the example because using a port below 1024 requires special OS level privileges, and ports like 8080 might already be in use. Visiting http://localhost:1701 with a browser yields the Zn welcome page. The Transcript produces output related to the server's activities, for example:

```
2015-06-11 18:06:31 001 565881 Server Socket Bound 0.0.0.0:1701
2015-06-11 18:06:31 002 275888 Started ZnManagingMultiThreadedServer
    HTTP port 1701
2015-06-11 18:06:35 003 565881 Connection Accepted 127.0.0.1
2015-06-11 18:06:35 004 097901 Request Read a ZnRequest(GET /) 0ms
2015-06-11 18:06:35 005 097901 Request Handled a ZnRequest(GET /) 0ms
2015-06-11 18:06:35 006 097901 Response Written a ZnResponse(200 OK
    text/html;charset=utf-8 977B) 2ms
2015-06-11 18:06:35 007 097901 GET / 200 977B 2ms
2015-06-11 18:06:35 008 097901 Request Read a ZnRequest(GET
    /favicon.ico) 129ms
2015-06-11 18:06:35 009 097901 Request Handled a ZnRequest(GET
    /favicon.ico) 0ms
2015-06-11 18:06:35 010 097901 Response Written a ZnResponse(200 OK
    image/vnd.microsoft.icon 318B) 2ms
2015-06-11 18:06:35 011 097901 GET /favicon.ico 200 318B 2ms
2015-06-11 18:06:35 012 097901 Request Read a ZnRequest(GET
    /favicon.ico) 32ms
2015-06-11 18:06:35 013 097901 Request Handled a ZnRequest(GET
    /favicon.ico) 0ms
2015-06-11 18:06:35 014 097901 Response Written a ZnResponse(200 OK
    image/vnd.microsoft.icon 318B) 0ms
2015-06-11 18:06:35 015 097901 GET /favicon.ico 200 318B 0ms
2015-06-11 18:07:05 016 097901 Server Read Error ConnectionTimedOut:
    Data receive timed out.
2015-06-11 18:07:05 017 097901 Server Connection Closed 127.0.0.1
```

You can see the server starting and initializing its server socket on which it listens for incoming connections. When a connection comes in, it starts executing its request-response loop. Then it gets a GET request for / (the home page), to which it answers a 200 OK response with 997 bytes of HTML. The browser also asks for a favicon.ico, which the server supplies. The request-response loop is kept alive for some time and usually closes when the other end does. Although it looks like an error, it actually is normal, expected behavior.

The example uses the default server: Zn manages a default server to ease interactive experimentation. The server object is obtained by: ZnServer default. The default server also survives image save and restart cycles and needs to be stopped with ZnServer stopDefault. The Transcript output will confirm what happens:

```
2015-06-11 18:11:07 018 565881 Server Socket Released 0.0.0.0:1701
2015-06-11 18:11:07 019 275888 Stopped ZnManagingMultiThreadedServer
    HTTP port 1701
```

> **Note** Due to its implementation, the server will print a debug notification: Wait for accept timed out, every 5 minutes. Again, although it looks like an error, it is by design and normal, expected behavior.

5.2 Server Delegate, Testing and Debugging

The functional behavior of a ZnServer is defined by an object called its delegate. A delegate implements the key method handleRequest: which gets the incoming request as parameter and has to produce a response as result. The delegate only needs to reason in terms of a ZnRequest and a ZnResponse. The technical side of being an HTTP server, like the protocol itself, the networking and the (optional) multiprocessing, is handled by the server object.

This allows us to write what is arguably the simplest possible HTTP server behavior:

```
(ZnServer startDefaultOn: 1701)
   onRequestRespond: [ :request |
      ZnResponse ok: (ZnEntity text: 'Hello World!') ].
```

Now go to http://localhost:1701 or do:

```
ZnEasy get: 'http://localhost:1701'.
```

This server does not look at the incoming request. It always answers 200 OK with a text/plain string Hello World!. The onRequestRespond: method accepts a block that takes a request and that should produce a response. It is implemented using the helper object ZnValueDelegate, which converts handleRequest: to value: on a wrapped block.

The Default Server Delegate

Out of the box, a ZnServer will have a certain functionality that is related to testing and debugging. The ZnDefaultServerDelegate object implements this behavior. Assuming a server is running locally on port 1701, this is the list of URLs that are available.

- http://localhost:1701/ the default for /, equivalent to /welcome
- http://localhost:1701/bytes a collection of bytes
- http://localhost:1701/dw-bench a dynamically generated page for benchmarking
- http://localhost:1701/echo a textual response echoing the request
- http://localhost:1701/favicon.ico nice Zn favicon used by browsers
- http://localhost:1701/form-test-1 to /form-test-3 are form test pages
- http://localhost:1701/help this list of URLs
- http://localhost:1701/random a random string of characters
- http://localhost:1701/session information about the session

- http://localhost:1701/status a textual page showing some server internals
- http://localhost:1701/unicode a UTF-8 encoded page listing the first 591 Unicode characters
- http://localhost:1701/welcome the standard Zn greeting page

The random handler normally returns 64 characters, you can specify your own size as well. For example, /random/1024 will respond with a 1Kb random string. The random pattern consists of hexadecimal digits and ends with a linefeed. The standard, slower UTF-8 encoding is used instead of the faster LATIN-1 encoding.

The bytes handler has a similar size option. Its output is in the form of a repeating BCDA pattern. When requesting equally sized byte patterns repeatably, some extra server side caching will improve performance.

Testing and Debugging

The echo handler is used extensively by the unit tests. It not only lists the request headers as received by the server, but even the entity if there is one. In case of a non-binary entity, the textual contents will be included. This is really useful to debug PUT or POST requests.

In general, to help in debugging a server, enabling logging is important to learn what is going on. Breakpoints can be put anywhere in the server, but interrupting a running server can sometimes be a bit hard or produce strange results. This is because the server and its spawned handler subprocesses are different from the UI process.

When logging is enabled, the server will also keep track of the last request and response it processed. You can inspect these to find out what happened, even if there was no debugger raised.

5.3 Server Authenticator

Similar to the delegate, a ZnServer also has an authenticator object whose function is to authenticate requests. An authenticator has to implement the authenticateRequest:do: method whose first argument is the incoming request and second argument a block. This method has to produce a response, like handleRequest: does. If the request is allowed, the block should be evaluated, which will produce the response. If the request is denied, the authenticator should generate a 401 Unauthorized response. One simple authenticator is available to add basic HTTP authentication:

```
(ZnServer startDefaultOn: 1701)
    authenticator: (ZnBasicAuthenticator username: 'admin' password:
    'secret').
```

Now, when you try to visit the server at http://localhost:1701 you will have to provide a username and password. Note that it is also possible to use ZnEasy to send a get request to this URL with these credentials.

```
ZnEasy
    get: 'http://localhost:1701'
    username: 'admin'
    password: 'secret'.
```

> **Note** Using ZnBasicAuthenticator or implementing an alternative authenticator is only one of several possibilities to address the problem of adding security to a web site or web application.

5.4 Logging

Log output consists of a log message preceded by a number of fixed fields. Here is an example of a server log.

```
2015-06-11 10:19:59 001 220937 Server Socket Bound 0.0.0.0:1701
2015-06-11 10:19:59 002 233075 Started ZnManagingMultiThreadedServer
    HTTP port 1701
2015-06-11 10:25:36 003 220937 Connection Accepted 127.0.0.1
2015-06-11 10:25:36 004 879540 Request Read a ZnRequest(GET /help)
    2ms
2015-06-11 10:25:36 005 879540 Request Handled a ZnRequest(GET
    /help) 0ms
2015-06-11 10:25:36 006 879540 Response Written a ZnResponse(200 OK
    text/html;charset=utf-8 867B) 0ms
2015-06-11 10:25:36 007 879540 GET /help 200 867B 0ms
2015-06-11 10:25:38 008 879540 Request Read a ZnRequest(GET /help)
    1770ms
2015-06-11 10:25:38 009 879540 Request Handled a ZnRequest(GET
    /help) 0ms
2015-06-11 10:25:38 010 879540 Response Written a ZnResponse(200 OK
    text/html;charset=utf-8 867B) 0ms
2015-06-11 10:25:38 011 879540 GET /help 200 867B 0ms
2015-06-11 10:25:44 012 879540 Request Read a ZnRequest(GET
    /unicode) 6082ms
2015-06-11 10:25:44 013 879540 Request Handled a ZnRequest(GET
    /unicode) 5ms
2015-06-11 10:25:44 014 879540 Response Written a ZnResponse(200 OK
    text/html;charset=utf-8 11454B) 2ms
2015-06-11 10:25:44 015 879540 GET /unicode 200 11454B 7ms
```

The first two fields are the date and time in a fixed sized format. The next field is the id of the log entry. The next number is a fixed sized hash of the process ID. Note how 3 different processes are involved: the one starting the server (probably the UI process), the actual server listening process, and the client worker process spawned to handle the request.

Both ZnClient and ZnServer implement logging using a similar mechanism based on the announcements framework. ZnLogEvents are subclasses of the Announcement class and are sent by an HTTP server or client containing logging information. A log event has a TimeStamp, an id, and a message.

To log something, a server or client uses its own log methods. For example, a server receives a logConnectionAccepted: message with the socket that will process the request as argument. In ZnSingleThreadedServer, the implementation of logConnectionAccepted: is:

```
logConnectionAccepted: socket
    logLevel < 3 ifTrue: [ ^ nil ].
    ^ (self newLogEvent: ZnConnectionAcceptedEvent)
        address: ([ socket remoteAddress ] on: Error do: [ nil ]);
        emit
```

This logging mechnism can be easily customized by implementing subclasses of ZnLogEvent. For example, ZnConnectionAcceptedEvent is a subclass of ZnLogEvent customized for connection acceptation.

You can also provide your own listener for ZnLogEvents. The following example shows how to log events in a file named zn.log, next to the image.

```
| logger |
loggerStream := (Smalltalk imageDirectory / 'zn.log') writeStream.
ZnLogEvent announcer
    when: ZnLogEvent
    do: [ :event | loggerStream lf; print: event ].
(ZnServer defaultOn: 1701) start.
```

5.5 Server Variants and Life Cycle

The class side of ZnServer is actually a factory to instantiate a particular concrete ZnServer subclass, as can be seen in defaultServerClass. The hierarchy looks as follows.

```
ZnServer
    + ZnSingleThreadedServer
        + ZnMultiThreadedServer
            + ZnManagedMultiThreadedServer
```

ZnServer is an abstract class. ZnSingleThreadedServer implements the core server functionality. It runs in one single process, which means it can only handle one request at a time, making it easier to understand and debug. ZnMultiThreadedServer spawns a new process on each incoming request, possibly handling multiple request/response cycles on the same connection. ZnManagedMultiThreadedServers keeps explicit track of which connections are alive so that they can be stopped when the server stops instead of letting them die out.

Server instances can be started and stopped using start and stop. By registering a server instance, by sending it register, it becomes managed. That means it will survive image save and restart. This only happens automatically with the default server, for other server instances it needs to be enabled manually.

The main parameter a server needs is the port on which it will listen. Additionally, you can restrict the network interface the server should listen on by setting its bindingAddress: to some IP address. The default, which is nil or #[0 0 0 0], means to listen on all interfaces. With #[127 0 0 1], the server will not respond to requests over its normal network, but only to requests coming from the same host. This is often used to increase security while proxying.

```
(ZnServer defaultOn: 1701)
    bindingAddress: #[127 0 0 1];
    logToTranscript;
    start.
```

5.6 Static File Server

When most people think about a web server, they imagine what is technically called static file serving. There is a directory full of HTML, image, CSS, and other files, somewhere on a machine, and the web server serves these files over HTTP to web browser clients anywhere on the network. This is indeed what Apache does in its most basic form.

Zn can do this by using a ZnStaticFileServerDelegate. Given a directory and an optional prefix, this delegate will serve all files it finds in that directory, for example:

```
(ZnServer startDefaultOn: 1701)
    delegate: (
      ZnStaticFileServerDelegate new
          directory: '/var/www' asFileReference;
          prefixFromString: 'static-files';
          yourself).
```

If we suppose the contents of /var/www is

- index.html
- small.html

You can access these files with these URLs

- http://localhost:1701/static-files/index.html
- http://localhost:1701/static-files/small.html

The prefix is added in front of all files being served, the actual directory where the files reside is of course invisible to the end web user. If no prefix is specified, the files will be served directly.

Note how all other URLs result in a 404 Not found error. Note that while the ZnStaticFileServerDelegate is very simple, it does have a couple of capabilities. Most importantly, it will do what most people expect with respect to directories. Consider the following URLs:

- http://localhost:1701/static-files
- http://localhost:1701/static-files/

The first URL above will result in a redirect to the second. The second URL will look for either an index.html or index.htm file and serve that. Automatic generation of an index page when there is no index file is not implemented.

As a static file server, the following features are implemented:

- automatic determination of the content mime-type based on the file extension
- correct setting of the content length based on the file length
- usage of streaming
- addition of correct modification date based on the files' last modification date
- correct reaction to the if-modified-since protocol
- optional expiration and caching control

Here is a more complex example:

```
(ZnServer startDefaultOn: 1701)
    logToTranscript;
    delegate: (
        ZnStaticFileServerDelegate new
            directory: '/var/www' asFileReference;
            mimeTypeExpirations: ZnStaticFileServerDelegate
        defaultMimeTypeExpirations;
            yourself);
    authenticator: (
        ZnBasicAuthenticator username: 'admin' password: 'secret').
```

In the above example, we add the optional expiration and caching control based on default settings. Note that it is easy to combine static file serving with logging and authentication.

5.7 Dispatching

Dispatching or routing is HTTP application server speak for deciding what part of the software will handle an incoming request. This decision can be made on any of the properties of the request: the HTTP method, the URL or part of it, the query parameters, the meta headers and the entity body. Different applications will prefer different kinds of solutions to this problem.

Zinc HTTP Components is a general framework that offers all the necessary components to build your own dispatcher. Out of the box, there are the different delegates that we discussed before. Most of these have hand coded dispatching in their handleRequest: method.

ZnDefaultServerDelegate can be configured to perform dispatching as it uses a prefix map internally that maps URI prefixes to internal methods. Configuration is by installing a block as the value to a prefix, which accepts the request and produces a response. Here is an example of using that capability:

```
| staticFileServerDelegate |

ZnServer startDefaultOn: 8080.

(staticFileServerDelegate := ZnStaticFileServerDelegate new)
    prefixFromString: 'zn';
    directory: '/home/ubuntu/zn' asFileReference.

ZnServer default delegate prefixMap
    at: 'zn'
    put: [ :request | staticFileServerDelegate handleRequest: request
      ];
    at: 'redirect-to-zn'
    put: [ :request | ZnResponse redirect: '/zn/index.html' ];
    at: '/'
    put: 'redirect-to-zn'.
```

This is taken from the configuration of what runs at http://zn.stfx.eu. A static web server is set up under the zn prefix pointing to the directory /home//ubuntu/zn. The prefix map of the default delegate is kept as is, with its standard functionality, but is modified, such that

- anything with a zn prefix is directly forwarded to the static file server
- a special redirect-to-zn prefix is set up which will issue a redirect to /zn/index.html
- the default / handler is linked to redirect-to-zn instead of the default welcome:

Another option is to use ZnDispatcherDelegate.

```
(ZnServer startDefaultOn: 9090) delegate: (
   ZnDispatcherDelegate new
      map: '/hello'
      to: [ :request :response |
            response entity: (ZnEntity html: '<h1>hello!</h1>') ]).
```

You configure the dispatcher using map:to: methods. First argument is the prefix, second argument is a block taking two arguments: the incoming request and an already instantiated response.

5.8 Character Encoding

Proper character encoding and decoding is crucial in today's international world. Pharo Smalltalk encodes characters and strings using Unicode. The primary internet encoding is UTF-8, but a couple of others are used as well. To translate between these two, a concrete ZnCharacterEncoding subclass like ZnUTF8Encoder is used.

ZnCharacterEncoding is an extension and reimplementation of regular TextConverter. It only works on binary input and generated binary output and it adds the ability to compute the encoded length of a source character, a crucial operation for HTTP. It is more correct and will throw proper exceptions when things go wrong.

Character encoding is mostly invisible. Here are some code snippets using the encoders directly, feel free to substitute any Unicode character to make the test more interesting.

```
| encoder string |
encoder := ZnUTF8Encoder new.
string := 'any Unicode'.
self assert: (encoder decodeBytes: (encoder encodeString: string))
      equals: string.
encoder encodedByteCountForString: string.
```

There are no automatic conversions in Zinc, so no defaults are assumed. Instead you should specify a proper Content-Type header including the charset information. Otherwise Zinc has no chance of knowing what to use and the default NullEncoder will make your string wrong.

Consider the following example:

```
ZnServer startDefaultOn: 1701.

ZnClient new
   url: 'http://localhost:1701/echo';
   entity: (ZnEntity with: 'An der schönen blauen Donau');
   post.

ZnClient new
```

```
    url: 'http://localhost:1701/echo';
    entity: (
       ZnEntity
          with: 'An der schönen blauen Donau'
          type: (ZnMimeType textPlain charSet: #'iso-8859-1';
    yourself));
    post;
    yourself.
```

In the first case, a UTF-8 encoded string is POST-ed and correctly returned (in a UTF-8 encoded response).

In the second case, an ISO-8859-1 encoded string is POST-ed and correctly returned (in a UTF-8 encoded response).

In both cases the decoding was done correctly, using the specified charset (if that is missing, the ZnNullEncoder is used). Now, ö is not a perfect test example because its Unicode encoding value is 246 in decimal, U+00F6 in hex, still fits in 1 byte and hence survives null encoding/decoding (it would not be the case with € for example). That is why the following still works, although it is wrong to drop the charset.

```
ZnClient new
    url: 'http://localhost:1701/echo';
    entity: (
       ZnEntity
          with: 'An der schönen blauen Donau'
          type: (ZnMimeType textPlain clearCharSet; yourself));
    post;
    yourself.
```

5.9 Resource Protection Limits, Content and Transfer Encoding

Internet facing HTTP servers will come under attack by malicious clients. Good security is thus important. The first step is a correct and safe implementation of the HTTP protocol. Another way a server protects itself is by implementing some resource limits.

Zinc HTTP Components currently implements and enforces the following limits:

- maximumLineLength (4Kb), impacting mainly the size of a header pair
- maximumEntitySize (16Mb), the size of incoming entities
- maximumNumberOfDictionaryEntries (256), which is used in headers, URLs and some entities

Of course these values may be customized if one needs to.

Also, Zn implements two important techniques used by HTTP servers when they send entity bodies to clients: Gzip encoding and chunked transfer encoding. The first one adds compression. The second one is used when the size of an entity is not known up front. Instead chunks of certain sizes are sent until the entity is complete.

All this is handled internally and invisibly. The main object dealing with content and transfer encoding is ZnEntityReader. When necessary, the binary socket stream is wrapped with either a ZnChunkedReadStream and/or a GZipReadStream. Zn also makes use of a ZnLimitedReadStream to make sure there is no read beyond the boundaries of one single request's body, provided the content length is set.

5.10 Seaside Adaptor

Seaside[1] is a well known, cross platform, advanced Smalltalk web application framework. It does not provide its own HTTP server but relies on an existing one by means of an adaptor. It works well with Zn, through the use of a ZnZincServerAdaptor. It comes already included with certain Seaside distributions and on Pharo Smalltalk it is the default.

Starting this adaptor can be done using the Seaside Control panel in the normal way. Alternatively, the adaptor can be started programmatically.

```
ZnZincServerAdaptor startOn: 8080.
```

Since Seaside does its own character conversions, the Zn adaptor is configured to work in binary mode for maximum efficiency. There is complete support for POST and PUT requests with entities in form URL, multipart or raw encoding.

There is even a special adaptor that combines being a Seaside adaptor with static file serving, which is useful if you don't like the WAFileLibrary machinery and prefer plain static files served directly.

```
ZnZincStaticServerAdaptor startOn: 8080 andServeFilesFrom:
    '/var/www/'.
```

5.11 Scripting a REST Web Service with Zinc

As a last example of the use of Zinc HTTP, we now show the implementation of REST web services, both the client and the server parts. REST or Representational State Transfer[2] is an architectural style most easily described as using HTTP verbs and URIs to deal with encoded resources. Some kind of framework is needed to successfully implement a non-trivial REST service.

---

[1] http://www.seaside.st/
[2] http://en.wikipedia.org/wiki/Representational_state_transfer

5.11 Scripting a REST Web Service with Zinc

There is one available in the Zinc-REST-Server package, for example. Here we will implement a very small, simplified example by hand, for educational purposes.

The service will allow arbitrary JSON[3] objects to be stored on the server, each identified by an URI allocated by the server. Here is the REST API exposed by the server:

GET / Returns a list of all known stored object URIs;

GET /n Returns the JSON object known under URI /n;

POST / Creates a new entry with JSON as contents, returns the new URI;

PUT /n Updates (replaces) the contents of an existing JSON object known under URI /n;

DELETE /n Removes the JSON object known under URI /n.

The Server Code

A proper implementation should best use a couple of classes. However for brevity, the following implementation is written in a workspace, not using any classes. It requires STON (see Chapter STON) and starts by creating two global variables to hold the stored objects and the last ID used. The former is a standard dictionary mapping string URIs to objects.

```
JSONStore := Dictionary new.
ServerLastId := 0.
```

The server implementation uses two helper objects: a jsonEntityBuilder and a mapper. Both make use of block closures.

```
| jsonEntityBuilder mapper |

jsonEntityBuilder := [ :object |
   ZnEntity
      with: ((String streamContents: [ :stream |
         STON jsonWriter
            on: stream;
            prettyPrint: true;
            nextPut: object.
         stream cr ])
         replaceAll: Character cr with: Character lf)
      type: ZnMimeType applicationJson ].
```

The jsonEntityBuilder block helps in transforming Smalltalk objects to a JSON entity. We use the STON writer and reader here because they are backwards compatible with JSON. We use linefeeds to improve compatibility with

---
[3] http://www.json.org/

internet conventions as well as pretty printing to help human interpretation of the data.

```
mapper := {
   [ :request |
      request uri isSlash and: [ request method = #GET ] ]
   ->
   [ :request |
      ZnResponse
         ok: (jsonEntityBuilder value: JSONStore keys asArray) ].
"-----------------------------------------------------------------"
   [ :request |
      request uri pathSegments size = 1 and: [ request method = #GET
      ] ]
   ->
   [ :request | | uri |
      uri := request uri pathPrintString.
      JSONStore
         at: uri
         ifPresent: [ :object |
            ZnResponse ok: (jsonEntityBuilder value: object) ]
         ifAbsent: [ ZnResponse notFound: uri ] ].
"-----------------------------------------------------------------"
   [ :request |
      (request uri isSlash
         and: [ request method = #POST ])
         and: [ request contentType = ZnMimeType applicationJson ] ]
   ->
   [ :request | | uri |
      uri := '/', (ServerLastId := ServerLastId + 1) asString.
      JSONStore at: uri put: (STON fromString: request contents).
      (ZnResponse created: uri)
         entity: (jsonEntityBuilder value: 'Created ', uri);
         yourself ].
"-----------------------------------------------------------------"
   [ :request |
      (request uri pathSegments size = 1
         and: [ request method = #PUT ])
         and: [ request contentType = ZnMimeType applicationJson ]]
   ->
   [ :request | | uri |
      uri := request uri pathPrintString.
      (JSONStore includesKey: uri)
         ifTrue: [
            JSONStore
               at: uri
               put: (STON fromString: request contents).
            ZnResponse ok: (jsonEntityBuilder value: 'Updated') ]
         ifFalse: [ ZnResponse notFound: uri ] ].
"-----------------------------------------------------------------"
```

```
    [ :request |
      request uri pathSegments size = 1
          and: [ request method = #DELETE ] ]
    ->
    [ :request | | uri |
      uri := request uri pathPrintString.
      (JSONStore removeKey: uri ifAbsent: [ nil ])
         ifNil: [ ZnResponse notFound: uri ]
         ifNotNil: [
            ZnResponse ok: (jsonEntityBuilder value: 'Deleted') ] ].
}.
```

The mapper is a dynamically created array of associations (not a dictionary). Each association consists of two blocks. The first block is a condition: it tests a request and returns true when it matches. The second block is a handler that is evaluated with the incoming request to produce a response (if and only if the first condition matched).

The associations in the mapper follow exactly the list of the REST API as shown earlier. The server is set up with a block based delegate using the on-RequestRespond: method. Again, a more object-oriented implementation would use a proper delegate object here, but for this example, the block is sufficient.

The server logic thus becomes: find a matching entry in the mapper and invoke it. If no matching entry is found, we have a bad request. Error handling is of course rather limited in this small example.

```
(ZnServer startDefaultOn: 1701)
    logToTranscript;
    onRequestRespond: [ :request |
       (mapper
            detect: [ :each | each key value: request ]
            ifNone: [ nil ])
         ifNil: [ ZnResponse badRequest: request ]
         ifNotNil: [ :handler | handler value value: request ] ].
```

Using the Server

Here is an example command line session using the Unix utility curl[4], interacting with the server.

```
$ curl http://localhost:1701/
[ ]

$ curl -X POST -d '[1,2,3]' -H'Content-type:application/json'
    http://localhost:1701/
"Created /1"
```

---

[4] http://en.wikipedia.org/wiki/CURL

```
$ curl http://localhost:1701/1
[
    1,
    2,
    3
]

$ curl -X POST -d '{"bar":-2}' -H'Content-type:application/json'
    http://localhost:1701/
"Created /2"

$ curl http://localhost:1701/2
{
    "bar" : -2
}

$ curl -X PUT -d '{"bar":-1}' -H'Content-type:application/json'
    http://localhost:1701/2
"Updated /2"

$ curl http://localhost:1701/2
{
    "bar" : -1
}

$ curl http://localhost:1701/
[
    "/1",
    "/2"
]

$ curl -X DELETE http://localhost:1701/2
"Deleted /2"

$ curl http://localhost:1701/2
Not Found /2
```

A Zinc Client

It is trivial to use ZnClient to have the same interaction. But we can do better: using a contentWriter and contentReader, we can customise the client to do the JSON conversions automatically.

```
| client |

client := ZnClient new
    url: 'http://localhost:1701';
    enforceHttpSuccess: true;
    accept: ZnMimeType applicationJson;
```

```
    contentWriter: [ :object |
       ZnEntity
          with: (String streamContents: [ :stream |
                   STON jsonWriter on: stream; nextPut: object ])
          type: ZnMimeType applicationJson ];
    contentReader: [ :entity |   STON fromString: entity contents ];
    yourself.
```

Now we can hold the same conversation as above, only in this case in terms of real Smalltalk objects.

```
client get: '/'
--> #()

client post: '/' contents: #(1 2 3)
--> 'Created /1'

client get: '/1'
--> #(1 2 3)

client post: '/' contents: (Dictionary with: #bar -> -2)
---> 'Created /2'

client put: '/2' contents: (Dictionary with: #bar -> -1)
--> 'Updated'

client get: '/2'
--> a Dictionary('bar'->-1 )

client get: '/'
--> #('/1' '/2')

client delete: '/2'
--> 'Deleted'

client get: '/2'
--> throws a ZnHttpUnsuccessful exception
```

5.12 Conclusion

Zinc HTTP Components was written with the explicit goal of allowing users to explore the implementation. The test suite contains many examples that can serve as learning material. This carefulness while writing Zinc HTTP Components code now enable users to customize it to their need or to build on top of it. Zinc is indeed an extremely malleable piece of software.

CHAPTER 6

WebSockets

Sven Van Caekenberghe with Luc Fabresse

The WebSocket protocol defines a full-duplex single socket connection over which messages can be sent between a client and a server. It simplifies much of the complexity around bi-directional web communication and connection management. WebSocket represents the next evolutionary step in Web communication compared to Comet and Ajax. And of course, Zinc HTTP Components supports Web sockets as you will discover throughout this chapter.

6.1 An Introduction to WebSockets

HTTP, one of the main technologies of the internet, defines a communication protocol between a client and a server where the initiative of the communication lies with the client and each interaction consists of a client request and a server response. When correctly implemented and used, HTTP is enormously scaleable and very flexible.

With the arrival of advanced Web applications mimicking regular desktop applications with rich user interfaces, as well as mobile Web applications, it became clear that HTTP was not suitable or not a great fit for two use cases:

- When the server wants to take the initiative and send the client a message. In the HTTP protocol, the server cannot take the initiative to send a message, the only workaround is for the client to do some form of polling.

- When the client wants to send (many) (possibly asynchronous) short messages with little overhead. For short messages, the HTTP protocol adds quite a lot of overhead in the form of meta data headers. For many applications, the response (and the delay waiting for it) are not needed.

Previously, Comet and Ajax were used as (partial) solutions to these use cases. The WebSocket protocol defines a reliable communication channel between two equal parties, typically, but not necessarily, a Web client and a Web server, over which asynchronous messages can be send with very little overhead. Messages can be any String or ByteArray. Overhead is just a couple of bytes. There is no such thing as a direct reply or a synchronous confirmation.

Using WebSockets, a server can notify a client instantly of interesting events, and clients can quickly send small notifications to a server, possibly multiplexing many virtual communications channels over a single network socket.

6.2 The WebSocket Protocol

Zinc WebSockets implements RFC 6455[1], not any of the previous development versions. For an introduction, both the WebSocket Wikipedia article[2] and websocket.org[3] are good starting points.

As a protocol, WebSocket starts with an initial setup handshake that is based on HTTP. The initiative for setting up a WebSocket lies with the client, who is sending a so called connection upgrade request. The upgrade request contains a couple of special HTTP headers. The server begins as a regular HTTP server accepting the connection upgrade request. When the request conforms to the specification, a 101 Switching Protocols response is sent. This response also contains a couple of special HTTP headers. From that point on, the HTTP conversation over the network socket stops and the WebSocket protocol begins.

WebSocket messages consist of one or more frames with minimal encoding. Behind the scenes, a number of control frames are used to properly close the WebSocket and to manage keeping alive the connection using ping and pong frames.

6.3 Source Code

The code implementing Zinc WebSockets resides in a single package called 'Zinc-WebSocket-Core' in the Zinc HTTP Components repository. There is also an accompanying 'Zinc-WebSocket-Tests' package containing the unit tests. The ConfigurationOfZincHTTPComponents has a 'WebSocket' group that you can load separately. Here is the loading code snippet:

```
Gofer new
    smalltalkhubUser: 'SvenVanCaekenberghe' project:
    'ZincHTTPComponents';
```

---
[1] http://tools.ietf.org/html/rfc6455
[2] http://en.wikipedia.org/wiki/WebSocket
[3] http://www.websocket.org

```
package: 'ConfigurationOfZincHTTPComponents';
    load.
(Smalltalk globals at: #ConfigurationOfZincHTTPComponents) project
    latestVersion load: 'WebSocket'.
```

6.4 Using Client Side WebSockets

An endpoint for a WebSocket is specified using an URL:

```
ws://www.example.com:8088/my-app
```

Two new schemes are defined, `ws://` for regular WebSockets and `wss://` for the secure (TLS/SSL) variant. Zinc WebSockets supports the usage of client side WebSockets of both the regular and secure variants. Note that the secure variant requires loading the Zodiac TLS/SSL Pharo project[4]. The Zinc WebSockets API is really simple: you use `sendMessage:`, `readMessage` and finally `close` on an open socket.

Here is a client-side example talking to a public echo service:

```
| webSocket |
webSocket := ZnWebSocket to: 'ws://echo.websocket.org'.
[ webSocket
    sendMessage: 'Pharo Smalltalk using Zinc WebSockets !';
    readMessage ] ensure: [ webSocket close ].
```

Note that `readMessage` is blocking. It always returns a complete `String` or `ByteArray`, possible assembled out of multiple frames. Inside `readMessage` control frames will be handled automagically. Reading and sending are completely separate and independent.

For sending very large messages, there are `sendTextFrames:` and `sendByteFrames:` that take a collection of `Strings` or `ByteArrays` to be sent as different frames of the same message. At the other end, these will be joined together and seen as a single message.

In any non-trivial application, you will have to add your own encoding and decoding to messages. In many cases, JSON will be the obvious choice as the client end is often JavaScript. A modern, standalone JSON parser and writer is NeoJSON.

To use secure Web sockets, just use the proper URL scheme `wss://` as in the following example:

```
| webSocket |
webSocket := ZnWebSocket to: 'wss://echo.websocket.org'.
[ webSocket
    sendMessage: 'Pharo Smalltalk using Zinc WebSockets & Zodiac !';
    readMessage ] ensure: [ webSocket close ].
```

---

[4] http://smalltalkhub.com/#!/~SvenVanCaekenberghe/Zodiac

Of course, your image has to contain Zodiac and your VM needs access to the proper plugin. That should not be a problem with the latest Pharo releases.

6.5 Using Server-Side WebSockets

Since the WebSocket protocol starts off as HTTP, it is logical that a ZnServer with a special delegate is the starting point. ZnWebSocketDelegate implements the standard handleRequest: to check if the incoming request is a valid WebSocket connection upgrade request. If so, the matching 101 switching protocols response is constructed and sent. From that moment on, the network socket stream is handed over to a new, server side ZnWebSocket object.

ZnWebSocketDelegate has two properties. An optional prefix implements a specific path, like /my-ws-app. The required handler is any object implementing value: with the new Web socket as argument.

Let's implement the echo service that we connected to as a client in the previous section. In essence, we should go in a loop, reading a message and sending it back. Here is the code:

```
ZnServer startDefaultOn: 1701.
ZnServer default delegate: (ZnWebSocketDelegate handler:
   [ :webSocket |
      [ | message |
         message := webSocket readMessage.
         webSocket sendMessage: message ] repeat ]).
```

We start a default server on port 1701 and replace its delegate with an instance of ZnWebSocketDelegate. This instance will pass each correct web socket request on to its handler. In this example, a block is used as handler. The handler is given a new connected ZnWebSocket instance. For the echo service, we go into a repeat loop, reading a message and sending it back.

Finally, you can stop the server using:

```
ZnServer stopDefault.
```

The code above works but will eventually encounter two NetworkErrors:

```
ConnectionTimedOut
ConnectionClosed (or its more specific subclass ZnWebSocketClosed)
```

The readMessage call blocks on the socket stream waiting for input until its timeout expires, which will be signaled with a ConnectionTimedOut exception. In most applications, you should just keep on reading, essentially ignoring the timeout for an infinite wait on incoming messages.

This behavior is implemented in the ZnWebSocket>>runWith: convenience method: it enters a loop reading messages and passing them to a block, continuing on timeouts. This simplifies our example:

6.5 Using Server-Side WebSockets

```
ZnServer startDefaultOn: 1701.
ZnServer default delegate: (ZnWebSocketDelegate handler:
  [ :webSocket |
    webSocket runWith: [ :message |
      webSocket sendMessage: message ] ]).
```

That leaves us with the problem of ConnectionClosed. This exception can occur at the lowest level when the underlying network connection closes unexpectedly, or at the WebSocket protocol level when the other end sends a close frame. In either case we have to deal with it as a server. In our trivial echo example, we can catch and ignore any ConnectionClosed exception or log it as follows:

```
ZnServer stopDefault.
ZnServer startDefaultOn: 1701.
ZnServer default delegate: (ZnWebSocketDelegate handler:
  [ :webSocket |
    [ webSocket runWith: [ :message |
        webSocket sendMessage: message ]
    ]
    on: ConnectionClosed
    do: [ self crLog: 'Ignoring connection close, done' ] ]).
```

Although using a block as handler is convenient, for non-trivial examples a regular object implementing value: will probably be better. You can find such an implementation in ZnWebSocketEchoHandler.

```
ZnServer stopDefault.
ZnServer startDefaultOn: 1701.
ZnServer default
  delegate: (
    ZnWebSocketDelegate
      handler: ZnWebSocketEchoHandler new).
```

The current process (thread) as spawned by the server can be used freely by the handler code, for as long as the web socket connection lasts. The responsibility for closing the connection lies with the handler, although a close from the other side will be handled correctly.

To test the service, you can use a client-side web socket, like we did in the previous section. This is what the unit test ZnWebSocketTests>>testEcho does. Another solution is to run some JavaScript code in a web browser. You can find the necessary HTML page containing JavaScript code invoking the echo service on the class side of ZnWebSocketEchoHandler. The following setup will serve this code:

```
ZnServer stopDefault.
ZnServer startDefaultOn: 1701.
ZnServer default logToTranscript.
ZnServer default delegate
  map: 'ws-echo-client-remote'
```

```
    to: [ :request | ZnResponse ok: (ZnEntity html:
      ZnWebSocketEchoHandler clientHtmlRemote) ];
    map: 'ws-echo-client'
    to: [ :request | ZnResponse ok: (ZnEntity html:
      ZnWebSocketEchoHandler clientHtml) ];
    map: 'ws-echo'
    to: (ZnWebSocketDelegate map: 'ws-echo' to:
      ZnWebSocketEchoHandler new).
```

Now, you can try the following URLs in your Web browser:

- http://localhost:1701/ws-echo-client-remote
- http://localhost:1701/ws-echo-client

The first one will connect to ws://echo.websocket.org as a reference, the second one will connect to our implementation at ws://localhost:1701/ws-echo.

6.6 Building a Pharo Statistics Web Page

Another simple example is available in ZnWebSocketStatusHandler where a couple of Smalltalk image statistics are emitted every second for an efficient live view in your browser. In this scenario, the server accepts each incoming web socket connection and starts streaming to it, not interested in any incoming messages. Here is the core loop:

```
ZnWebSocketStatusHandler>>value: webSocket
    [
        self crLog: 'Started status streaming'.
        [
            webSocket sendMessage: self status.
            1 second asDelay wait.
            webSocket isConnected ] whileTrue
    ]
    on: ConnectionClosed
    do: [ self crLog: 'Ignoring connection close' ].
    self crLog: 'Stopping status streaming'
```

Here is code to setup all examples:

```
ZnServer stopDefault.
ZnServer startDefaultOn: 1701.
ZnServer default logToTranscript.
ZnServer default delegate
    map: 'ws-status-client'
    to: [ :request | ZnResponse ok: (ZnEntity html:
      ZnWebSocketStatusHandler clientHtml) ];
    map: 'ws-status'
    to: (ZnWebSocketDelegate map: 'ws-status' to:
      ZnWebSocketStatusHandler new).
```

Visit http://localhost:1701/ws-status-client to see statistics (uptime, memory...) of your running Pharo lively refreshed in a Web page.

What happened is that your Web browser contacted the Zinc server at the URL http://localhost:1701/ws-status-client and got back the HTML and Javascript code in ZnWebSocketStatusHandler class>>clientHtml. The execution of this Javascript code by the Web browser sent an HTTP request to the Zinc server on http://localhost:1701/ws-status asking for an upgrade to up a Web socket connection. Then, the ZnWebSocketStatusHandler object can send status updates through this Web socket connection directly to the Javascript code that refreshes the HTML page content.

6.7 Building a Web Chat

Another available example is ZnWebSocketChatroomHandler. It implements the core logic of a chatroom: clients can send messages to the server which distributes them to all connected clients. In this case, the handler has to manage a collection of all connected client Web sockets. Here is the core loop:

```
ZnWebSocketChatroomHandler>>value: webSocket
    [
        self register: webSocket.
        webSocket runWith: [ :message |
            self crLog: 'Received message: ', message printString.
            self distributeMessage: message ]
    ]
    on: ConnectionClosed
    do: [
        self crLog: 'Connection close, cleaning up'.
        self unregister: webSocket ]
```

Distributing a message basically means iterating over each client:

```
ZnWebSocketChatroomHandler>>distributeMessage: message
    clientWebSockets do: [ :each |
        each sendMessage: message ].
```

Here is code to start this Web chat app:

```
ZnServer stopDefault.
ZnServer startDefaultOn: 1701.
ZnServer default logToTranscript.
ZnServer default delegate
    map: 'ws-chatroom-client'
    to: [ :request | ZnResponse ok: (ZnEntity html:
      ZnWebSocketChatroomHandler clientHtml) ];
    map: 'ws-chatroom'
    to: (ZnWebSocketDelegate map: 'ws-chatroom' to:
      ZnWebSocketChatroomHandler new).
```

Visit http://localhost:1701/ws-chat-client to access your Web chat application. You can open multiple tabs on this same URL to simulate multiple users on the Chat. You can also send chat messages directly from Pharo, much like a moderator:

```
(ZnServer default delegate prefixMap at: 'ws-chatroom')
   handler distributeMessage: 'moderator>>No trolling please!'.
```

6.8 A Quick Tour of Zinc WebSocket Implementation

All code resides in the 'Zinc-WebSocket-Core' package. The wire level protocol, the encoding and decoding of frames is in ZnWebSocketFrame. The key methods are writeOn: and readFrom: as well as the instance creation protocol. Together with the testing protocol and printOn: these should give enough information to understand the implementation.

ZnWebSocket implements the protocol above frames, either from a server or a client perspective. The key methods are readMessage and readFrame, sending is quite simple. Client-side setup can be found on the class side of ZnWebSocket. Server-side handling of the setup is implemented in the class ZnWebSocketDelegate. Two kinds of exceptions, ZnWebSocketFailed and ZnWebSocketClosed and a shared ZnWebSocketUtils class round out the core code.

6.9 Live Demo

There is a live demo available at http://websocket.stfx.eu with the basic Zinc-WebSocket demos: echo, status & chatroom. A starting point to learn how these demos were set up is the method installExamplesInServer: in the ZnWebSocketDelegate class. Setting up a production demo is complicated by the fact that most proxies and load balancers, most notably the market leader Apache, do not (yet) deal correctly with the WebSocket protocol. It is thus easier to organize things such that your client directly talks to your Smalltalk image.

6.10 Conclusion

WebSockets integrate smoothly with Zinc HTTP Components to form another part of the Pharo Web stack. It provides support for building modern single page Web applications in Pharo. The implementation of Zinc WebSockets as an add-on to Zinc HTTP Components was made possible in part through financial backing by Andy Burnett of Knowinnovation Inc. and ESUG.

Part III

Data

CHAPTER 7

NeoCSV

Sven Van Caekenberghe with Damien Cassou and Stéphane Ducasse

CSV (Comma-Separated Values) is a popular data-interchange format. This chapter presents NeoCSV, a library to parse and export CSV files. This chapter has originally been written by Sven Van Caekenberghe the author of NeoCSV and many other nicely designed Pharo libraries.

7.1 NeoCSV

NeoCSV is an elegant and efficient standalone Pharo library to read (resp. write) CSV files converting to (resp. from) Pharo objects.

An Introduction to CSV

CSV is a lightweight text-based *de facto* standard for human-readable tabular data interchange. Essentially, the key characteristics are that CSV (or more generally, delimiter-separated text data):

- is text-based (ASCII, Latin1, Unicode);
- consists of records, 1 per line (any line ending convention);
- where *records* consist of *fields* separated by a *delimiter* (comma, tab, semicolon);
- where every record has the same number of fields; and
- where fields can be quoted should they contain separators or line endings.

> **Note** References: http://en.wikipedia.org/wiki/Comma-separated_values, http://tools.ietf.org/html/rfc4180

Note that there is not one single official standard specification.

Hands On NeoCSV

NeoCSV contains a reader (`NeoCSVReader`) and a writer (`NeoCSVWriter`) to parse and generate delimiter-separated text data to and from Smalltalk objects. The goals of NeoCSV are:

- to be standalone (have no dependencies and little requirements);
- to be small, elegant and understandable;
- to be efficient (both in time and space); and
- to be flexible and non-intrusive.

To load NeoCSV, evaluate the following or use the Configuration Browser:

```
Gofer it
   smalltalkhubUser: 'SvenVanCaekenberghe' project: 'Neo';
   configurationOf: 'NeoCSV';
   loadStable.
```

To use either the reader or the writer, you instantiate them on a character stream and use standard stream access messages.

The first example reads a sequence of data separated by , and containing line breaks. The reader produces arrays corresponding to the lines with the data (the `withCRs` method converts backslashes to new lines).

```
(NeoCSVReader on: '1,2,3\4,5,6\7,8,9' withCRs readStream) upToEnd.
   -->   #(#('1' '2' '3') #('4' '5' '6') #('7' '8' '9'))
```

The second proceeds from the inverse: given a set of data as arrays it produces comma separated lines.

```
String streamContents: [ :stream |
  (NeoCSVWriter on: stream)
    nextPutAll: #( (x y z) (10 20 30) (40 50 60) (70 80 90) ) ].
  -->
'"x","y","z"
"10","20","30"
"40","50","60"
"70","80","90"
'
```

7.2 Generic Mode

NeoCSV can operate in generic mode without any further customization. While writing,

- record objects should respond to the do: protocol,
- fields are always sent asString and quoted, and
- CRLF line ending is used.

While reading,

- records become arrays,
- fields remain strings,
- any line ending is accepted, and
- both quoted and unquoted fields are allowed.

The standard delimiter is a comma character. Quoting is always done using a double quote character. A double quote character inside a field will be escaped by repeating it. Field separators and line endings are allowed inside a quoted field. Any whitespace is significant.

7.3 Customizing NeoCSVWriter

Any character can be used as field separator, for example:

```
[ neoCSVWriter separator: Character tab
```

or

```
[ neoCSVWriter separator: $;
```

Likewise, any of the three common line end conventions can be set. In the following example we set carriage return:

```
[ neoCSVWriter lineEndConvention: #cr
```

There are 3 mechanisms that the writer may use to write a field (in increasing order of efficiency):

quoted converting it with asString and quoting it (the default);

raw converting it with asString but not quoting it; and

object not quoting it and using printOn: directly on the output stream.

When disabling quoting, you have to be sure your values do not contain embedded separators or line endings. If you are writing arrays of numbers for example, this would be the fastest way to do it:

```
neoCSVWriter
    fieldWriter: #object;
    nextPutAll: #( (100 200 300) (400 500 600) (700 800 900) )
```

The `fieldWriter` option applies to all fields.

Writing Objects

If your data is in the form of regular domain-level objects it would be wasteful to convert them to arrays just for writing them as CSV. NeoCSV has a non-intrusive option to map your domain object's fields: You add field specifications based on accessors. This is how you would write an array of Points.

```
String streamContents: [ :stream |
   (NeoCSVWriter on: stream)
      nextPut: #('x field' 'y field');
      addFields: #(x y);
      nextPutAll: { 1@2. 3@4. 5@6 } ].
   -->
'"x field","y field"
"1","2"
"3","4"
"5","6"
'
```

Note how `nextPut:` is used to first write the header (*i.e.*, the first line). After printing the header, the writer is customized: the messages `addField:` and `addFields:` arrange for the specified selectors (here x and y) to be sent on each incoming object to produce fields that will be written.

To change the writing behavior for a specific field, you have to use `addQuotedField:`, `addRawField:` and `addObjectField:`.

To specify different field writers for an array (actually any subclass of SequenceableCollection), you can use the `first`, `second`, `third`, etc. methods as selectors:

```
String streamContents: [ :stream |
   (NeoCSVWriter on: stream)
      addFields: #(first third second);
      nextPutAll: { 'acb' . 'dfe' . 'gih' }].
   -->
'"a","b","c"
"d","e","f"
"g","h","i"
'
```

7.4 Customizing NeoCSVReader

The parser is flexible and forgiving. Any line ending will do, quoted and non-quoted fields are allowed.

Any character can be used as field separator, for example:

```
neoCSVReader separator: Character tab
```

or

```
neoCSVReader separator: $;
```

NeoCSVReader will produce records that are instances of its `recordClass`, which defaults to `Array`. All fields are always read as Strings. If you want, you can specify converters for each field, to convert them to integers, floats or any other object. Here is an example:

```
(NeoCSVReader on: '1,2.3,abc,2015/07/07' readStream)
    separator: $,;
    addIntegerField;
    addFloatField;
    addField;
    addFieldConverter: [ :string | Date fromString: string ];
    upToEnd.
    --> an Array(an Array(1 2.3 'abc' 7 July 2015))
```

Here we specify 4 fields: an integer, a float, a string and a date field. Field conversions specified this way only work on indexable record classes, like `Array`.

Ignoring Fields

While reading from a CSV file, you can ignore fields using `addIgnoredField`. In the following example, the third field of each record is ignored:

```
| input |
(NeoCSVReader on: '1,2,a,3\1,2,b,3\1,2,c,3\' withCRs readStream)
    addIntegerField;
    addIntegerField;
    addIgnoredField;
    addIntegerField;
    upToEnd
    --> #(#(1 2 3) #(1 2 3) #(1 2 3))
```

Adding ignored field(s) requires adding field types on all other fields.

Creating Objects

In many cases you will probably want your data to be returned as one of your domain objects. It would be wasteful to first create arrays and then convert all those. NeoCSV has non-intrusive options to create instances of your own classes and to convert and set fields on them directly. This is done by specifying accessors and converters. Here is an example for reading Associations of Floats.

```
(NeoCSVReader on: '1.5,2.2\4.5,6\7.8,9.1' withCRs readStream)
   recordClass: Association;
   addFloatField: #key: ;
   addFloatField: #value: ;
   upToEnd.
   --> {1.5->2.2. 4.5->6. 7.8->9.1}
```

For each field you have to give the mutating accessor to use. You might also want to pass a conversion block using addField:converter:.

Reading many Objects

Handling large CSV files is possible with NeoCVS. In the following, we first create a large CSV file then read it partly (this takes a bit of time, be patient).

```
'paul.csv' asFileReference writeStreamDo: [ :file |
   ZnBufferedWriteStream on: file do: [ :out | | writer |
      writer := (NeoCSVWriter on: out).
      writer writeHeader: { #Number. #Color. #Integer. #Boolean}.
      1 to: 1e7 do: [ :each |
         writer nextPut: {
            each.
            #(Red Green Blue) atRandom.
            1e6 atRandom.
            #(true false) atRandom } ] ] ].
```

Above code results in a 300Mb file:

```
$ ls -lah paul.csv
-rw-r--r--@ 1 sven   staff    327M Nov 14 20:45 paul.csv
$ wc paul.csv
10000001 10000001 342781577 paul.csv
```

The following code selectively collects every record with a third field lower than 1000 (this takes a bit of time, be patient):

```
Array streamContents: [ :out |
  'paul.csv' asFileReference readStreamDo: [ :input |
     (NeoCSVReader on: (ZnBufferedReadStream on: in))
        skipHeader;
        addIntegerField;
        addSymbolField;
        addIntegerField;
        addFieldConverter: [ :x | x = #true ];
        do: [ :each |
           each third < 1000
              ifTrue: [ out nextPut: each ] ] ] ].
```

CHAPTER 8

NeoJSON

Sven Van Caekenberghe with Damien Cassou and Stéphane Ducasse

JSON (JavaScript Object Notation) is a popular data-interchange format. NeoJSON is an elegant and efficient standalone Smalltalk library to read and write JSON converting to and from Smalltalk objects. The library is developed and actively maintained by Sven Van Caekenberghe.

8.1 An Introduction to JSON

JSON is a lightweight text-based open standard designed for human-readable data interchange. It was derived from the JavaScript scripting language for representing simple data structures and associative arrays, called objects. Despite its relationship to JavaScript, it is language independent, with parsers available for many languages.

> **Note** References: http://www.json.org/, http://en.wikipedia.org/wiki/Json and http://www.ietf.org/rfc/rfc4627.txt?number=4627.

There are only a couple of primitive types in JSON:

- numbers (integer or floating point)
- strings
- the boolean constants `true` and `false`
- `null`

Only two composite types exist:

- lists (an ordered sequenece of values)

- maps (an unordered associative array, mapping string property names to values)

That is really all there is to it. No options or additions are defined in the standard.

8.2 NeoJSON

To load NeoJSON, evaluate the following:

```
Gofer it
    smalltalkhubUser: 'SvenVanCaekenberghe' project: 'Neo';
    configurationOf: 'NeoJSON';
    loadStable.
```

The NeoJSON library contains a reader (the class NeoJSONReader) and a writer (the class NeoJSONWriter) to parse, respectively generate, JSON to and from Pharo objects. The goals of NeoJSON are:

- to be standalone (have no dependencies and little requirements);
- to be small, elegant and understandable;
- to be efficient (both in time and space);
- to be flexible and non-intrusive.

Compared to other Smalltalk JSON libraries, NeoJSON

- has less dependencies and little requirements;
- can be more efficient (be faster and use less memory);
- allows for the use of schemas and mappings.

8.3 Primitives

Obviously, the primitive types are mapped to corresponding Pharo classes. While reading:

- JSON numbers become instances of Integer or Float
- JSON strings become instances of String
- JSON booleans become instances of Boolean
- JSON null becomes nil

While writing:

- Pharo numbers are converted to floats, except for instances of Integer that become JSON integers

- Pharo strings become JSON strings
- Pharo booleans become JSON booleans
- Pharo nil becomes JSON null

8.4 Generic Mode

NeoJSON can operate in a generic mode that requires no further configuration.

Reading from JSON

While reading:

- JSON maps become instances of mapClass, Dictionary by default;
- JSON lists become instances of listClass, Array by default.

The following example creates a Pharo array from a JSON expression:

```
NeoJSONReader fromString: ' [ 1,2,3 ] '.
```

This expression can be decomposed to better control the reading process:

```
(NeoJSONReader on: ' [ 1,2,3 ] ' readStream)
    listClass: OrderedCollection;
    next.
```

The above expression is equivalent to the previous one except that a Pharo ordered collection will be used in place of an array.

The next example creates a Pharo dictionary (with 'x' and 'y' keys):

```
NeoJSONReader fromString: ' { "x" : 1, "y" : 2 } '.
```

To automatically convert keys to symbols, pass true to propertyNamesAsSymbols: like this:

```
(NeoJSONReader on: ' { "x" : 1, "y" : 2 } ' readStream)
    propertyNamesAsSymbols: true;
    next
```

The result of this expression is a dictionary with #x and #y as keys.

Writing to JSON

While writing:

- instances of Dictionary and SmallDictionary become maps;
- all other collections become lists;

- all other non-primitive objects are rejected.

Here are some examples writing in generic mode:

```
NeoJSONWriter toString: #(1 2 3).
NeoJSONWriter toString: { Float pi. true. false. 'string' }.
NeoJSONWriter toString: { #a -> '1' . #b -> '2' } asDictionary.
```

Above expressions return a compact string (*i.e.*, with neither indentation nor new lines). To get a nicely formatted output, use `toStringPretty:` like this:

```
NeoJSONWriter toStringPretty: #(1 2 3).
```

In order to use the generic mode, you have to convert your domain objects to and from `Dictionary` and `SequenceableCollection`. This is relatively easy but not very efficient, depending on the use case.

8.5 Schemas and Mappings

NeoJSON allows for the optional specification of schemas and mappings to be used when writing or reading.

When writing, mappings are used when arbitrary objects are seen. For example, in order to write an array of points, you could do as follows:

```
String streamContents: [ :stream |
    (NeoJSONWriter on: stream)
        prettyPrint: true;
        mapInstVarsFor: Point;
        nextPut: (Array with: 1@3 with: -1@3) ].
```

Collections are handled automatically, like in the generic case. As a result, the above expression returns a string containing:

```
[
    {
        "x" : 1,
        "y" : 3
    },
    {
        "x" : -1,
        "y" : 3
    }
]
```

When reading, a mapping is used to specify what Pharo object to instantiate and how to instantiate it. Here is a very simple case, reading a map as a point:

```
(NeoJSONReader on: ' { "x" : 1, "y" : 2 } ' readStream)
    mapInstVarsFor: Point;
    nextAs: Point.
```

8.5 Schemas and Mappings

Since JSON lacks a universal way to specify the class of an object, we have to specify the target schema that we want to use as an argument to `nextAs:`.

To define the schema of the elements in a list, write something like the following:

```
(NeoJSONReader
    on: ' [{ "x" : 1, "y" : 2 },
           { "x" : 3, "y" : 4 }] ' readStream)
    mapInstVarsFor: Point;
    for: #ArrayOfPoints
        customDo: [ :mapping | mapping listOfElementSchema: Point ];
    nextAs: #ArrayOfPoints.
```

The above expression returns an array of 2 points. As you can see, the argument to `nextAs:` can be a class (as seen previously) or any symbol, provided the mapper knows about it.

To get an `OrderedCollection` instead of an array as output, you should use the `listOfType:` message:

```
(NeoJSONReader on: ' [ 1, 2 ] ' readStream)
    for: #Collection
        customDo: [ :mapping | mapping listOfType: OrderedCollection ];
    nextAs: #Collection.
```

To specify how values in a map should be instantiated, use the `mapWithValueSchema::`

```
(NeoJSONReader on: ' { "point1" : {"x" : 1, "y" : 2 } }' readStream)
    mapInstVarsFor: Point;
    for: #DictionaryOfPoints
        customDo: [ :mapping | mapping mapWithValueSchema: Point ];
    nextAs: #DictionaryOfPoints.
```

The above expression returns a `Dictionary` with 1 key-value pair `'point1'` -> (1@2).

You can go beyond pre-defined messages and specify a decoding block:

```
(NeoJSONReader on: ' "2015/06/19" ' readStream)
    for: DateAndTime
        customDo: [ :mapping |
            mapping decoder: [ :string |
                DateAndTime fromString: string ] ];
    nextAs: DateAndTime.
```

The above expression returns an instance of `DateAndTime`. The message `encoder:` is used to do the opposite, *i.e.* convert from a Smalltalk object to JSON:

```
String streamContents: [ :stream |
    (NeoJSONWriter on: stream)
```

```
    for: DateAndTime
        customDo: [ :mapping | mapping encoder: #printString ];
    nextPut: DateAndTime now ].
```

The above expression returns a string representing the current date and time.

NeoJSON deals efficiently with mappings: the minimal amount of intermediary structures are created. On modern hardware, NeoJSON can write or read tens of thousands of small objects per second. Several benchmarks are included in the unit tests package.

8.6 Emitting null Values

For efficiency reasons, by default, `NeoJSONWriter` does not write `nil` values:

```
String streamContents: [ :stream |
    (NeoJSONWriter on: stream)
        mapAllInstVarsFor: Point;
        nextPut: Point new ].
```

The above expression returns the '{}' string. If you want to see the uninitialized instance properties, pass `true` to the `writeNil:` message:

```
String streamContents: [ :stream |
    (NeoJSONWriter on: stream)
        mapAllInstVarsFor: Point;
        writeNil: true;
        nextPut: Point new ].
```

The above expression returns the '{"x":null,"y":null}' string.

8.7 Conclusion

NeoJSON is a powerful library to convert objects. Sven, the author of NeoJSON, also developed STON (Smalltalk object notation) which is closer to Pharo syntax and handles cycles and references between serialized objects.

CHAPTER 9

STON: a Smalltalk Object Notation

Sven Van Caekenberghe with Stéphane Ducasse and Johan Fabry

STON (for *Smalltalk Object Notation*) is a lightweight, text-based, and human-readable data-interchange format. STON is developed by Sven Van Caekenberghe. STON can be used to serialize domain level objects, either for persistency or for network transport. As its name suggests, it is based on JSON (see also Chapter NeoJSON). It adds symbols as a primitive value, and class tags for object values and references. Implementations for Pharo Smalltalk, Squeak and Gemstone Smalltalk are available.

9.1 Introduction

JSON is very simple, yet just powerful enough to represent some of the most common data structures across many different languages. JSON is very readable and relatively easy to type. If you have ever seen JSON Javascript Object Notation[1], you will be instantly familiar with STON as it uses similar primitive values, with the addition of a symbol type. Some details are slightly different though.

Some of these differences are due to the fact that JSON knows only about lists and maps, which means that there is no concept of object types or classes. As a result it is not easy to encode arbitrary objects, and some of the possible solutions are quite verbose. For example, the type or class is encoded as a property and/or an indirection to encode the object's contents is added. To address this, STON extends JSON by adding a primitive value, and 'class' tags for object values and references, as we will see next.

---

[1] http://www.json.org

STON Features and Limitations

STON offers three main features:

- Symbols: STON extends JSON by adding symbols as a primitive value, and class tags for object values and references. Adding a symbol (a globally unique string) primitive type is a very useful addition. This is because symbols help to represent constant values in a readable way that is compact and fast, and because symbols allow for simpler and more readable map keys.
- Circular structures: Allowing shared and circular object structures is also ueseful simply because these structures are widely used and because they allow for naturally efficient object graphs.
- JSON backward compatible: Additionally, the current STON implementation is backward compatible with standard JSON.

Limitations of STON are that in its current form it cannot serialize a number of objects that are more system or implementation than domain oriented, such as Blocks and classes. STON is also less efficient than a binary encoding such as Fuel.

Loading STON

A reference implementation for STON was implemented in Pharo and works in versions 1.3, 1.4, 2.0, 3.0 and 4.0. The project contains a full complement of unit tests.

STON is hosted on SmalltalkHub. To load STON, execute the following code snippet:

```
Gofer new
    smalltalkhubUser: 'SvenVanCaekenberghe' project: 'STON';
    configurationOf: 'Ston';
    loadStable.
```

You can also add the following repository to your package browser:

```
MCHttpRepository
    location:
      'http://smalltalkhub.com/mc/SvenVanCaekenberghe/STON/main'
    user: ''
    password: ''
```

A Gemstone (http://gemtalksystems.com/products/) port implemented by Dale Henrichs is available at https://github.com/dalehenrich/ston .

Serializing and Materializing Objects

We now show how to serialize and materialize objects, starting with a simple rectangle and then continuing with more complex objects.

9.1 Introduction

Serializing a Rectangle

To generate a STON representation for an object, STON provides two messages toString: and toStringPretty:. The first message generates a compact version and the second displays the serialized version in a more readable way. For example:

```
STON toString: (Rectangle origin: 10@10 corner: 100@50)
  --> 'Rectangle{#origin:Point[10,10],#corner:Point[100,50]}'
```

```
STON toStringPretty: (Rectangle origin: 10@10 corner: 100@50)
  -->
  'Rectangle {
      #origin : Point [ 10, 10 ],
      #corner : Point [ 100, 50 ]
  }'
```

What is shown above follows the default representation scheme for objects. Each class can define its own custom representation, as discussed in section 9.3.

Materializing a Rectangle

Once you have the textual representation of an object you can obtain the encoded objects using the STONReader class as follows:

```
(STONReader on: ( 'Rectangle {
    #origin : Point [ -40, -15 ],
    #corner : Point [ 60, 35 ]
    }') readStream) next
    -->  (-40@ -15) corner: (60@35)
```

Alternatively, you can also use the STON facade as follows

```
(STON reader on: ( 'Rectangle {
    #origin : Point [ -40, -15 ],
    #corner : Point [ 60, 35 ]
    }') readStream) next
    -->  (-40@ -15) corner: (60@35)
```

Serialization of Maps, Lists and Class Tags

This example shows how more complex data structures are represented in STON. Maps are represented by curly braces { and }, with keys and values separated by a colon : and items are separated by a comma , . Lists are delimited by [and] and their items are separated by a comma. Class tags are represented by ClassName [...] or ClassName {...}.

Next is an example of what pretty printed STON for a simple object looks like. Even without further explanation, the semantics should be clear.

STON: a Smalltalk Object Notation

```
[TestDomainObject {
    #created : DateAndTime [ '2012-02-14T16:40:15+01:00' ],
    #modified : DateAndTime [ '2012-02-14T16:40:18+01:00' ],
    #integer : 39581,
    #float : 73.84789359463944,
    #description : 'This is a test',
    #color : #green,
    #tags : [
       #two,
       #beta,
       #medium
    ],
    #bytes : ByteArray [ 'afabfdf61d030f43eb67960c0ae9f39f' ],
    #boolean : false
 }
```

A Large Example: an HTTP Response

Here is a more complex example: a ZnResponse object. It is the result of serializing the result of the following HTTP request (using Zinc, see Chapters Zinc Client and Zinc Server). It also shows that curly braces are for dictionaries and square brackets are for lists.

```
[ZnResponse {
    #headers : ZnHeaders {
       #headers : ZnMultiValueDictionary {
          'Date' : 'Sat, 21 Mar 2015 20:09:23 GMT',
          'Modification-Date' : 'Thu, 10 Feb 2011 08:32:30 GMT',
          'Content-Length' : '113',
          'Server' : 'Zinc HTTP Components 1.0',
          'Vary' : 'Accept-Encoding',
          'Connection' : 'close',
          'Content-Type' : 'text/html;charset=utf-8'
       }
    },
    #entity : ZnStringEntity {
       #contentType : ZnMimeType {
          #main : 'text',
          #sub : 'html',
          #parameters : {
             'charset' : 'utf-8'
          }
       },
       #contentLength : 113,
       #string :
'<html>\n<head><title>Small</title></head>\n<body><h1>Small</h1>
<p>This is a small HTML document</p></body>\n</html>\n',
       #encoder : ZnUTF8Encoder { }
    },
```

```
    #statusLine : ZnStatusLine {
        #version : 'HTTP/1.1',
        #code : 200,
        #reason : 'OK'
    }
}
```

Note that when encoding regular objects, STON uses Symbols as keys. For Dictionaries, you can use Symbols, Strings and Numbers as keys.

9.2 How Values are Encoded

We will now go into detail on how the notation encodes Smalltalk values. Values are either a primitive value or an object value. Note that the undefined object `nil` and a reference to an already encountered object are considered values as well.

Primitive Values

The kinds of values which are considered as primitives are numbers, strings, symbols, booleans and `nil`. We talk about each of these next, and we show an example of their encoding.

Numbers

Numbers are either integers or floats.

- Integers can be of infinite precision.
- Floats can be simple fractions or use the full scientific base 10 exponent notation.

```
(STON reader on: '123' readStream) next.
    --> 123
```

```
(STON reader on: '-10e6' readStream) next.
    --> -10000000
```

Strings

Strings are enclosed using single quotes and backslash is used as the escape character. A general Unicode escape mechanism using four hexadecimal digits can be used to encode any character. Some unreadable characters have their own escape code, like in JSON. STON conventionally encodes all non-printable non-ASCII characters.

```
(STON reader on: '''a simple string''' readStream) next.
    --> 'a simple string'
```

```
(STON reader on: '''\u00E9l\u00E8ves Fran\u00E7aises''' readStream)
    next.
    --> 'élèves Françaises'
```

```
(STON reader on: '''a newline \n and \t a tab''' readStream) next.
    -->
'a newline
and     a tab'
```

Symbols

Symbols are preceded by a #. Symbols consisting of a limited character set (letters, numbers, a dot, underscore, dash or forward slash) are written literally. Symbols containing characters outside this limited set are encoded like strings, enclosed in single quotes.

```
(STON reader on: '#foo' readStream) next.
    --> #foo
```

```
(STON reader on: '#''Foo-bar''' readStream) next.
    --> #'Foo-bar'
```

Booleans

Booleans consist of the constants `true` and `false`.

```
(STON reader on: 'true' readStream) next.
    --> true
```

The UndefinedObject

The undefined object is represented by the constant `nil`

```
(STON reader on: 'nil' readStream) next.
    --> nil
```

Object Values

Values that are not primitives can be three kinds of objects. The first kind is a collection of values: lists or maps, the second kind is a non-collection object, and the last kind is a reference to another value.

Like in JSON, STON uses two primitive composition mechanisms: lists and maps. Lists consist of an ordered collection of arbitrary objects. Maps consist of an unordered collection of key-value pairs. Keys can be strings, symbols or numbers, and values are arbitrary objects.

Lists

Lists are delimited by [and]. Items are separated by a comma ,.

For example the following expression is a list with two numbers -40 and -15.

```
[ -40, -15 ]
```

The serialization of an array is represented by a list.

```
STON toString: #(20 30 40)
    --> '[20,30,40]'
```
```
STON toString:  { 1. 0. -1. true. false. nil }.
    --> '[1,0,-1,true,false,nil]'
```

Lists are also used to represent values of certain object instance variables, as discussed in section 9.3.

```
STON toString: 20@30
    --> 'Point[20,30]'
```
```
STON toString: Date today
    --> 'Date[''2015-03-21'']'
```

Maps

Maps are delimited by { and }. Keys and values are separated by a colon : and items are separated by a comma ,. Dictionaries are serialized as maps, for example as below:

```
STON toStringPretty: (
    Dictionary new
        at: #blue
        put: 'bluish';
        at: #green
        put: 'greenish';
        yourself)
    -->
'{
    #green : ''greenish'',
    #blue : ''bluish''
}'
```

Objects

An object in STON has a class tag and a representation. A class tag starts with an alphabetic uppercase letter and contains alphanumeric characters only. A representation is either a list or a map. The next example shows an instance of the class ZnMimeType:

```
ZnMimeType {
   #main : 'text',
   #sub : 'html',
   #parameters : {
      'charset' : 'utf-8'
   }
}
```

This is a generic way to encode arbitrary objects. Non-collection classes are encoded using a map of their instance variables: instance variable name (a symbol) mapped to instance variable value. Collection classes are encoded using a list of their values.

For the list like collection subclass Array, the class tag is optional, given a list representation. The following pairs are thus equivalent:

```
[1, 2, 3]  =  Array [1, 2, 3]
```

Also, for the map like collection subclass Dictionary the class tag is optional, given a map representation:

```
{#a : 1, #b : 2} = Dictionary {#a : 1, #b : 2}
```

References

To support shared objects and cycles in the object graph, STON adds the concept of references to JSON. Each object value encountered during a depth first traversal of the graph is numbered from 1 up. If a object is encountered again, only a reference to its number is recorded. References consist of the @ sign followed by a positive integer. When the data is materialized, references are resolved after reconstructing the object graph.

Here is an OrderedCollection that shares a Point object three times:

```
| pt ar |
pt := 10@20.
ar := { pt . pt . pt }.
STON toString: ar
   --> '[Point[10,20],@2,@2]'
```

A two element Array that refers to itself in its second element will look like this:

```
[ #foo, @1 ]
```

Note that strings are not treated as objects and are consequently never shared.

9.3 Custom Representations of Objects

In the current reference implementation in Pharo, a number of classes received a special, custom representation, often chosen for compactness and

9.3 Custom Representations of Objects

readability. We give a list of them here and then discuss on how to implement such a custom representation.

Default Custom Representations

Time

`Time` is represented by a one element array with an ISO style `HH:MM:SS` string

```
STON toString: Time now
   --> 'Time[''17:06:41.489009'']'
```

Date

`Date` is represented as a one element array with an ISO style `YYYYMMDD` string

```
STON toString: Date today
   --> 'Date[''2015-03-21'']'
```

Date and Time

`DateAndTime`, `TimeStamp` is represented as a one element array with an ISO style `YYYY-MM-DDTHH:MM:SS.N+TZ.TZ` string

```
STON toString: DateAndTime now
   --> 'DateAndTime[''2015-03-21T17:46:01.751981-03:00'']'
```

Point

`Point` is represented as a two element array with the x and y values

```
STON toString: 100@200
   --> 'Point[100,200]'
```

ByteArray

`ByteArray` is represented as a one element array with a hex string

```
STON toString: #( 10 20 30) asByteArray
   --> 'ByteArray[''0a141e'']'
```

Character

`Character` is represented as a one element array with a one element string

```
STON toString: $a
   --> 'Character[''a'']'
```

Associations

Associations are represented as a pair separated by :.

```
STON toString: (42 -> #life)
   --> '42:#life'
```

Nesting is also possible #foo : 1 : 2 means #foo->(1->2).

Note that this custom representation does not change the way maps (either for dictionaries or for arbitrary objects) work. In practice, this means that there are now two closely related expressions:

```
STON fromString: '[ #foo:1, #bar:2 ]'.
   --> { #foo->1. #bar->2 }
```

```
STON fromString: '{ #foo:1, #bar:2 }'.
   --> a Dictionary(#bar->2 #foo->1 )
```

In the first case you get an Array of explicit Associations, in the second case you get a Dictionary (which uses Associations internally).

Creating a Custom Representation

The choice of using a default STON mapping for objects or to prefer a custom representation is up to you and your application. In the generic mapping instance variable names (as symbols) and their values become keys and values in a map. This is flexible: it won't break when instance variables are added or removed. It is however more verbose and exposes all internals of an object, including ephemeral ones. Custom representations are most useful to increase the readability of small, simple objects.

The key methods are instance method stonOn: and class or instance method fromSton:. The former produces a STON representation of the object and the latter creates a new object from a STON representation. If fromSton: is implemented at instance side, STON will first create an instance of the object before calling fromSton: e.g. as in Point. If implemented at class side, the creation of the instance is the responsibility of the fromSton: method, e.g. as in ByteArray.

During encoding, classes can output a one-line representation of themselves by sending either the message #writeObject:listSingleton: or the message #writeObject:streamShortList: to an instance of STONWriter. The first argument of the message should be self and the second argument a single element, or a collection of elements respectively.

Examples of this are below:

```
Date>>stonOn: stonWriter
   "Use an ISO style YYYYMMDD representation"
   stonWriter writeObject: self listSingleton: self yyyymmdd
```

```
Point>>stonOn: stonWriter
    stonWriter writeObject: self streamShortList: [ :array |
        array add: x; add: y ]
```

An instance of STONWriter also understands the #writeObject:stream-
List: and #writeObject:streamMap: messages, which generate a multi-
line representation. Also, classes can use another external name by overriding Object class>>stonName.

STON offers a way to control which instance variables get written and the
order in which they get written. This can be done by overwriting Object
class>>#stonAllInstVarNames to return an array of symbols. Each symbol is the name of a variable and the order of the symbols determines write
order. Also, having Object>>#stonShouldWriteNilInstVars return true
causes instance variables to be written out when they are nil (the default is
to omit them).

Lastly, postprocessing on instance variables for resolving references is real-
ized by the Object>>stonProcessSubObjects: method. If custom postprocessing is required, this method should be overwritten.

9.4 Usage

This section lists some code examples on how to use the current implementation and its API. The class STON acts as a class facade API to read/write
to/from streams/strings while hiding the actual parser or writer classes. It is
a central access point, but it is very thin: using the reader or writer directly
is perfectly fine, and offers some more options as well.

Simple Reading and Writing

Parsing is the simplest operation, use either the fromString: or from-
Stream: method, like this:

```
STON fromString: 'Rectangle { #origin : Point [ -40, -15 ],
    #corner : Point [ 60, 35 ]}'.
```

```
'/Users/sven/Desktop/foo.ston' asReference
    fileStreamDo: [ :stream | STON fromStream: stream ].
```

Invoking the reader (parser) directly goes like this:

```
(STON reader on:
    'Rectangle{#origin:Point[0,0],#corner:Point[1440,846]}'
        readStream) next.
```

Writing has two variants: the regular compact representation or the pretty
printed one. The methods to use are toString: and toStringPretty: or
put:onStream: and put:onStreamPretty:, like this:

```
STON toString: World bounds.
STON toStringPretty: World bounds.
'/Users/sven/Desktop/bounds.ston' asReference
   fileStreamDo: [ :str |
      STON put: World bounds onStream: str ].
'/Users/sven/Desktop/bounds.ston' asReference
   fileStreamDo: [ :str |
      STON put: World bounds onStreamPretty: str ].
```

Supporting Comments

Like JSON, STON does not allow comments of any kind in its format. However, STON offers the possibility to handle comments using a special stream named STONCStyleCommentsSkipStream. The following snippets illustrate two ways to use this stream:

```
STON fromStream: (STONCStyleCommentsSkipStream on:
   'Point[/* this is X*/ 1, /* this is Y*/ 2] // Nice huh ?'
   readStream).
   --> 1@2
```

```
STON fromStringWithComments: '// Here is how you create a point:
Point[
   // this is X
   1,
   // this is Y
   2 ]
// Nice huh ?'.
   --> 1@2
```

This helper class is useable in other contexts too, like for NeoJSON. The advantage is that it does not change the STON (or JSON) syntax itself, it just adds some functionality on top.

Configuring the Writer

The writer can be created explicitly as follows:

```
String streamContents: [ :stream |
   (STON writer on: stream) nextPut: World bounds ].
```

When created, the reference policy of the writer can be set. The default for STON is to track object references and generate references when needed. Other options are to signal an error on shared references by sending the writer referencePolicy: #error, or to ignore them (referencePolicy: #ignore) with the risk of going into an infinite loop. An example of the error reference policy is below:

```
| pt ar |
pt := 10@20.
```

```
ar := { pt . pt . pt }.
String streamContents: [ :stream |
   (STON writer on: stream)
      referencePolicy: #error;
      nextPut: ar]
   --> STONWriterError: 'Shared reference detected'
```

Compatibility with JSON

The current STON implementation has a very large degree of JSON compatibility. Valid JSON input is almost always valid STON. The only exceptions are the string delimiters (single quotes for STON, double quotes for JSON) and nil versus null. The STON parser accepts both variants for full compatibility.

The STON writer has a jsonMode option so that generated output conforms to standard JSON. That means the use of single quotes as string delimiters, null instead of nil, and the treatment of symbols as strings. When using JSON mode the reference policy should be set to #error or #ignore for full JSON compatibility. Also, as JSON does not understand non-primitive values outside of arrays or dictionaries, it is necessary to convert data structures to an Array or Dictionary first. Attempting to write non primitive instances that are not arrays or dictionaries will throw an error.

Next is an example of how to use the STON writer to generate JSON output.

```
| bounds json |
bounds := World bounds.
json := Dictionary
   with: #origin -> (
      Dictionary
         with: #x -> bounds origin x
         with: #y -> bounds origin y)
   with: #corner -> (
      Dictionary
         with: #x -> bounds corner x
         with: #y -> bounds corner y).
String streamContents: [ :stream |
   (STON writer on: stream)
      prettyPrint: true;
      jsonMode: true;
      referencePolicy: #error;
      nextPut: json ].
```

9.5 Handling CR, LF inside Strings

STON also supports the conversion or not of CR, LF, or CRLF characters inside strings and symbols as one chosen canonical newLine.

The message `STONReader>>convertNewLines: aBoolean` and the message `STONReader>>newLine: aCharacter` read and convert CR, LF, or CRLF inside strings and symbols as one chosen canonical newLine. When true, any newline CR, LF or CRLF read unescaped inside strings or symbols will be converted to the newline convention chosen, see `newLine:`. The default is false, not doing any convertions.

In the following example, any CR, LF or CRLF seen while reading Strings will all be converted to the same EOL, CRLF.

```
(STON reader on: ..)
    newLine: String crlf;
    convertNewLines: true;
    next.
```

The message `STONWriter>>keepNewLines: aBoolean` works as follows: If true, any newline CR, LF or CRLF inside strings or symbols will not be escaped but will instead be converted to the newline convention chosen, see `newLine:`. The default is false, where CR, LF or CRLF will be enscaped unchanged.

```
(STON writer on: ...)
    newLine: String crlf;
    keepNewLines: true;
    nextPut: ...
```

Any CR, LF or CRLF inside any String will no longer be written as \r, \n or \r\n but all as CRLF, a normal EOL.

9.6 Conclusion

STON is a practical and simple text-based object serializer based on JSON (see also Chapter NeoJSON). We have shown how to use it, how values are encoded and how to define a custom representation for a given class.

9.7 Appendix: BNF

```
value
    primitive-value
    object-value
    reference
    nil
primitive-value
    number
    true
    false
    symbol
    string
```

9.7 Appendix: BNF

```
object-value
   object
   map
   list
object
   classname map
   classname list
reference
   @ int-index-previous-object-value
map
   {}
   { members }
members
   pair
   pair , members
pair
   string : value
   symbol : value
   number : value
list
   []
   [ elements ]
elements
   value
   value , elements
string
   ''
   ' chars '
chars
   char
   char chars
char
   any-printable-ASCII-character-except-'-"-or-\
   \'
   \"
   \\
   \/
   \b
   \f
   \n
   \r
   \t
   \u four-hex-digits
symbol
   # chars-limited
   # ' chars '
chars-limited
   char-limited
   char-limited chars-limited
char-limited
```

```
    a-z A-Z 0-9 - _ . /
classname
    uppercase-alpha-char alphanumeric-char
number
    int
    int frac
    int exp
    int frac exp
int
    digit
    digit1-9 digits
    - digit
    - digit1-9 digits
frac
    . digits
exp
    e digits
digits
    digit
    digit digits
e
    e
    e+
    e-
    E
    E+
    E-
```

CHAPTER 10

Serializing Complex Objects with Fuel

Martín Dias, Stéphane Ducasse, Mariano Martinez Peck and Max Leske with Johan Fabry

Fuel is a fast open-source general-purpose binary object serialization framework developed by Mariano Martinez-Peck, Martìn Dias and Max Leske. It is robust and used in many industrial cases. A fundamental reason for the creation of Fuel was speed: while there is a plethora of frameworks to serialize objects based on recursive parsing of the object graphs in textual format as XML, JSON, or STON, these approaches are often slow. (For JSON and STON see also Chapters STON and NeoJSON.)

Part of the speed of Fuel comes from the idea that objects are loaded more often than stored. This makes it worth to spend more time while storing to yield faster loading. Also, its storage scheme is based on the pickle format that puts similar objects into groups for efficiency and performance. As a result, Fuel has been shown to be one of the fastest object loaders, while still being a really fast object saver. Moreover, Fuel can serialize nearly any object in the image, it can even serialize a full execution stack and later reload it!

The main features of Fuel are as follows:

- It has an object-oriented design.
- It does not need special VM-support.
- It is modularly packaged.
- It can serialize/materialize not only plain objects but also classes, traits, methods, closures, contexts, packages, etc.
- It supports global references.

- It is very customizable: you can ignore certain instance variables, substitute objects by others, define pre and post serialization and materialization actions, etc.
- It supports class renaming and class reshaping.
- It has good test coverage and a large suite of benchmarks.

10.1 General Information

Fuel has been developed and maintained over the years by the following people: Martin Dias, Mariano Martinez Peck, Max Leske, Pavel Krivanek, Tristan Bourgois and Stéphane Ducasse (as PhD advisor and financer).

The idea of Fuel was developed by Mariano Martinez Peck based on the work by Eliot Miranda who worked on the "parcels" implementation for VisualWorks. Eliot's work again was based on the original "parcels" implementation by David Leib. "Parcels" demonstrates very nicely that the binary pickle format can be a good alternative to textual storage and that grouping of objects makes a lot of sense in object oriented systems.

Before going into details we present the ideas behind Fuel and it's main features and give basic usage examples.

Goals

Concrete Fuel doesn't aspire to have a dialect-interchange format. This makes it possible to serialize special objects like contexts, block closures, exceptions, compiled methods and classes. Although there are ports to other dialects, most notably Squeak, Fuel development is Pharo-centric.

Flexible Depending on the context, there can be multiple ways of serializing the same object. For example, a class can be considered either a global or a regular object. In the former case, references to the class will be encoded by name and the class is expected to be part of the environment upon materialization; in the latter case, the class will be encoded in detail, with its method dictionary, etc.

Fast Fuel has been designed for performance. Fuel comes with a complete benchmark suite to help analyse the performance with diverse sample sets, as well as to compare it against other serializers. Fuel's pickling algorithm achieves outstanding materialization performance, as well as very good serialization performance, even when compared to other binary formats such as ImageSegment.

Object-Oriented A requirement from the onset was to have a good object-oriented design and to avoid special support from the virtual machine.

Maintainable Fuel has a complete test suite (over 600 unit tests), with a high degree of code coverage. Fuel also has well-commented classes and methods.

Installation and Demo

Fuel 1.9 is available by default in Pharo since version 2.0 of Pharo. Therefore you do not need to install it. The **default packages** work out of the box in Pharo 1.1.1, 1.1.2, 1.2, 1.3, 1.4, 2.0, 3.0 and 4.0 and Squeak 4.1, 4.2, 4.3, 4.4, 4.5. The stable version at the time of writing is 1.9.4.

Open the Transcript and execute the code below in a Playground. This example serializes a set, the default Transcript (which is a global) and a block. On materialization it shows that

- the set is correctly recreated,
- the global Transcript is still the same instance (hasn't been modified)
- and the block can be evaluated properly.

```
| arrayToSerialize materializedArray |
arrayToSerialize :=
    Array
        with: (Set with: 42)
        with: Transcript
        with: [ :aString | Transcript show: aString; cr ].

"Store (serialize)"
FLSerializer serialize: arrayToSerialize toFileNamed: 'demo.fuel'.

"Load (materialize)"
materializedArray := FLMaterializer materializeFromFileNamed:
    'demo.fuel'.

Transcript
    show: 'The sets are equal: ';
    show: arrayToSerialize first = materializedArray first;
    cr;
    show: 'But not the same: ';
    show: arrayToSerialize first ~~ materializedArray first;
    cr;
    show: 'The global value Transcript is the same: ';
    show: arrayToSerialize second == materializedArray second;
    cr.

materializedArray third
    value: 'The materialized block closure can be properly
        evaluated.'.
```

Some Links

- The home page is http://rmod.inria.fr/web/software/Fuel.
- The source code is at http://smalltalkhub.com/#!/~Pharo/Fuel.
- The CI job is at https://ci.inria.fr/pharo-contribution/job/Fuel-Stable/.

10.2 Getting Started

Basic Examples

Fuel offers some class-side messages to ease more common uses of serialization (the `serialize:toFileNamed:` message) and materialization (the message `materializeFromFileNamed:`). The next example writes to and reads from a file:

```
FLSerializer serialize: 'stringToSerialize' toFileNamed: 'demo.fuel'.
materializedString := FLMaterializer materializeFromFileNamed:
    'demo.fuel'.
```

Fuel also provides messages for storing into a ByteArray, namely the messages `serializeToByteArray:` and `materializeFromByteArray:`. This can be interesting, for example, for serializing an object graph as a blob of data into a database when using Voyage (see Chapter Voyage).

```
anArray := FLSerializer serializeToByteArray: 'stringToSerialize'.
materializedString := FLMaterializer materializeFromByteArray:
    anArray.
```

FileStream

In the following example we work with file streams. Note that the stream needs to be set to binary mode:

```
'demo.fuel' asFileReference writeStreamDo: [ :aStream |
   FLSerializer newDefault
      serialize: 'stringToSerialize'
      on: aStream binary ].

'demo.fuel' asFileReference readStreamDo: [ :aStream |
   materializedString := (FLMaterializer newDefault
      materializeFrom: aStream binary) root ].
```

In this example, we are no longer using the class-side messages. Now, for both `FLSerializer` and `FLMaterializer`, we first create instances by sending the `newDefault` message and then perform the desired operations. As we will see in the next example, creating the instances allows for more flexibility on serialization and materialization.

10.2 Getting Started

Compression

Fuel does not care to what kind of stream it writes its data. This makes it easy to use stream compressors. An example of use is as follows:

```
'number.fuel.zip' asFileReference writeStreamDo: [ :aFileStream |
   |gzip|
   aFileStream binary.
   gzip := GZipWriteStream on: aFileStream.
   FLSerializer newDefault serialize: 123 on: gzip.
   gzip close ].

'number.fuel.zip' asFileReference readStreamDo: [ :aFileStream |
   |gzip|
   aFileStream binary.
   gzip := GZipReadStream on: aFileStream.
   materializedString := (FLMaterializer newDefault
      materializeFrom: gzip) root.
   gzip close ].
```

Showing a Progress Bar

Sometimes it is nice to see progress updates on screen. Use the message showProgress in this case. The progress bar functionality is available from the FuelProgressUpdate package, so load that first:

```
Gofer it
   url: 'http://smalltalkhub.com/mc/Pharo/Fuel/main';
   package: 'ConfigurationOfFuel';
   load.

(ConfigurationOfFuel project  version: #stable)
   load: 'FuelProgressUpdate'.
```

The following example uses the message showProgress to display a progress bar during operations.

```
'numbers.fuel' asFileReference writeStreamDo: [ :aStream |
   FLSerializer newDefault
      showProgress;
      serialize: (1 to: 200000) asArray
      on: aStream binary ].

'numbers.fuel' asFileReference readStreamDo: [ :aStream |
   materializedString :=
      (FLMaterializer newDefault
         showProgress;
         materializeFrom: aStream binary) root ].
```

10.3 Managing Globals

Sometimes we may be interested in storing just the name of a reference, because we know it will be present when materializing the graph. For example when the current processor scheduler `Processor` is referenced from the graph we do not want to serialize it as it does not make sense to materialize it. Hence Fuel considers some objects as globals that may not be serialized. It also allows for you to add to this set and lastly to use a different environment when materializing globals.

Default Globals

By default, Fuel considers the following objects as globals, i.e., it will store just their name:

- `nil`, `true`, `false`, and `Smalltalk globals`.
- Any `Class`, `Trait`, `Metaclass` or `ClassTrait`.
- Any `CompiledMethod`, except when either it answers false to the message `isInstalled` or true to the message `isDoIt`. The latter happens, for example, if this is code evaluated from a Workspace.
- Some well-known global variables: `Smalltalk`, `SourceFiles`, `Transcript`, `Undeclared`, `Display`, `TextConstants`, `ActiveWorld`, `ActiveHand`, `ActiveEvent`, `Sensor`, `Processor`, `ImageImports`, `SystemOrganization` and `World`.

Duplication of Custom Globals

With this following code snippet, we show that by default a Smalltalk global value is not serialized as a global. In such a case it is duplicated on materialization.

```
"Define a global variable named SomeGlobal."
SomeGlobal := Set new.

"Serialize and materialize the value of SomeGlobal."
FLSerializer
    serialize: SomeGlobal
    toFileNamed: 'g.fuel'.

"The materialized object *is not* the same as the global instance."
[ (FLMaterializer materializeFromFileNamed: 'g.fuel') ~~ SomeGlobal
    ] assert.
```

We can tell Fuel to handle a new global and how to avoid global duplication on materialization. The message `considerGlobal:` is used to specify that an object should be stored as global, i.e. it should only be referenced by name.

10.3 Managing Globals

```
| aSerializer |

"Define a global variable named SomeGlobal."
SomeGlobal := Set new.

aSerializer := FLSerializer newDefault.

"Tell the serializer to consider SomeGlobal as global."
aSerializer analyzer considerGlobal: #SomeGlobal.

aSerializer
    serialize: SomeGlobal
    toFileNamed: 'g.fuel'.

"In this case, the materialized object *is* the same as the global
    instance."
[ (FLMaterializer materializeFromFileNamed: 'g.fuel') == SomeGlobal
    ] assert.
```

Changing the Environment

The default lookup location for globals is Smalltalk globals. This can be changed by using the message globalEnvironment: during serialization and materialization.

The following example shows how to change the globals environment during materialization. It creates a global containing the empty set, tells Fuel to consider it as a global and serializes it to disk. A new environment is then created with a different value for the global: 42 and the global is then materialized in this environment. We see that the materialized global has as value 42, i.e. the value of the environment in which it is materialized.

```
| aSerializer aMaterializer anEnvironment |

"Define a global variable named SomeGlobal."
SomeGlobal := Set new.

"Tell the serializer to consider SomeGlobal as global."
aSerializer := FLSerializer newDefault.
aSerializer analyzer considerGlobal: #SomeGlobal.
aSerializer
    serialize: SomeGlobal
    toFileNamed: 'g.fuel'.

"Override value for SomeGlobal."
anEnvironment := Dictionary newFrom: Smalltalk globals.
anEnvironment at: #SomeGlobal put: {42}.

"In this case, the materialized object *is the same* as the global
```

```
    instance."
'g.fuel' asFileReference readStreamDo: [ :aStream |
    | materializedGlobal |
    aStream binary.
    aMaterializer := FLMaterializer newDefault.

    "Set the environment"
    aMaterializer globalEnvironment: anEnvironment.

    materializedGlobal := (aMaterializer materializeFrom: aStream)
        root.

    [ materializedGlobal = {42} ] assert.
    [ materializedGlobal == (anEnvironment at: #SomeGlobal) ] assert
    ].
```

10.4 Customizing the Graph

When serializing an object you often want to select which part of the object's state should be serialized. To achieve this with Fuel you can selectively ignore instance variables.

Ignoring Instance Variables

Under certain conditions it may be desirable to prevent serialization of certain instance variables for a given class. A straightforward way to do this is to override the hook method fuelIgnoredInstanceVariableNames, at class side of the given class. It returns an array of instance variable names (as symbols) and **all** instances of the class will be serialized without these instance variables.

For example, let's say we have the class User and we do not want to serialize the instance variables 'accumulatedLogins' and 'applications'. So we implement:

```
User class>>fuelIgnoredInstanceVariableNames
    ^ #('accumulatedLogins' 'applications')
```

Post-Materialization Action

When materialized, ignored instance variables will be nil. To re-initialize and set values to those instance variables, send the fuelAfterMaterialization message.

The message fuelAfterMaterialization lets you execute some action once an object has been materialized. For example, let's say we would like to set back the instance variable 'accumulatedLogins' during materialization. We can implement:

10.4 Customizing the Graph

```
User>>fuelAfterMaterialization
    accumulatedLogins := 0.
```

Substitution on Serialization

Sometimes it is useful to serialize something different than the original object, without altering the object itself. Fuel proposes two different ways to do this: dynamically and statically.

Dynamically

You can establish a specific substitution for a particular serialization. Let's illustrate with an example, where the graph includes a `Stream` and you want to serialize `nil` instead.

```
objectToSerialize := { 'hello' . '' writeStream}.

'demo.fuel' asFileReference writeStreamDo: [ :aStream |
    aSerializer := FLSerializer newDefault.
    aSerializer analyzer
        when: [ :object | object isStream ]
        substituteBy: [ :object | nil ].
    aSerializer
        serialize: objectToSerialize
        on: aStream binary ].

'demo.fuel' asFileReference readStreamDo: [ :aStream |
    materializedObject := (FLMaterializer newDefault
        materializeFrom: aStream binary) root]
```

After executing this code, `materializedObject` will contain `#('hello' nil)`, i.e. without the instance of a `Stream`.

Statically

You can also do substitution for each serialization of an object by overriding its `fuelAccept:` method. Fuel visits each object in the graph by sending this message to determine how to trace and serialize it. The argument of the message is an instance of a `FLMapper` subclass.

As an example, imagine we want to replace an object directly with nil. In other words, we want to make all objects of a class transient, for example all `CachedResult` instances. For that, we should implement:

```
CachedResult>>fuelAccept: aGeneralMapper
    ^ aGeneralMapper
        visitSubstitution: self
        by: nil
```

As another example, we have a `Proxy` class and when serializing we want to serialize its `target` instead of the proxy. So we redefine `fuelAccept:` as follows:

```
Proxy>>fuelAccept: aGeneralMapper
    ^ aGeneralMapper
        visitSubstitution: self
        by: target
```

The use of `fuelAccept:` also allows for deciding about serialization conditionally. For example, we have the class `User` and we want to `nil` the instance variable `history` when its size is greater than 100. A naive implementation is as follows:

```
User>>fuelAccept: aGeneralMapper
    ^ self history size > 100
        ifTrue: [
            aGeneralMapper
                visitSubstitution: self
                by: (self copy history: #()) ].
        ifFalse: [ super fuelAccept: aGeneralMapper ]
```

> **Note** We are substituting the original user by another instance of `User`, which Fuel will visit with the same `fuelAccept:` method. Because of this we fall into an infinite sequence of substitutions!

Using `fuelAccept:` we can easily fall into an infinite sequence of substitutions. To avoid this problem, the message `visitSubstitution:by:onRecursionDo:` should be used. In it, an alternative mapping is provided for the case of mapping an object which is already a substitute of another one. The example above should be written as follows:

```
User>>fuelAccept: aGeneralMapper
    aGeneralMapper
        visitSubstitution: self
        by: (self copy history: #())
        onRecursionDo: [ super fuelAccept: aGeneralMapper ]
```

In this case, the substituted user (i.e., the one with the empty history) will be visited via its super implementation.

Substitution on Materialization

In the same way that we may want to customize object serialization, we may want to customize object materialization. This can be done either by treating an object as a globally obtained reference, or by hooking into instance creation.

10.4 Customizing the Graph

Global References

Suppose we have a special instance of User that represents the admin user, and it is a unique instance in the image. In the case that the admin user is referenced in our graph, we want to get that object from a global when the graph is materialized. This can be achieved by modifying the **serialization** process as follows:

```
User>>fuelAccept: aGeneralMapper
   ^ self == User admin
      ifTrue: [
         aGeneralMapper
            visitGlobalSend: self
            name: #User
            selector: #admin ]
      ifFalse: [ super fuelAccept: aGeneralMapper ]
```

During serialization the admin user won't be serialized but instead its global name and selector are stored. Then, at materialization time, Fuel will send the message admin to the class User, and use the returned value as the admin user of the materialized graph.

Hooking into Instance Creation

Fuel provides two hook methods to customise how instances are created: fuelNew and fuelNew:.

For (regular) fixed objects, the method fuelNew is defined in Behavior as:

```
fuelNew
   ^ self basicNew
```

But we can override it to our needs, for example:

```
fuelNew
   ^ self uniqueInstance
```

This similarly applies to variable sized objects through the method fuelNew: which by default sends basicNew:.

Not Serializable Objects

You may want to make sure that some objects are not part of the graph during serialization. Fuel provides the hook method named visitNotSerializable: which signals an FLNotSerializable exception if such an object is found in the graph that is to be serialized.

```
MyNotSerializableObject>>fuelAccept: aGeneralMapper
   aGeneralMapper visitNotSerializable: self
```

10.5 Errors

We provide a hierarchy of errors which allows one to clearly identify the problem when something went wrong:

- FLError
    - FLSerializationError
        * FLNotSerializable
        * FLObjectNotFound
        * FLObsolete
    - FLMaterializationError
        * FLBadSignature
        * FLBadVersion
        * FLClassNotFound
        * FLGlobalNotFound
        * FLMethodChanged
        * FLMethodNotFound

As most classes of Fuel, they have class comments that explain their purpose:

FLError I represent an error produced during Fuel operation.

FLSerializationError I represent a serialization error.

FLNotSerializable I represent an error which may happen while tracing in the graph an object that is forbidden of being serialized.

FLObjectNotFound I represent an error which may happen during serialization, when trying to encode on the stream a reference to an object that should be encoded before, but it is not. This usually happens when the graph changes during serialization. Another possible cause is a bug in the analysis step of serialization.

FLObsolete I am an error produced during serialization, signaled when trying to serialize an obsolete class as global. It is a prevention, because such class is likely to be absent during materialization.

FLMaterializationError I represent a materialization error.

FLBadSignature I represent an error produced during materialization when the serialized signature doesn't match the materializer's signature (accessible via FLMaterializer>>signature). A signature is a byte prefix that should prefix a well-serialized stream.

FLBadVersion I represent an error produced during materialization when the serialized version doesn't match the materializer's version (accessible via FLMaterializer>>version). A version is encoded in 16 bits and is encoded heading the serialized stream, after the signature.

10.6 Object Migration

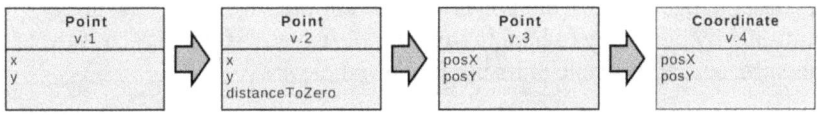

Figure 10-1 Example of changes to a class

FLClassNotFound I represent an error produced during materialization when a serialized class or trait name doesn't exist.

FLGlobalNotFound I represent an error produced during materialization when a serialized global name doesn't exist (at Smalltalk globals).

FLMethodChanged I represent an error produced during materialization when a change in the bytecodes of a method serialized as global is detected. This error was born when testing the materialization of a BlockClosure defined in a method that changed. The test produced a VM crash.

FLMethodNotFound I represent an error produced during materialization when a serialized method in a class or trait name doesn't exist (in Smalltalk globals).

10.6 Object Migration

We often need to load objects whose class has changed since it was saved. For example, figure 10-1 illustrates typical changes that can happen to the class shape. Now imagine we previously serialized an instance of Point and we need to materialize it after Point class has changed.

Let's start with the simple cases. If a variable was **inserted**, its value will be nil. If it was **removed**, it is also obvious: the serialized value will be ignored. The **change of Order** of instance variables is handled by Fuel automatically.

A more interesting case is when a variable was **renamed**. Fuel cannot automatically guess the new name of a variable, so the change will be understood by Fuel as two independent operations: an insertion and a removal. To resolve this problem, the user can tell the Fuel materializer which variables are renamed by using the message migratedClassNamed:variables:. It takes as first argument the name of the class and as second argument a mapping from old names to new names. This is illustrated in the following example:

```
FLMaterializer newDefault
    migrateClassNamed: #Point
    variables: {'x' -> 'posX'. 'y' -> 'posY'}.
```

The last change that can happen is a **class rename**. Again the Fuel materializer provides a way to handle this: the migrateClassNamed:toClass: message, and an example of its use is shown below:

```
FLMaterializer newDefault
    migrateClassNamed: #Point
    toClass: Coordinate.
```

Lastly, Fuel defines the message migrateClassNamed:toClass:variables: that combines both **class and variable rename**.

Additionally, the method globalEnvironment:, shown in Section 10.3, is useful for migration of global variables: you can prepare an ad-hoc environment dictionary with the same keys that were used during serialization, but with the new classes as values.

> **Note** A class could also change its **layout**. For example, Point could change from being **fixed** to **variable**. Layout changes from fixed to variable format are automatically handled by Fuel. Unfortunately, the inverse (variable to fixed) is not supported yet.

10.7 Fuel Format Migration

Until now, each Fuel version has used its own stream format, which is **not** compatible with the format of other versions. This means that when upgrading Fuel, we will need to convert our serialized streams. This is done by using the old version of Fuel to materialize a stream, keeping a reference to this object graph, and then loading the new version of Fuel and serializing the object graph back to a file.

We include below an example of such a format migration. Let's say we have some files serialized with Fuel 1.7 in a Pharo 1.4 image and we want to migrate them to Fuel 1.9.

```
| oldVersion newVersion fileNames objectsByFileName
    materializerClass serializerClass |
oldVersion := '1.7'.
newVersion := '1.9'.
fileNames := #('a.fuel' 'b.fuel' 'c.fuel' 'd.fuel' 'e.fuel').
objectsByFileName := Dictionary new.

(ConfigurationOfFuel project version: oldVersion) load.
"Need to do it like this otherwise
    the class is decided at compile time."
materializerClass := Smalltalk at: #FLMaterializer.

fileNames do: [ :fileName |
    objectsByFileName
        at: fileName
```

```
        put: (materializerClass materializeFromFileNamed: fileName) ].


(ConfigurationOfFuel project version: newVersion) load.
"Need to do it like this otherwise
    the class is decided at compile time."
serializerClass := Smalltalk at: #FLSerializer.

objectsByFileName keysAndValuesDo: [ :fileName :objects |
    serializerClass
        serialize: objects
        toFileNamed: 'migrated-', fileName ].
```

We assume in this example that the number of objects to migrate can be materialized all together at the same time. This assumption may be wrong. In such case, you could adapt the script to split the list of files and do the migration in parts.

> **Note** This script should be evaluated in the original image. We don't guarantee that Fuel 1.7 loads in Pharo 2.0, but we do know that Fuel 1.9 loads in Pharo 1.4.

10.8 Built-in Header Support

It can be useful to store additional information with the serialized graph or perform pre and post materialization actions. To achieve this, Fuel supports the possibility to customize the header, an instance of `FLHeader`.

The following example shows these features: first we add a property called timestamp to the header using the message `at:putAdditionalObject:`. We then define some pre and post actions using `addPreMaterializationAction:` and `addPostMaterializationAction:`, respectively. In the latter we show how we can retrieve the property value by using the `additionalObjectAt:` message.

```
| serializer |
serializer := FLSerializer newDefault.

serializer header
    at: #timestamp
    putAdditionalObject: DateAndTime now rounded.

serializer header
    addPreMaterializationAction: [
        Transcript show: 'Before serializing'; cr ].

serializer header
    addPostMaterializationAction: [ :materialization |
        Transcript
```

```
            show: 'Serialized at ';
            show: (materialization additionalObjectAt: #timestamp).
        Transcript cr;
            show: 'Materialized at ';
            show: DateAndTime now rounded;
            cr ].
serializer
    serialize: 'a big amount of data'
    toFileNamed: 'demo.fuel'
```

Then, you can materialize the header info only, and obtain the timestamp property, as follows:

```
| aHeader |
aHeader := FLMaterializer materializeHeaderFromFileNamed:
    'demo.fuel'.
aHeader additionalObjectAt: #timestamp.
```

If we materialize the whole file, as below, the print string of the results is: 'a big amount of data'.

```
FLMaterializer materializeFromFileNamed: 'demo.fuel'
```

And something similar to the following is shown in Transcript:

```
Before serializing
Serialized at 2015-05-24T22:39:18-03:00
Materialized at 2015-05-24T22:39:37-03:00
```

10.9 Conclusion

Fuel is a fast and stable binary object serializer for Pharo and is available by default in Pharo since 2.0. It can serialize to and materialize from any stream and the graph of objects to be serialized can be customized in multiple ways. It can serialize nearly any object in the system. For example, cases are known of an error occurring in a deployed application, the full stack being serialized and later materialized on a development machine for debugging.

CHAPTER 11

Persisting Objects with Voyage

Johan Fabry and Esteban Lorenzano with Damien Cassou and Norbert Hartl

Voyage is a small persistence framework developed by Esteban Lorenzano, constructed as a small layer between the objects and a persistency mechanism. It is purely object-oriented and has as a goal to present a minimal API to most common development usages. Voyage is a common layer for different backends but currently it supports just two: an *in-memory* layer and a backend for the MongoDB database (http://mongodb.org[1]).

The in-memory layer is useful to prototype applications quickly and for initial development without a database back-end, for example using the Smalltalk image as the persistency mechanism.

The MongoDB database backend stores the objects in a document-oriented database. In MongoDB each stored entity is a JSON-style document. This document-centric nature allows for persisting complex object models in a fairly straightforward fashion. MongoDB is not an object database, like Gemstone, Magma or Omnibase, so there still is a small gap to be bridged between objects and documents. To bridge this gap, Voyage contains a mapper converting objects to and from documents. This mapper is equivalent to an Object-Relational Mapper (ORM) when using relational databases. While this mapper does not solve all the known impedance mismatch issues when going from objects to a database, we find that using a document database fits better with the object world than a combination of a ORM and a relational database. This is because document databases tend to provide better support for the dynamic nature of the object world.

Voyage provides a default way in which objects are stored in the database. Fine-grained configuration of this can be performed using Magritte descriptions. Voyage also includes a query API, which allows specific objects to be

---

[1] http://mongodb.org/

retrieved from a MongoDB database. We will discuss each of these features in this text.

This text started as a number of blog posts by Esteban Lorenzano, which have been extensively reworked by Johan Fabry, and including additional information shared by Sabine Manaa and Norbert Hartl.

11.1 Setup

Load Voyage

To install Voyage, including support for the MongoDB database, go to the Configurations Browser (in the World Menu/Tools) and load ConfigurationOfVoyageMongo. Or alternatively execute in a workspace:

```
Gofer it
    url: 'http://smalltalkhub.com/mc/estebanlm/Voyage/main';
    configurationOf: 'VoyageMongo';
    loadStable.
```

This will load all that is needed to persist objects into a Mongo database.

Install MongoDB

Next is to install the MongoDB database. How to do this depends on the operating system, and is outside of the scope of this text. We refer to the MongoDB website[2] for more information.

Create A repository

In Voyage, all persistent objects are stored in a repository. The kind of repository that is used determines the storage backend for the objects.

To use the in-memory layer for Voyage, an instance of VOMemoryRepository needs to be created, as follows:

```
repository := VOMemoryRepository new
```

In this text, we shall however use the MongoDB backend. To start a new MongoDB repository or connect to an existing repository create an instance of VOMongoRepository, giving as parameters the hostname and database name. For example, to connect to the database databaseName on the host mongo.db.url execute the following code:

```
repository := VOMongoRepository
    host: 'mongo.db.url'
    database: 'databaseName'.
```

---

[2]http://www.mongodb.org/downloads

11.1 Setup

Alternatively, using the message host:port:database: allows to specify the port to connect to. Lastly, if authentication is required, this can be done using the message host:database:username:password: or the message host:port:database:username:password:.

Singleton Mode and Instance Mode

Voyage can work in two different modes:

- Singleton mode: There is an unique repository in the image, which works as a singleton keeping all the data. When you use this mode, you can program using a "behavioral complete" approach where instances respond to a certain vocabulary (see below for more details about vocabulary and usage).
- Instance mode: You can have an undetermined number of repositories living in the image. Of course, this mode requires you to make explicit which repositories you are going to use.

By default, Voyage works in instance mode: the returned instance has to be passed as an argument to all database API operations. Instead of having to keep this instance around, a convenient alternative is to use Singleton mode. Singleton mode removes the need to pass the repository as an argument to all database operations. To use Singleton mode, execute:

```
repository enableSingleton.
```

> **Note** Only one repository can be the singleton, hence executing this line will remove any other existing repositories from Singleton mode! In this document, we cover Voyage in Singleton mode, but using it in Instance mode is straightforward as well. See the protocol persistence of VORepository for more information.

Voyage API

The following two tables show a representative subset of the API of Voyage. These methods are defined on Object and Class, but will only truly perform work if (instances of) the receiver of the message is a Voyage root. See the voyage-model-core-extensions persistence protocol on both classes for the full API of Voyage.

First we show Singleton mode:

save	stores an object into repository (insert or update)
remove	removes an object from repository
removeAll	removes all objects of class from repository
selectAll	retrieves all objects of some kind
selectOne:	retrieves first object that matches the argument
selectMany:	retrieves all objects that matches the argument

Second is Instance mode. In Instance mode, the first argument is always the repository on which to perform the operation.

save:	stores an object into repository (insert or update)
remove:	removes an object from repository
removeAll:	removes all objects of class from repository
selectAll:	retrieves all objects of some kind
selectOne:where:	retrieves first object that matches the where clause
selectMany:where:	retrieves all objects that matches the where clause

Resetting or Dropping the Database Connection

In a deployed application, there should be no need to close or reset the connection to the database. Also, Voyage re-establishes the connection when the image is closed and later reopened.

However, when developing, resetting the connection to the database may be needed to reflect changes. This is foremost required when changing storage options of the database (see section 11.3). Performing a reset is achieved as follows:

```
VORepository current reset.
```

In case the connection to the database needs to be dropped, this is performed as follows:

```
VORepository setRepository: nil.
```

11.2 Storing Objects

To store objects, the class of the object needs to be declared as being a *root of the repository*. All repository roots are points of entry to the database. Voyage stores more than just objects that contain literals. Complete trees of objects can be stored with Voyage as well, and this is done transparently. In other words, there is no need for a special treatment to store trees of objects. However, when a graph of objects is stored, care must be taken to break loops. In this section we discuss such basic storage of objects, and in section 11.3 on Enhancing Storage we show how to enhance and/or modify the way objects are persisted.

Basic Storage

Let's say we want to store an Association (i.e. a pair of objects). To do this, we need to declare that the class Association is storable as a root of our repository. To express this we define the class method isVoyageRoot to return true.

11.2 Storing Objects

```
Association class>>isVoyageRoot
    ^ true
```

We can also define the name of the collection that will be used to store documents with the voyageCollectionName class method. By default, Voyage creates a MongoDB collection for each root class with name the name of the class.

```
Association class>>voyageCollectionName
    ^ 'Associations'
```

Then, to save an association, we need to just send it the save message:

```
anAssociation := #answer->42.
anAssociation save.
```

This will generate a collection in the database containing a document of the following structure:

```
{
    "_id" : ObjectId("a05feb6300000000000000000"),
    "#instanceOf" : "Association",
    "#version" : NumberLong("3515916499"),
    "key" : 'answer',
    "value" : 42
}
```

The stored data keeps some *extra information* to allow the object to be correctly reconstructed when loading:

- instanceOf records the class of the stored instance. This information is important because the collection can contain subclass instances of the Voyage root class.

- version keeps a marker of the object version that is committed. This property is used internally by Voyage for refreshing cached data in the application. Without a version field, the application would have to refresh the object by frequently querying the database.

Note that the documents generated by Voyage are not directly visible using Voyage itself, as the goal of Voyage is to abstract away from the document structure. To see the actual documents you need to access the database directly. For MongoDB this can be done through Mongo Browser, which is loaded as part of Voyage (World->Tools->Mongo Browser). Other options for MongoDB are to use the mongo command line interface or a GUI tool such as RoboMongo[3] (Multi-Platform) or MongoHub[4] (for Mac).

---

[3] http://robomongo.org
[4] http://mongohub.todayclose.com/

Embedding Objects

Objects can be as simple as associations of literals or more complex: objects can contain other objects, leading to a tree of objects. Saving such objects is as simple as sending the `save` message to them. For example, let's say that we want to store rectangles and that each rectangle contains two points. To achieve this, we specify that the `Rectangle` class is a document root as follows:

```
Rectangle class>>isVoyageRoot
    ^ true
```

This allows rectangles to be saved to the database, for example as shown by this snippet:

```
aRectangle := 42@1 corner: 10@20.
aRectangle save.
```

This will add a document to the `rectangle` collection of the database with this structure:

```
{
    "_id" : ObjectId("ef72b58100000000000000000"),
    "#instanceOf" : "Rectangle",
    "#version" : NumberLong("2460645040"),
    "origin" : {
        "#instanceOf" : "Point",
        "x" : 42,
        "y" : 1
    },
    "corner" : {
        "#instanceOf" : "Point",
        "x" : 10,
        "y" : 20
    }
}
```

Referencing other Roots

Sometimes the objects are trees that contain other root objects. For instance, you could want to keep users and roles as roots, i.e. in different collections, and a user has a collection of roles. If the embedded objects (the roles) are root objects, Voyage will store references to these objects instead of including them in the document.

Returning to our rectangle example, let's suppose we want to keep the points in a separate collection. In other words, now the points will be referenced instead of embedded.

After we add `isVoyageRoot` to `Point class`, and save the rectangle, in the `rectangle` collection, we get the following document:

```
{
   "_id" : ObjectId("7c5e772b00000000000000000"),
   "#instanceOf" : "Rectangle",
   "#version" : 423858205,
   "origin" : {
      "#collection" : "point",
      "#instanceOf" : "Point",
      "__id" : ObjectId("7804c56c0000000000000000")
   },
   "corner" : {
      "#collection" : "point",
      "#instanceOf" : "Point",
      "__id" : ObjectId("2a731f3100000000000000000")
   }
}
```

In addition to this, in the collection `point` we also get the two following entities:

```
{
   "_id" : ObjectId("7804c56c0000000000000000"),
   "#version" : NumberLong("4212049275"),
   "#instanceOf" : "Point",
   "x" : 42,
   "y" : 1
}

{
   "_id" : ObjectId("2a731f3100000000000000000"),
   "#version" : 821387165,
   "#instanceOf" : "Point",
   "x" : 10,
   "y" : 20
}
```

Breaking Cycles in Graphs

When the objects to be stored contain a graph of embedded objects instead of a tree, i.e. when there are cycles in the references that the embedded objects have between them, the cycles between these embedded objects must be broken. If not, storing the objects will cause an infinite loop. The most straightforward solution is to declare one of the objects causing the cycle as a Voyage root. This effectively breaks the cycle at storage time, avoiding the infinite loop.

For example, in the rectangle example say we have a label inside the rectangle, and this label contains a piece of text. The text also keeps a reference to the label in which it is contained. In other words there is a cycle of references between the label and the text. This cycle must be broken in order to persist the rectangle. To do this, either the label or the text must be declared as a Voyage root.

An alternative solution to break cycles, avoiding the declaration of new voyage roots, is to declare some fields of objects as transient and define how the graph must be reconstructed at load time. This will be discussed in the following section.

Storing Instances of Date in Mongo

A known issue of mongo is that it does not make a difference between Date and DateAndTime, so even if you store a Date instance, you will retrieve a DateAndTime instance. You will have to transform it back to Date manually when materializing the object.

11.3 Enhancing Storage

How objects are stored can be changed by adding Magritte descriptions to their classes. In this section, we first talk about configuration options for the storage format of the objects. Then we treat more advanced concepts such as loading and saving of attributes, which can be used, for example, to break cycles in embedded objects.

Configuring Storage

Consider that, continuing with the rectangle example but using embedded points, we add the following storage requirements:

- We need to use a different collection named rectanglesForTest instead of rectangle.
- We only store instances of the Rectangle class in this collection, and therefore the instanceOf information is redundant.
- The origin and corner attributes are always going to be points, so the instanceOf information there is redundant as well.

To implement this, we use Magritte descriptions with specific pragmas to declare properties of a class and to describe both the origin and corner attributes.

The method mongoContainer is defined as follows: First it uses the pragma <mongoContainer> to state that it describes the container to be used for this class. Second it returns a specific VOMongoContainer instance. This instance is configured such that it uses the rectanglesForTest collection in the database, and that it will only store Rectangle instances.

11.3 Enhancing Storage

Note that it is not required to specify both configuration lines. It is equally valid to only declare that the collection to be used is `rectanglesForTest`, or only specify that the collection contains just `Rectangle` instances.

```
Rectangle class>>mongoContainer
    <mongoContainer>

    ^ VOMongoContainer new
        collectionName: 'rectanglesForTest';
        kind: Rectangle;
        yourself
```

The two other methods use the pragma `<mongoDescription>` and return a Mongo description that is configured with their respective attribute name and kind, as follows:

```
Rectangle class>>mongoOrigin
    <mongoDescription>

    ^ VOMongoToOneDescription new
        attributeName: 'origin';
        kind: Point;
        yourself
```

```
Rectangle class>>mongoCorner
    <mongoDescription>

    ^ VOMongoToOneDescription new
        attributeName: 'corner';
        kind: Point;
        yourself
```

After resetting the repository with:

```
VORepository current reset
```

a saved rectangle, now in the `rectanglesForTest` collection, will look more or less as follows:

```
{
    "_id" : ObjectId("ef72b58100000000000000000"),
    "#version" : NumberLong("2460645040"),
    "origin" : {
        "x" : 42,
        "y" : 1
    },
    "corner" : {
        "x" : 10,
        "y" : 20
    }
}
```

Other configuration options for attribute descriptions are:

- **beEager** declares that the referenced instance is to be loaded eagerly (the default is lazy).
- **beLazy** declares that referenced instances are loaded lazily.
- **convertNullTo:** when retrieving an object whose value is Null (nil), instead return the result of evaluating the block passed as argument.

For attributes which are collections, the VOMongoToManyDescription needs to be returned instead of the VOMongoToOneDescription. All the above configuration options remain valid, and the kind: configuration option is used to specify the kind of values the collection contains.

VOMongoToManyDescription provides a number of extra configuration options:

- **kindCollection:** specifies the class of the collection that is contained in the attribute.
- **convertNullToEmpty** when retrieving a collection whose value is Null (nil), it returns an empty collection.

Custom Loading and Saving of Attributes

It is possible to write specific logic for transforming attributes of an object when written to the database, as well as when read from the database. This can be used, e.g., to break cycles in the object graph without needing to declare extra Voyage roots. To declare such custom logic, a MAPluggableAccessor needs to be defined that contains Smalltalk blocks for reading the attribute from the object and writing it to the object. Note that the names of these accessors can be counter-intuitive: the read: accessor defines the value that will be **stored** in the database, and the write: accessor defines the transformation of this **retrieved** value to what is placed in the object. This is because the accessors are used by the Object-Document mapper when **reading the object** to store it to the database and when **writing the object** to memory, based on the values obtained from the database.

Defining accessors allows, for example, a Currency object that is contained in an Amount to be written to the database as its' three letter abbreviation (EUR, USD, CLP, ...). When loading this representation, it needs to be converted back into a Currency object, e.g. by instantiating a new Currency object. This is achieved as follows:

```
Amount class>>mongoCurrency
    <mongoDescription>

    ^ VOMongoToOneDescription new
        attributeName: 'currency';
        accessor: (MAPluggableAccessor
            read: [ :amount | amount currency abbreviation ]
            write: [ :amount :value | amount currency: (Currency
```

11.3 Enhancing Storage

```
    fromAbbreviation: value) ]);
      yourself
```

Also, a post-load action can be defined for an attribute or for the containing object, by adding a `postLoad:` action to the attribute descriptor or the container descriptor. This action is a one-parameter block, and will be executed after the object has been loaded into memory with as argument the object that was loaded.

Lastly, attributes can be excluded from storage (and hence retrieval) by returning a `VOMongoTransientDescription` instance as the attribute descriptor. This allows to place cut-off points in the graph of objects that is being saved, i.e. when an object contains a reference to data that should not be persisted in the database. This may also be used to break cycles in the stored object graph. It however entails that when retrieving the graph from the database, attributes that contain these objects will be set to `nil`. To address this, a post-load action can be specified for the attribute descriptor or the container descriptor, to set these attributes to the correct values.

A few Words Concerning the OID

The mongo ObjectId (OID) is a unique field acting as a primary key. It is a 12-byte BSON type, constructed using:

- a 4-byte value representing seconds passed since the Unix epoch,
- a 3-byte machine identifier,
- a 2-byte process id,
- a 3-byte counter, starting with a random value.

Objects which are added into a mongo root collection get a unique id, instance of `OID`. If you create such an object and then ask it for its OID by sending it `voyageId`, you get the OID. The instance variable `value` of the OID contains a `LargePositiveInteger` that corresponds to the mongo ObjectId.

It is possible to create and use your own implementation of OIDs and put these objects into the mongo database. But this is not recommended as you possibly may no longer be able to query these objects by their OID (by using `voyageId`), since mongo expects a certain format. If you do, you should check your format by querying for it in the mongo console, for example as below. If you get the result `Error: invalid object id: length`, then you will not be able to query this object by id.

```
> db.Trips.find({"person.__id" : ObjectId("190372")})
Fri Aug 28 14:21:10.815 Error: invalid object id: length
```

An extra advantage of the OID in the mongo format is that these are ordered by creation date and time and as a result you have an indexed "creationDate-

AndTime" attribute for free (since there is a non deletable index on the field of the OID _id).

11.4 Querying in Voyage

Voyage allows to selectively retrieve object instances though queries on the database. When using the in-memory layer, queries are standard Smalltalk blocks. When using the MongoDB back-end, the MongoDB query language is used to perform the searches. To specify these queries, MongoDB uses JSON structures, and when using Voyage there are two ways in which these can be constructed. MongoDB queries can be written either as blocks or as dictionaries, depending on their complexity. In this section, we first discuss both ways in which queries can be created, and we end the section by talking about how to execute these queries.

Basic Object Retrieval using Blocks or MongoQueries

The most straightforward way to query the database is by using blocks when using the in-memory layer or MongoQueries when using the MongoDB back-end. In this discussion we will focus on the use of MongoQueries, as the use of blocks is standard Smalltalk.

MongoQueries is not part of Voyage itself but part of the MongoTalk layer that Voyage uses to talk to MongoDB. MongoTalk was made by Nicolas Petton and provides all the low-level operations for accessing MongoDB. MongoQueries transforms, within certain restrictions, regular Pharo blocks into JSON queries that comply to the form that is expected by the database. In essence, MongoQueries is an embedded Domain Specific Language to create MongoDB queries. Using MongoQueries, a query looks like a normal Pharo expression (but the language is much more restricted than plain Smalltalk).

Using MongoQueries, the following operators may be used in a query:

< <= > >= = ~=	Regular comparison operators
&	AND operator
|	OR operator
not	NOT operator
at:	Access an embedded document
where:	Execute a Javascript query

For example, a query that selects all elements in the database whose name is John is the following:

```
[ [ :each | each name = 'John' ]
```

A slightly more complicated query is to find all elements in the database whose name is John and the value in orders is greater than 10.

11.4 Querying in Voyage

```
[ [ :each | (each name = 'John') & (each orders > 10 ) ]
```

Note that this way of querying only works for querying values of the object but not values of references to other objects. For such case you should build your query using ids, as traditionally done in relational database, which we talk about next. However the best solution in the Mongo spirit of things is to revisit the object model to avoid relationships that are expressed with foreign keys.

Quering with Elements from another Root Document

With No-SQL databases, it is impossible to query on multiple collections (the equivalent of a JOIN statement in SQL). You have two options: alter your schema, as suggested above, or write application-level code to reproduce the JOIN behavior. The latter option can be done by sending the voyageId message to an object already returned by a previous query and using that id to match another object. An example where we match colors color to a reference color refCol is as follows:

```
[ [ :each | (each at: 'color.__id') = refCol voyageId ]
```

Using the at: Message to Access Embedded Documents

Since MongoDB stores documents of any complexity, it is common that one document is composed of several embedded documents, for example:

```
{
    "origin" : {
        "x" : 42,
        "y" : 1
    },
    "corner" : {
        "x" : 10,
        "y" : 20
    }
}
```

In this case, to search for objects by one of the embedded document elements, the message at:, and the field separator "." needs to be used. For example, to select all the rectangles whose origin x value is equal to 42, the query is as as follows.

```
[ [ :each | (each at: 'origin.x') = 42 ]
```

Using the where: Message to Perform Javascript Comparisons

To perform queries which are outside the capabilities of MongoQueries or even the MongoDB query language, MongoDB provides a way to write queries directly in Javascript using the $where operand. This is also possible in MongoQueries by sending the where: message:

In the following example we repeat the previous query with a Javascript expression:

```
[ :each | each where: 'this.origin.x == 42' ].
```

More complete documentation about the use of $where is in the MongoDB where documentation[5].

Using JSON Queries

When MongoQueries is not powerful enough to express your query, you can use a JSON query instead. JSON queries are the MongoDB query internal representation, and can be created straightforwardly in Voyage. In a nutshell: a JSON structure is mapped to a dictionary with pairs. In these pairs the key is a string and the value can be a primitive value, a collection or another JSON structure (i.e., another dictionary). To create a query, we simply need to create a dictionary that satisfies these requirements.

> **Note** The use of JSON queries is strictly for when using the MongoDB back-end. Other back-ends, e.g., the in-memory layer, do not provide support for the use of JSON queries.

For example, the first example of the use of MongoQueries is written as a dictionary as follows:

```
{ 'name' -> 'John' } asDictionary
```

Dictionary pairs are composed with AND semantics. Selecting the elements having John as name AND whose orders value is greater than 10 can be written like this:

```
{
    'name' -> 'John'.
    'orders' -> { '$gt' : 10 } asDictionary
} asDictionary
```

To construct the "greater than" statement, a new dictionary needs to be created that uses the MongoDB $gt query selector to express the greater than relation. For the list of available query selectors we refer to the MongoDB Query Selectors documentation[6].

Querying for an Object by OID

If you know the ObjectId for a document, you can create an OID instance with this value and query for it.

---

[5] http://docs.mongodb.org/manual/reference/operator/where/#op._S_where
[6] http://docs.mongodb.org/manual/reference/operator/query/#query-selectors

11.4 Querying in Voyage

```
[{('_id' -> (OID value: 16r55CDD2B6E9A87A520F000001))} asDictionary.
```

Note that both of the following are equivalent:

```
OID value: 26555050698940995562836590593. "dec"
OID value: 16r55CDD2B6E9A87A520F000001. "hex"
```

> **Note** If you have an instance which is in a root collection, then you can ask it for its voyageId and use that ObjectId in your query.

Using dot Notation to Access Embedded Documents

To access values embedded in documents with JSON queries, the dot notation is used. For example, the query representing rectangles whose origin have 42 as their x values can be expressed this way:

```
{
    'origin.x' -> {'$eq' : 42} asDictionary
} asDictionary
```

Expressing OR Conditions in the Query

To express an OR condition, a dictionary whose key is '$or' and whose values are the expression of the condition is needed. The following example shows how to select all objects whose name is John that have more than ten orders OR objects whose name is not John and has ten or less orders:

```
{ '$or' :
    {
        {
            'name' -> 'John'.
            'orders' -> { '$gt': 10 } asDictionary
        } asDictionary.
        {
            'name' -> { '$ne': 'John'} asDictionary.
            'orders' -> { '$lte': 10 } asDictionary
        } asDictionary.
    }.
} asDictionary.
```

Going Beyond MongoQueries Features

Using JSON queries allows to use features that are not present in Mongo-Queries, for example the use of regular expressions. Below is a query that searches for all documents with a fullname.lastName that starts with the letter D:

```
{
    'fullname.lastName' -> {
        '$regexp': '^D.*'.
```

```
        '$options': 'i'.
    } asDictionary.
} asDictionary.
```

The option i for a regular expression means case insensitivity. More options are described in the documentation of the $regex operator[7].

This example only briefly illustrates the power of JSON queries. Many more different queries can be constructed, and the complete list of operators and usages is in the MongoDB operator documentation[8]

Executing a Query

Voyage has a group of methods to perform searches. To illustrate the use of these methods we will use the stored Point example we have presented before. Note that all queries in this section can be written either as Mongo-Queries or as JSON queries, unless otherwise specified.

Basic Object Retrieval

The following methods provide basic object retrieval.

- **selectAll** Retrieves all documents in the corresponding database collection. For example, `Point selectAll` will return all Points.

- **selectOne:** Retrieves one document matching the query. This maps to a `detect:` method and takes as argument a query specification (either a MongoQuery or a JSON Query). For example, `Point selectOne: [:each | each x = 42]` or alternatively `Point selectOne: { 'x' -> 42 } asDictionary`.

- **selectMany:** Retrieves all the documents matching the query. This maps to a `select:` method and takes as argument a query specification, like above.

Limiting Object Retrieval and Sorting

The methods that query the database look similar to their equivalent in the Collection hierarchy. However unlike regular collections which can operate fully on memory, often Voyage collection queries need to be customized in order to optimize memory consumption and/or access speed. This is because there can be literally millions of documents in each collection, surpassing the memory limit of Pharo, and also the database searches have a much higher performance than the equivalent code in Pharo.

---

[7]http://docs.mongodb.org/manual/reference/operator/query/regex/#op._S_regex
[8]http://docs.mongodb.org/manual/reference/operator

11.4 Querying in Voyage

The first refinement to the queries consist in limiting the amount of results that are returned. Of the collection of all the documents that match, a subset is returned that starts at the index that is given as argument. This can be used to only retrieve the first N matches to a query, or go over the query results in smaller blocks, as will be shown next in the simple paginator example.

- selectMany:limit: Retrieves a collection of objects from the database that match the query, up to the given limit. An example of this is Point selectMany: [:each | each x = 42] limit: 10
- selectMany:limit:offset: Retrieves a collection of objects from the database that match the query. The first object retrieved will be at the offset position plus one of the results of the query, and up to limit objects will be returned. For example, if the above example matched 25 points, the last 15 points will be returned by the query Point selectMany: [:each | each x = 42] limit: 20 offset: 10 (any limit argument greater than 15 will do for this example).

The second customization that can be performed is to sort the results. To use this, the class VOOrder provides constants to specify ascending or descending sort order.

- selectAllSortBy: Retrieves all documents, sorted by the specification in the argument, which needs to be a JSON query. For example, Point selectAllSortBy: { #x -> VOOrder ascending} asDictionary returns the points in ascending x order.
- selectMany:sortBy: Retrieves all the documents matching the query and sorts them. For example to return the points where x is 42, in descending y order: Point selectMany: { 'x' -> 42 } asDictionary sortBy: { #y -> VOOrder descending } asDictionary.
- selectMany:sortBy:limit:offset: Provides for specifying a limit and offset to the above query.

A Simple Paginator Example

Often you want to display just a range of objects that belong to the collection, e.g. the first 25, or from 25 to 50, and so on. Here we present a simple paginator that implements this behavior, using the selectMany:limit:offset: method.

First we create a class named Paginator. To instantiate it, a Voyage root (aClass) and a query (aCondition) need to be given.

```
Object subclass: #Paginator
   instanceVariableNames: 'collectionClass where pageCount'
   classVariableNames: ''
   package: 'DemoPaginator'
```

```
Paginator class>>on: aClass where: aCondition
    ^ self basicNew
        initializeOn: aClass where: aCondition

Paginator>>initializeOn: aClass where: aCondition
    self initialize.
    collectionClass := aClass.
    where := aCondition
```

Then we define the arithmetic to get the number of pages for a page size and a given number of entities.

```
Paginator>>pageSize
    ^ 25

Paginator>>pageCount
    ^ pageCount ifNil: [ pageCount := self calculatePageCount ]

Paginator>>calculatePageCount
    | count pages |
    count := self collectionClass count: self where.
    pages := count / self pageSize.
    count \\ self pageSize > 0
        ifTrue: [ pages := pages + 1].
    ^ count
```

The query that retrieves only the elements for a given page is then implemented as follows:

```
Paginator>>page: aNumber
    ^ self collectionClass
        selectMany: self where
        limit: self pageSize
        offset: (aNumber - 1) * self pageSize
```

11.5 Creating and Removing Indexes

There are a number of useful features in MongoDB that are not present in Voyage but still can be performed from within Pharo, the most important one being the management of indexes.

Creating Indexes by using OSProcess

It is not yet possible to create and remove indexes from Voyage, but this can nonetheless be done by using OSProcess.

For example, assume there is a database named myDB with a collection named Trips. The trips have an embedded collection with receipts. The receipts

11.5 Creating and Removing Indexes

have an attribute named description. The following creates an index on description:

```
OSProcess command:
    '/{pathToMongoDB}/MongoDB/bin/mongo --eval ',
    '"db.getSiblingDB(''myDB'').Trips.',
    'createIndex({''receipts.description'':1})"'
```

Removing all indexes on the Trips collection can be done as follows:

```
OSProcess command:
    '/{pathToMongoDB}/MongoDB/bin/mongo --eval ',
    '"db.getSiblingDB(''myDB'').Trips.dropIndexes()"'
```

Verifying the use of an Index

To ensure that a query indeed uses the index, ".explain()" can be used in the mongo console. For example, if we add the index on description as above, run a query and add .explain() we see, that only a subset of documents were scanned.

```
> db.Trips.find({"receipts.description":"a"})
                .explain("executionStats")
{
    "cursor" : "BtreeCursor receipts.receiptDescription_1",
    "isMultiKey" : true,
    "n" : 2,
    "nscannedObjects" : 2,
    "nscanned" : 2,
    "nscannedObjectsAllPlans" : 2,
    "nscannedAllPlans" : 2,

    [...]
}
```

After removing the index, all documents are scanned (in this example there are 246):

```
> db.Trips.find({"receipts.description":"a"}
                ..explain("executionStats")
{
    "cursor" : "BasicCursor",
    "isMultiKey" : false,
    "n" : 2,
    "nscannedObjects" : 246,
    "nscanned" : 246,
    "nscannedObjectsAllPlans" : 246,
    "nscannedAllPlans" : 246,

    [...]
}
```

11.6 Conclusion

In this chapter we presented Voyage, a persistence programming framework. The strength of Voyage lies in the presence of the object-document mapper and MongoDB back-end. We have shown how to store objects in, and remove object from the database, and how to optimise the storage format. This was followed by a discussion of querying the database; showing the two ways in which queries can be constructed and detailing how queries are ran. We ended this chapter by presenting how we can construct indexes in MongoDB databases, even though Voyage does not provide direct support for it.

Part IV

Presentation

CHAPTER 12

Mustache Templates for Pharo

Stéphane Ducasse and Norbert Hartl with Johan Fabry

Mustache is a framework-agnostic, logic-free templating format that "emphasizes separating logic from presentation: it is impossible to embed application logic in this template language". It is supported in many programming languages, as shown at http://mustache.github.io. The full syntax documentation is available online at http://mustache.github.io/mustache.5.html.

Mustache is simple and versatile, its syntax is small and covers a wide range of use cases. Although it was designed to be a templating engine for HTML pages it is useful in different areas.

Norbert Hartl developed a Mustache package for Pharo. This chapter is an introduction to this package and a mini tutorial to get started with Mustache. This text is based on the original blog entries written by Norbert and extended to offer a larger covering of the Mustache features.

12.1 Getting Started

To install Mustache, execute the following expression in a workspace:

```
Gofer it
    smalltalkhubUser: 'NorbertHartl' project: 'Mustache';
    configuration;
    loadStable
```

A Mustache expression takes two arguments as input: (1) a template and (2) a context object (which is a list of bindings). The latter is called a hash in Mustache jargon.

Consider a simple Mustache template (taken literally from the documentation):

```
templateString := 'Hello {{ name }}
You have just won ${{value}}!
{{#in_ca}}
Well, ${{taxed_value}}, after taxes.
{{/in_ca}}'.
```

The expression {{}} delimits a *tag* or variable inside a template. In the above example, {{ name }} represents the variable name. When the template is evaluated with a context, variables are replaced by their values given by a context. A possible context for the template above is the following:

```
context := {
    'name' -> 'Chris'.
    'value' -> 10000.
    'taxed_value' -> (10000 - (10000 * 0.4)).
    'in_ca' -> true } asDictionary
```

Given a context object with some bindings, we can evaluate a template in two different ways. The first one is as follows:

```
(MustacheTemplate on: templateString) value: context
```

The second way is through the asMustacheTemplate message:

```
templateString asMustacheTemplate value: context
```

For the above example, we get the following output in both cases:

```
'Hello Chris
You have just won $10000!

Well, $6000.0, after taxes.
'
```

As context object we can use Dictionaries and Objects. Dictionaries need to have a key that is used in the template and Objects need a selector with the same name. In this chapter we use Dictionaries for brevity.

12.2 Tags as Variables

Tags can be of different types: The first and simplest type is *variable*. We explain its working with an example: a {{age}} tag in a basic template tries to find the age key in the current context. If there is no age key, the parent contexts are looked up recursively. If the top context is reached and the age key is still not found, nothing will be rendered.

The following example illustrates this. Since age is not defined, nothing is present in the output (included below after the -->).

```
'* {{name}}
* {{age}}
```

```
* {{company}}' asMustacheTemplate value:
{
    'name' -> 'Chris' .
    'company' -> '<b>GitHub</b>'
} asDictionary

    -->
'* Chris
*
* &lt;b&gt;GitHub&lt;/b&gt;'
```

The last line above shows that all variables are HTML escaped by default, e.g. if a binding for that variable contains a < character it will be converted to <. To return unescaped HTML, the triple mustache expression must be used: {{{name}}}. Also, the character & can be used to unescape a variable as in {{& name}}. This can be useful when changing delimiters, which is discussed later in this chapter. The template below shows the different ways in which company is escaped in the output (included below after the -->).

```
'* {{name}}
* {{age}}
* {{&company}}
* {{company}}
* {{{company}}}' asMustacheTemplate value:
{
'age' -> 33 .
    'name' -> 'Chris' .
    'company' -> '<b>GitHub</b>'
} asDictionary

    -->
'* Chris
* 33
* <b>GitHub</b>
* &lt;b&gt;GitHub&lt;/b&gt;
* <b>GitHub</b>'
```

12.3 Sections

Sections render blocks of text a number of times if their key is present in the context. A section is delimited by a hash sign and a slash. For example, {{#number}} begins a section for the *number* variable while {{/number}} ends it.

When a variable is not present in the context the section is not present in the output:

```
| templateString context |
templateString := 'Shown.
```

```
{{#number}}
    Shown too!
{{/number}}'.
context := { 'foo' -> 'true' } asDictionary.
(MustacheTemplate on: templateString) value: context

    -->
'Shown.
'
```

When the variable is set, the output depends on the contents of the variable and there are three distinct cases, as we discuss next.

With the Variable Value being a 'simple' Object

For values that are not collections nor blocks, the output will be present once. For example, below `number` is bound to `true` which renders the text `'Shown too'`. The same will happen when `number` is bound to another value, e.g. 42.

```
| templateString context |
templateString := 'Shown.
{{#number}}
    Shown too!
{{/number}}'.
context := { 'number' -> true } asDictionary.
(MustacheTemplate on: templateString) value: context

    -->
'Shown.

    Shown too!
'
```

There is one exception to this rule: when the variable is bound to `false` the section is not present in the output:

```
| templateString context |
templateString := 'Shown.
{{#number}}
    Shown too!
{{/number}}'.
context := { 'number' -> false } asDictionary.
(MustacheTemplate on: templateString) value: context

    -->
'Shown.
'
```

12.3 Sections

With the Variable Value being a Collection

We can use collections to create loop constructs in templates. If a section key is present in the context and it has a collection as a value, the text of the section is present as many times as there are items in the collection. Keep in mind that Strings are collections of characters.

```
| templateString context |
templateString := 'Shown.
{{#list}}
   Shown too!
{{/list}}'.
context := { 'list' -> #(1 2 3) } asDictionary.
(MustacheTemplate on: templateString) value: context

   -->
'Shown.

  Shown too!

  Shown too!

  Shown too!
'
```

> **Note** Consequently, if the collection is empty (or if it is the empty string), the output is present 0 times, i.e. it is absent.

When processing collections, Mustache iterates over them and for each element of the collection the context of the section is set to the current item. This allows a section to use variables that are contained in the elements of the collection. For example, below we define a *list* binding that contains multiple *number* bindings. The section *list* is evaluated for each of the its *number* bindings.

```
| templateString context |
templateString :=  'A {{ label }} list of numbers
{{# list }}
Number: {{ number }}
{{/ list }}'.
context := {
   'label' -> 'fine'.
   'list' -> {
      { 'number' -> 1 } asDictionary.
      { 'number' -> 2 } asDictionary.
   }
} asDictionary.
(MustacheTemplate on: templateString) value: context

   -->
```

```
'A fine list of numbers

Number: 1

Number: 2
'
```

With such behavior we can easily generate menus and lists in html, for example:

```
'<ul>
   {{#entries}}<li class="menuEntry{{#active}}
     active{{/active}}">{{label}}</li>
   {{/entries}}
</ul>' asMustacheTemplate
    value: { 'entries' -> {
       { 'label' -> 'first' } asDictionary.
       { 'label' -> 'second' . 'active' -> true } asDictionary.
       { 'label' -> 'third' } asDictionary } } asDictionary.

   -->
'<ul>
   <li class="menuEntry">first</li>
   <li class="menuEntry active">second</li>
   <li class="menuEntry">third</li>
</ul>'
```

```
'{{#coolBooks}}
   <b>{{name}}</b>
{{/coolBooks}}' asMustacheTemplate
    value: {'coolBooks' -> {
       { 'name' -> 'Pharo By Example' } asDictionary.
       { 'name' -> 'Deep Into Pharo' } asDictionary.
       { 'name' -> 'Fun Wih Pharo' } asDictionary }
       } asDictionary

   -->
'
   <b>Pharo By Example</b>

   <b>Deep Into Pharo</b>

   <b>Fun Wih Pharo</b>
'
```

With the Variable Value being a Block

We can use Pharo blocks in context objects as well. They are evaluated at the time the template is filled out. For example,

```
'The alphabet: {{ alphabet }}' asMustacheTemplate
   value: { 'alphabet' -> [ Character alphabet ] } asDictionary
   -->
The alphabet: abcdefghijklmnopqrstuvwxyz
```

Now there is another interesting way of using blocks. With a block we can get access to the value of a section and perform some operations on it.

This example shows that we can access the value of a section. Here the block is expecting one argument: the value of this argument will be the section with subsituted variables.

```
'{{#wrapped}} {{name}} is awesome {{/wrapped}}' asMustacheTemplate
   value: {
      'name' -> 'Willy'.
      'wrapped' -> [ :render | '<b>',  render value, '</b>' ] }
     asDictionary.
   -->
'<b> Willy is awesome </b>'.
```

Inverted Sections

A last use of sections is inverted sections. An inverted section begins with a caret and ends with a slash: for example, {{^list}} begins a an inverted section and {{/list}} ends it. While sections are used to render text one or more times based on the value of the key, inverted sections may render text once based on the *inverse* value of the key. That is, they will be rendered if the key doesn't exist, is false, or is an empty collection:

```
'list{{^ list }} is {{/ list}}displayed' asMustacheTemplate
   value: { 'list' -> false } asDictionary.
   -->
'list is displayed'
```

```
'list{{^ list }} is {{/ list}}displayed' asMustacheTemplate
   value: { 'list' -> { } } asDictionary.
   -->
'list is displayed'
```

```
'list{{^ list }} is {{/ list}}displayed' asMustacheTemplate
   value: { 'list' -> { 1 } } asDictionary.
   -->
'listdisplayed'
```

12.4 Partial templates

Mustache templates have a notion of sub-templates that are called partials. Partial templates are useful for reusing and composing templates out of simpler ones. Partials begin with a greater than sign, such as {{> user}}.

Mustache Templates for Pharo

The following example shows that the partial is replaced by its definition which is then expanded.

```
| template |
template := 'This is a test for {{> partial }} .' asMustacheTemplate.
template
    value: { 'name' -> 'partial template' } asDictionary
    partials: { 'partial' -> '{{name}} rendering' } asDictionary.
-->
'This is a test for partial template rendering .'
```

Partials work similarly with lists:

```
| template |
template := MustacheTemplate on:
    'We can have a list ({{# list}} [ {{> partial }} ] {{/ list}}) .'.
template
    value: { 'list' -> {
        { 'name' -> 'first AAA' } asDictionary.
        { 'name' -> 'last BBB' } asDictionary } } asDictionary
    partials:
        (Dictionary new
            at: 'partial' put: (MustacheTemplate on: 'including {{name}} item');
            yourself).
-->
'We can have a list ( [ including first AAA item ] [ including last BBB item ] ) .'
```

The values of dictionary used as template are supposed to be MustacheTemplates. However, when strings are used instead of MustacheTemplates, strings are transparently converted, as is the case for '{{name}}' below:

```
| template |
template := '<h2>Names</h2>
{{# names }}
   {{> user }}
{{/ names }}' asMustacheTemplate.
template
    value: {
        'names' -> {
            { 'name' -> 'Username' } asDictionary } } asDictionary
    partials: {'user' -> '<strong>{{name}}</strong>'} asDictionary
    -->
'<h2>Names</h2>

   <strong>Username</strong>
'
```

12.5 Miscellaneous

When you want to use Mustache to generate LaTeX you face the problem that LaTeX may need to contain {{ and }}, which conflicts with the Mustache set delimiters. To avoid such conflicts the delimiters can be changed using the =   characters separated by a space. For example, {{=<% %>=}} defines <% and %> as new delimiters. To replace the default separators, we can simply use the previously defined ones: <%={{ }}=%>:

```
'{{ number }}
{{=<% %>=}}
<% number %>
<%={{ }}=%>
{{ number }}' asMustacheTemplate
    value: { 'number' -> 42 } asDictionary
  -->
'42

42

42'
```

Also, JSON is really easy to apply to the templates once NeoJSON is installed (see Chapter NeoJSON.) After that it is just as simple as in the following example:

```
'I can use {{name}} easily with {{format}}' asMustacheTemplate
    value: (NeoJSONReader fromString:
        '{ "name" : "Mustache", "format" : "JSON" }')
    -->
'I can use Mustache easily with JSON'
```

12.6 Templates made Easy

Mustache can make template dependent tasks very easy from a simple token replacement up to nested structures to create HTML pages. We use them e.g., for generating SOAP templates. The strength of Mustache lays in the syntax and the combination of context objects. So, there is more for you to find what can be done with it. Happy templating !

CHAPTER 13

Cascading Style Sheets with RenoirSt

Gabriel Omar Cotelli with Damien Cassou

RenoirST is a DSL enabling programmatic cascading style sheet generation for Pharo developed by Gabriel Omar Cotelli.

RenoirST aims to improve CSS integration with existing web frameworks. To do that, RenoirST generates CSS out of Pharo code. Renoir features are: common properties declaration, CSS3 selector support, important rules, font face rules and media queries support. In this tutorial we will present the key features of RenoirSt with a large set of examples. This tutorial assumes some knowledge of CSS and Pharo. For a little introduction about CSS you can read the Seaside's book CSS chapter[1].

13.1 Getting Started

To load the library in your image, evaluate:

```
Metacello new
    configuration: 'RenoirSt';
    githubUser: 'gcotelli' project: 'RenoirSt' commitish: 'master'
      path: 'source';
    load
```

download a ready to use image from the Pharo contribution CI Server[2] or install it using the Catalog/Configuration Browser.

---

[1] http://book.seaside.st/book/fundamentals/css
[2] https://ci.inria.fr/pharo-contribution/job/RenoirSt

The main entry point for the library is the class `CascadingStyleSheet-Builder`. In a workspace or playground, inspect the result of the following expression:

```
CascadingStyleSheetBuilder new build
```

You now have an inspector on your first (empty and useless) style sheet. Real stylesheets are composed of rules (or rule-sets), where each one has a selector and a declaration group. The selector determines if the rule applies to some element in the DOM, and the declaration group specifies the style to apply.

Our first useful style sheet will simply assign a margin to every div element in the DOM.

```
CascadingStyleSheetBuilder new
    declareRuleSetFor: [ :selector | selector div ]
    with: [ :style | style margin: 2 px ];
    build
```

the expected result in CSS is:

```
div
{
    margin: 2px;
}
```

The message `declareRuleSetFor:with:` is used to configure a rule-set in the builder. The message requires two blocks: the first block defines the selector and the second defines the style to apply to elements matching the selector. The `selector` argument of the first block is an entry point to construct the selector (more on this later). The `style` argument of the second block is an entry point to declare CSS properties and values.

The properties API is mostly defined following this rules:

- Properties without dashes in the name are directly mapped: the margin CSS property is mapped to a `margin:` message send.
- Properties with one or more dashes are mapped using camel case: the margin-top CSS property is mapped to the `marginTop:` message send.

13.2 Defining the Rules

We now present how the various CSS rules can be expressed with RenoirSt. RenoirSt supports many CSS types, comments, and even functional notation.

Basic CSS Types

Lengths, Angles, Times and Frequencies

The library provides out-of-the-box support for the length, angle, time and frequency units in the CSS spec. There are extensions for `Integer` and `Float` classes allowing to obtain lengths.

The supported length units are:

- `em` relative to font size
- `ex` relative to "x" height
- `ch` relative to width of the zero glyph in the element's font
- `rem` relative to font size of root element
- `vw` 1% of viewport's width
- `vh` 1% of viewport's height
- `vmin` 1% of viewport's smaller dimension
- `vmax` 1% of viewport's larger dimension
- `cm` centimeters
- `mm` millimeteres
- `in` inches
- `pc` picas
- `pt` points
- `px` pixels (note that CSS has some special definition for pixel)

The supported angle units are:

- `deg` degrees
- `grad` gradians
- `rad` radians
- `turn` turns

The supported time units are:

- `s` seconds
- `ms` milliseconds

The supported frequency units are:

- `Hz` Hertz
- `kHz` KiloHertz

RenoirST also supports the creation of percentages: 50 percent is mapped to 50% in the resulting CSS.

Some properties require integer or floating point values. In these cases just use the standard Pharo integer and float support. For example:

```
CascadingStyleSheetBuilder new
   declareRuleSetFor: [ :selector | selector div ]
   with: [ :style | style zIndex: 2 ];
   build
```

Colors

The library supports abstractions for properties requiring color values. The shared pool CssSVGColors provides easy access to colors in the SVG 1.0 list, and the abstractions CssRGBColor and CssHSLColor allow the creation of colors in the RGB and HSL spaces including alpha support.

For example,

```
CascadingStyleSheetBuilder new
   declareRuleSetFor: [ :selector | selector div ]
   with: [ :style |
      style
         backgroundColor: CssSVGColors aliceBlue;
         borderColor: (CssRGBColor red: 0 green: 128 blue: 0 alpha: 0.5) ];
      build
```

evaluates to:

```
div
{
   background-color: aliceblue;
   border-color: rgba(0,128,0,0.5);
}
```

> **Note** In a real scenario you should avoid hard coding colors as in the examples. It is recommended to put colors in objects representing a theme or something that gives them a name related to your application.

RGB-Colors also support percentage values:

```
CascadingStyleSheetBuilder new
   declareRuleSetFor: [ :selector | selector div ]
   with: [ :style |
      style borderColor: (CssRGBColor red: 0 percent green: 50
   percent blue: 0 percent) ];
   build
```

evaluates to:

```
div
{
    border-color: rgb(0%,50%,0%);
}
```

Notice the difference in the used message because there is no alpha channel specification.

Constants

A lot of values for CSS properties are just keyword constants. This support is provided by the classes CssConstants and CssFontConstants.

```
CascadingStyleSheetBuilder new
    declareRuleSetFor: [ :selector | selector div ]
    with: [ :style | style textAlign: CssConstants justify ];
    build
```

evaluates to:

```
div
{
    text-align: justify;
}
```

Several Property Values

Some properties support a wide range of values. For example the margin property can have 1, 2 , 3 or 4 values specified. If you only need one value, just pass it as a parameter. For more than one value, use an array:

```
CascadingStyleSheetBuilder new
    declareRuleSetFor: [ :selector | selector div ]
    with: [ :style | style margin: { 2 px. 4 px } ];
    build
```

evaluates to:

```
div
{
    margin: 2px 4px;
}
```

URLs

ZnUrl instances can be used as the value for properties requiring an URI. Both relative and absolute URLs are accepted. A relative URL is considered by default relative to the site root.

```
CascadingStyleSheetBuilder new
    declareRuleSetFor: [ :selector | selector div class: 'logo' ]
```

```
    with: [ :style | style backgroundImage: 'images/logo.png' asZnUrl
      ];
    declareRuleSetFor: [ :selector | selector div class: 'logo' ]
    with: [ :style | style backgroundImage:
      'http://www.example.com/images/logo.png' asZnUrl ];
    build
```

Evaluates to:

```
div.logo
{
    background-image: url("/images/logo.png");
}

div.logo
{
    background-image: url("http://www.example.com/images/logo.png");
}
```

To use a URL relative to the style sheet, send to it the message `relative-ToStyleSheet`.

```
CascadingStyleSheetBuilder new
    declareRuleSetFor: [ :selector | selector div class: 'logo' ]
    with: [ :style | style backgroundImage: 'images/logo.png' asZnUrl
      relativeToStyleSheet];
    build
```

Evaluates to:

```
div.logo
{
    background-image: url("images/logo.png");
}
```

Comments

When declaring rule sets, the library supports attaching comments to them with the `declareRuleSetFor:with:andComment:` message:

```
CascadingStyleSheetBuilder new
    declareRuleSetFor: [ :selector | selector div ]
    with: [ :style | style margin: 2 pc ]
    andComment: 'Two picas margin';
    build
```

evaluates to:

```
/*Two picas margin*/
div
{
    margin: 2pc;
}
```

13.2 Defining the Rules

RenoirST also supports defining stand-alone comments (not attached to any rule):

```
CascadingStyleSheetBuilder new
    comment: 'A general comment';
    build
```

evaluates to:

```
/*A general comment*/
```

Functional Notation

A functional notation is a type of CSS component value that can represent complex types or invoke special processing. Mathematical expressions, toggling between values, attribute references, and gradients are all supported in RenoirST.

Mathematical Expressions

The library provides support for math expressions using the `CssMathExpression` abstraction:

```
CascadingStyleSheetBuilder new
    declareRuleSetFor: [ :selector | selector div ]
    with: [ :style | style margin: (CssMathExpression on: 2 pc) / 3 +
      2 percent ];
    build
```

evaluates to:

```
div
{
    margin: calc(2pc / 3 + 2%);
}
```

Toggling Between Values

To let descendant elements cycle over a list of values instead of inheriting the same value, one can use the `CssToggle` abstraction:

```
CascadingStyleSheetBuilder new
    declareRuleSetFor: [ :selector | selector unorderedList
      unorderedList ]
    with: [ :style | style listStyleType: (CssToggle cyclingOver: {
      CssConstants disc. CssConstants circle. CssConstants square}) ];
    build
```

evaluates to:

```
ul ul
{
```

```
    list-style-type: toggle(disc, circle, square);
}
```

Attribute References

The `attr()` function is allowed as a component value in properties applied to an element or pseudo-element. The function returns the value of an attribute on the element. If used on a pseudo-element, it returns the value of the attribute on the pseudo-element's originating element. This function is supported using the `CssAttributeReference` abstraction and can be used simply providing an attribute name:

```
CascadingStyleSheetBuilder new
   declareRuleSetFor: [ :selector | selector div before ]
   with: [ :style | style content: (CssAttributeReference
      toAttributeNamed: 'title') ];
   build
```

Evaluates to:

```
div::before
{
   content: attr(title string);
}
```

RenoirST allows for providing the type or unit of the attribute (if no type or unit is specified the `string` type is assumed):

```
CascadingStyleSheetBuilder new
   declareRuleSetFor: [ :selector | selector div ]
   with: [ :style |
      style width: (CssAttributeReference
         toAttributeNamed: 'height'
         ofType: CssLengthUnits pixel) ];
   build
```

evaluates to:

```
div
{
   width: attr(height px);
}
```

Additionally, it is possible to provide a value to use when the attribute is absent:

```
CascadingStyleSheetBuilder new
   declareRuleSetFor: [ :selector | selector div before ]
   with: [ :style |
      style content: (CssAttributeReference
      toStringAttributeNamed: 'title'
      withFallback: 'Missing title')
```

13.2 Defining the Rules

```
  ];
  build
```

evaluates to:

```
div::before
{
   content: attr(title string, "Missing title");
}
```

Gradients

A gradient is an image that smoothly fades from one color to another. Gradients are commonly used for subtle shading in background images, buttons, and many other places. The gradient notations described in this section allow an author to specify such an image in a terse syntax. This notation is supported using `CssLinearGradient` and `CssRadialGradient` abstractions.

To represent a simple linear gradient from a color to another, send the `fading:` message to `CssLinearGradient` with the two colors in an array as a parameter:

```
CascadingStyleSheetBuilder new
    declareRuleSetFor: [ :selector | selector div ]
    with: [ :style | style background: (CssLinearGradient
        fading: { CssSVGColors yellow. CssSVGColors blue }) ]
```

The above code evaluates to:

```
div
{
   background: linear-gradient(yellow, blue);
}
```

By default, a gradient's direction is from top to bottom. To specify a different direction, the author can use the `to:fading:` message instead:

```
CssLinearGradient
    to: CssConstants right
    fading: { CssSVGColors yellow. CssSVGColors blue }
```

The above code will result in a gradient with yellow on the left side and blue on the right side. The equivalent CSS is:

```
linear-gradient(to right, yellow, blue);
```

To specify a diagonal direction, an array must be passed as the `to:` argument:

```
CssLinearGradient
    to: { CssConstants top. CssConstants right }
    fading: { CssSVGColors yellow. CssSVGColors blue }
```

191

The above code will result in a gradient with blue in the top right corner and yellow in the bottom left one. The equivalent CSS is:

```
linear-gradient(to top right, yellow, blue);
```

Directions can also be specified as an angle by sending the `rotated:fading:` message:

```
CssLinearGradient
    rotated: 45 deg
    fading: { CssSVGColors yellow. CssSVGColors blue }
```

The above code maps to:

```
linear-gradient(45deg, yellow, blue);
```

Gradients can be fine-tuned by manipulating so-called color stops:

```
CssLinearGradient
    to: CssConstants right
    fading: {
        CssSVGColors yellow.
        CssColorStop for: CssSVGColors blue at: 30 percent }
```

The above code maps to:

```
linear-gradient(to right, yellow, blue 30%);
```

This results in a linear gradient from left to right with yellow at the left side and plain blue from 30% (of the horizontal line) to the right side. More than two colors can be passed as argument to `fading:`. This can be used to create rainbows:

```
CssLinearGradient
    to: CssConstants right
    fading: {
        CssSVGColors red.
        CssSVGColors orange.
        CssSVGColors yellow.
        CssSVGColors green.
        CssSVGColors blue.
        CssSVGColors indigo.
        CssSVGColors violet.
    }
```

This maps to:

```
linear-gradient(to right, red, orange, yellow, green, blue, indigo,
    violet);
```

To create radial gradients, the author must send messages to `CssRadialGradient`. For example,

13.2 Defining the Rules

```
[CssRadialGradient fading: { CssSVGColors yellow. CssSVGColors green }
```

maps to:

```
[radial-gradient(yellow,green)
```

This results in a radial gradient with yellow at the center and green all around. Coordinates can be passed to both the first and second parameters of the elliptical:at:fading: message:

```
(CssRadialGradient
    elliptical: {20 px. 30 px}
    at: { 20 px. 30 px}
    fading: { CssSVGColors red. CssSVGColors yellow. CssSVGColors
     green })
```

This maps to:

```
    background: radial-gradient(20px 30px ellipse at 20px 30px, red,
     yellow, green);
```

To make the gradient repeatable, just send to it the message beRepeating. For Example:

```
(CssRadialGradient fading: { CssSVGColors yellow. CssSVGColors green
     }) beRepeating
```

renders as:

```
[repeating-radial-gradient(yellow, green);
```

Box Shadows

Box Shadows are supported with CssBoxShadow abstraction. This abstraction simplifies the use of the box-shadow property.

```
CssBoxShadow
    horizontalOffset: 64 px
    verticalOffset: 64 px
    blurRadius: 12 px
    spreadDistance: 40 px
    color: (CssSVGColors black newWithAlpha: 0.4)
```

evaluates to:

```
[64px 64px 12px 40px rgba(0,0,0,0.4)
```

Several shadows can be combined:

```
(CssBoxShadow horizontalOffset: 64 px verticalOffset: 64 px
    blurRadius: 12 px  spreadDistance: 40 px color: (CssSVGColors
    black newWithAlpha: 0.4)) ,
(CssBoxShadow horizontalOffset: 12 px verticalOffset: 11 px
    blurRadius: 0 px  spreadDistance: 8 px color: (CssSVGColors
```

```
    black newWithAlpha: 0.4)) beInset
```

Evaluates to:

```
64px 64px 12px 40px rgba(0,0,0,0.4), inset 12px 11px 0px 8px
    rgba(0,0,0,0.4)
```

13.3 Defining the selectors

So far our focus was on the *style* part of the rule. Let's focus now on the available *selectors*. Remember that a CSS selector represents a structure used to match elements in the document tree. This chapter asume some familiarity with the CSS selectors and will not go in detail about the exact meaning of each one. For more details you can take a look at CSS3 selector documentation[3].

Type Selectors

These selectors match a specific element type in the DOM. The library provides out-of-the-box support for HTML elements. One example is the div selector used in the previous chapter:

```
CascadingStyleSheetBuilder new
    declareRuleSetFor: [ :selector | selector div ]
    with: [ :style | ... ];
    build
```

The following other example matches <ol> (ordered list) elements:

```
CascadingStyleSheetBuilder new
    declareRuleSetFor: [:selector | selector orderedList ]
    with: [ :style | ... ]
```

evaluating to:

```
ol
{
  ...
}
```

To get a list of the supported type selectors evaluate `CssSelector selectorsInProtocol: '*RenoirSt-HTML'`.

Combinators

Selectors can be combined to represent complex queries. One of the most common use cases is the *descendant combinator*:

---

[3] http://www.w3.org/TR/css3-selectors

13.3 Defining the selectors

```
CascadingStyleSheetBuilder new
    declareRuleSetFor: [:selector | selector div orderedList ]
    with: [:style | ... ]
```

evaluating to:

```
div ol
{
    ...
}
```

This only matches if an ol element is a descendant (direct or not) of a div element.

The *child combinator* only matches when an element is a direct child of another one:

```
CascadingStyleSheetBuilder new
    declareRuleSetFor: [:selector | selector div > selector
      orderedList ]
    with: [:style | ]
```

evaluates to

```
div > ol
{
    ...
}
```

Siblings combinators can be created using + and ~:

```
CascadingStyleSheetBuilder new
    declareRuleSetFor: [:selector | selector div + selector
      orderedList ]
    with: [:style | ]
    declareRuleSetFor: [:selector | selector div ~ selector
      orderedList ]
    with: [:style | ]
```

Class selectors can be created by sending class: and id selectors can be created by sending id:. For example,

```
CascadingStyleSheetBuilder new
    declareRuleSetFor: [:selector | (selector div class: 'pastoral')
      id: #account5 ]
    with: [:style | ]
```

evaluates to:

```
div.pastoral#account5
{
    ...
}
```

> **Note** You should not hardcode the classes and ids, they should be obtained from the same object that holds them for the HTML generation. You probably have some code setting the class(es) and/or id(s) to a particular HTML element.

A comma-separated list of selectors represents the union of all elements selected by each of the individual selectors in the list. For example, in CSS when several selectors share the same declarations, they may be grouped into a comma-separated list.

```
CascadingStyleSheetBuilder new
    declareRuleSetFor: [:selector | selector paragraph , selector div
      ]
    with: [:style | ... ]
```

evaluates to:

```
p, div
{
    ...
}
```

Attribute Selectors

Attribute selectors are useful to match an element based on its attributes and their values.

The *attribute presence* selector matches an element having an attribute (without considering the value of the attribute):

```
CascadingStyleSheetBuilder new
    declareRuleSetFor: [:selector | selector h1 havingAttribute:
      'title' ]
    with: [:style | style color: CssSVGColors blue ];
    build
```

evaluates to:

```
h1[title]
{
    color: blue;
}
```

The *attribute value exact matching* selectors matches an element having an attribute with a specific value:

```
CascadingStyleSheetBuilder new
    declareRuleSetFor: [:selector | selector span withAttribute:
      'class' equalTo: 'example' ]
    with: [:style | style color: CssSVGColors blue ];
    build
```

13.3 Defining the selectors

evaluates to:

```
span[class="example"]
{
    color: blue;
}
```

The *attribute value inclusion* selector matches an element having an attribute with a value including as a word the matching term:

```
CascadingStyleSheetBuilder new
    declareRuleSetFor: [:selector | selector anchor attribute: 'rel'
        includes: 'copyright' ]
    with: [:style | style color: CssSVGColors blue ];
    build
```

```
a[rel~="copyright"]
{
    color: blue;
}
```

Other attribute selectors are used for substring matching:

```
CascadingStyleSheetBuilder new
    declareRuleSetFor: [:selector | selector anchor
        firstValueOfAttribute: 'hreflang' beginsWith: 'en' ]
    with: [:style | style color: CssSVGColors blue ];
    build
```

```
a[hreflang|="en"]
{
    color: blue;
}
```

```
CascadingStyleSheetBuilder new
    declareRuleSetFor: [:selector | selector anchor attribute: 'type'
        beginsWith: 'image/' ]
    with: [:style | style color: CssSVGColors blue ];
    build
```

```
a[type^="image/"]
{
    color: blue;
}
```

```
CascadingStyleSheetBuilder new
    declareRuleSetFor: [:selector | selector anchor attribute: 'type'
        endsWith: '.html' ]
    with: [:style | style color: CssSVGColors blue ];
    build
```

```
a[type$=".html"]
{
    color: blue;
```

```
}
```

```
CascadingStyleSheetBuilder new
    declareRuleSetFor: [:selector | selector paragraph attribute:
      'title' includesSubstring: 'hello' ]
    with: [:style | style color: CssSVGColors blue ];
    build
```

```
p[title*="hello"]
{
    color: blue;
}
```

Pseudo-Classes

The pseudo-class concept is introduced to allow selection based on information that lies outside of the document tree or that cannot be expressed using the simpler selectors. Most pseudo-classes are supported just by sending one of the following messages link, visited, active, hover, focus, target, enabled, disabled or checked.

Here is a small example that uses the pseudo-classes:

```
CascadingStyleSheetBuilder new
    declareRuleSetFor: [:selector | selector anchor link ]
    with: [:style | style color: CssSVGColors blue ];
    declareRuleSetFor: [:selector | selector anchor visited active]
    with: [:style | style color: CssSVGColors green ];
    declareRuleSetFor: [:selector | selector anchor focus hover
      enabled]
    with: [:style | style color: CssSVGColors green ];
    declareRuleSetFor: [:selector | (selector paragraph class:
      'note') target disabled]
    with: [:style | style color: CssSVGColors green ];
    declareRuleSetFor: [:selector | selector input checked ]
    with: [:style | style color: CssSVGColors green ];
    build
```

evaluates to:

```
a:link
{
    color: blue;
}

a:visited:active
{
    color: green;
}

a:focus:hover:enabled
```

13.3 Defining the selectors

```
{
    color: green;
}

p.note:target:disabled
{
    color: green;
}

input:checked
{
    color: green;
}
```

Language Pseudo-Class:

The :lang(C) pseudo-class can be used by sending the message lang::

```
CascadingStyleSheetBuilder new
    declareRuleSetFor: [:selector | (selector lang: 'es') > selector
      div ]
    with: [:style | style quotes: { '"«"'. '"»"' } ];
    build
```

evaluates to:

```
:lang(es) > div
{
    quotes: "«" "»";
}
```

Negation Pseudo-Class:

The negation pseudo-class, :not(X), is a functional notation taking a simple selector (excluding the negation pseudo-class itself) as an argument. It represents an element that is not represented by its argument. For more information take a look at the CSS spec.

This selector is supported sending the message not:

```
CascadingStyleSheetBuilder new
    declareRuleSetFor: [:selector | selector button not: (selector
      havingAttribute: 'DISABLED') ]
    with: [:style | style color: CssSVGColors blue ];
    build
```

```
button:not([DISABLED])
{
    color: blue;
}
```

Structural Pseudo-Classes

These selectors allow selection based on extra information that lies in the document tree but cannot be represented by other simpler selectors nor combinators.

The :root pseudo-class represents an element that is the root of the document. To build this kind of selector just send the message root to another selector:

```
CascadingStyleSheetBuilder new
    declareRuleSetFor: [:selector | selector root ]
    with: [:style | style color: CssSVGColors grey ];
    build
```

evaluates to:

```
:root
{
    color: grey;
}
```

The :nth-child(an+b) pseudo-class notation represents an element that has an+b-1 siblings before it in the document tree, for any positive integer or zero value of n, and has a parent element. For values of a and b greater than zero, this effectively divides the element's children into groups of a elements (the last group taking the remainder), and selecting the bth element of each group. The a and b values must be integers (positive, negative, or zero). The index of the first child of an element is 1.

In addition to this, :nth-child() can take a number, odd and even as arguments. The value odd is equivalent to 2n+1, whereas even is equivalent to 2n.

```
CascadingStyleSheetBuilder new
    declareRuleSetFor: [:selector | selector childAt: 3 n + 1 ]
    with: [:style | style color: CssSVGColors blue ];
    declareRuleSetFor: [:selector | selector childAt: 5 ]
    with: [:style | style color: CssSVGColors blue ];
    declareRuleSetFor: [:selector | selector childAt: CssConstants
        even]
    with: [:style | style color: CssSVGColors blue ];
    build
```

evaluates to:

```
:nth-child(3n+1)
{
    color: blue;
}

:nth-child(5)
{
```

13.3 Defining the selectors

```
    color: blue;
}

:nth-child(even)
{
    color: blue;
}
```

All structural pseudo-classes can be generated using the following messages:

CSS pseudo-class	RenoirST selector message
root()	root
nth-child()	childAt:
nth-last-child()	childFromLastAt:
nth-of-type()	siblingOfTypeAt:
nth-last-of-type()	siblingOfTypeFromLastAt:
first-child	firstChild
last-child	lastChild
first-of-type	firstOfType
last-of-type	lastOfType
only-child	onlyChild
only-of-type	onlyOfType
empty	empty

Pseudo-Elements

Pseudo-elements create abstractions about the document tree beyond those specified by the document language. For instance, document languages do not offer mechanisms to access the first letter or first line of an element's content. Pseudo-elements allow authors to refer to this otherwise inaccessible information. Pseudo-elements may also provide authors a way to refer to content that does not exist in the source document.

The firstLine pseudo-element describes the contents of the first formatted line of an element.

```
CascadingStyleSheetBuilder new
    declareRuleSetFor: [:selector | selector paragraph firstLine ]
    with: [:style | style textTransform: CssConstants uppercase ];
    build
```

evaluates to:

```
p::first-line
{
    text-transform: uppercase;
}
```

The `firstLetter` pseudo-element represents the first letter of an element, if it is not preceded by any other content (such as images or inline tables) on its line.

```
CascadingStyleSheetBuilder new
    declareRuleSetFor: [:selector | selector paragraph firstLetter ]
    with: [:style | style fontSize: 200 percent ];
    build
```

evaluates to:

```
p::first-letter
{
    font-size: 200%;
}
```

The `before` and `after` pseudo-elements can be used to describe generated content before or after an element's content. The `content` property, in conjunction with these pseudo-elements, specifies what is inserted.

```
CascadingStyleSheetBuilder new
    declareRuleSetFor: [:selector | (selector paragraph class:
      'note') before ]
    with: [:style | style content: '"Note: "' ];
    declareRuleSetFor: [:selector | (selector paragraph class:
      'note') after ]
    with: [:style | style content: '"[*]"' ];
    build
```

evaluates to:

```
p.note::before
{
    content: "Note: ";
}

p.note::after
{
    content: "[*]";
}
```

13.4 Important Rules

CSS attempts to create a balance of power between author and user style sheets. By default, rules in an author's style sheet override those in a user's style sheet. However, for balance, an !important declaration takes precedence over a normal declaration. Both author and user style sheets may contain !important declarations, and user !important rules override author !important rules. This CSS feature improves accessibility of documents by giving users with special requirements control over presentation.

RenoirSt supports this feature through the beImportantDuring: message sent to the style.

```
CascadingStyleSheetBuilder new
    declareRuleSetFor: [:selector | selector paragraph ]
    with: [:style |
        style beImportantDuring: [:importantStyle |
            importantStyle
                textIndent: 1 em;
                fontStyle: CssConstants italic ].
        style fontSize: 18 pt ];
    build
```

evaluates to:

```
p
{
    text-indent: 1em !important;
    font-style: italic !important;
    font-size: 18pt;
}
```

Note that the important properties must be created by sending the messages to the inner argument importantStyle instead of the outer argument style.

13.5 Media Queries

A @media rule specifies the target media types of a set of statements. The @media construct allows style sheet rules that apply to various media in the same style sheet. Style rules outside of @media rules apply to all media types that the style sheet applies to. At-rules inside @media are invalid in CSS2.1.

The most basic media rule consists of specifying just a media type:

```
CascadingStyleSheetBuilder new
    declare: [ :cssBuilder |
        cssBuilder
            declareRuleSetFor: [ :selector | selector div ]
            with: [ :style | ] ]
    forMediaMatching: [ :queryBuilder |
        queryBuilder type: CssMediaQueryConstants print ];
    build
```

evaluates to:

```
@media print
{
    div { }
}
```

To use media queries in the library just send the message `declare:forMediaMatching:` to the builder. The first block is evaluated with an instance of a `CascadingStyleSheetBuilder` and the second one with a builder of media queries.

The media query builder will match any media type by default. To specify a media type just send it the message `type:` with the corresponding media type. The class `CssMediaQueryConstants` provides easy access to the following media types: `braille`, `embossed`, `handheld`, `print`, `projection`, `screen`, `speech`, `tty` and `tv`.

The media query builder supports a variety of messages for additional conditions (called media features). Media features are used in expressions to describe requirements of the output device.

The following media feature messages are supported:

- Accepting a `CssMeasure` with length units: `width:`, `minWidth:`, `maxWidth:`, `height:`, `minHeight:`, `maxHeight:`, `deviceWidth:`, `minDeviceWidth:`, `maxDeviceWidth:`, `deviceHeight:`, `minDeviceHeight:`, `maxDeviceHeight:`;

- `orientation:` accepting `CssMediaQueryConstants portrait` or `CssMediaQueryConstants landscape`;

- Accepting fractions as aspect ratios: `aspectRatio:`, `minAspectRatio:`, `maxAspectRatio:`, `deviceAspectRatio:`, `minDeviceAspectRatio:`, `maxDeviceAspectRatio:`;

- Accepting integers: `color:` (the argument describes the number of bits per color component of the output device), `minColor:`, `maxColor:`, `colorIndex:` (the argument describes the number of entries in the color lookup table of the output device), `minColorIndex:`, `maxColorIndex:`, `monochrome:` (the argument describes the number of bits per pixel in a monochrome frame buffer), `minMonochrome:`, `maxMonochrome:`, `grid:` (the argument must be 1 or 0);

- Accepting a `CssMeasure` with resolution units: `resolution:`, `minResolution:`, `maxResolution:`;

- `scan:` accepting `CssMediaQueryConstants progressive` or `CssMediaQueryConstants interlace`.

New units for resolutions are added using the `CssMeasure` abstraction. This kind of measures can be created sending the messages `dpi` (dots per inch), `dpcm` (dots per centimeter) or `dppx` (dots per pixel unit) to an integer or float.

Here is a final example to better understand the media features support:

```
CascadingStyleSheetBuilder new
  declare: [ :cssBuilder |
    cssBuilder
```

```
            declareRuleSetFor: [ :selector | selector id: #oop ]
            with: [ :style | style color: CssSVGColors red ] ]
    forMediaMatching: [ :queryBuilder |
      queryBuilder
            orientation: CssMediaQueryConstants landscape;
            resolution: 300 dpi ];
    build
```

evaluates to:

```
@media all and (orientation: landscape) and (resolution: 300dpi)
{
    #oop
    {
        color: red;
    }
}
```

13.6 Vendor-Specific Extensions

The library doesn't provide out of the box support for non standard properties. Nevertheless, the message vendorPropertyAt:put: is available to ease the creation of this kind of properties by the end user:

```
CascadingStyleSheetBuilder new
    declareRuleSetFor: [:selector | selector div ]
    with: [:style | style vendorPropertyAt: 'crazy-margin' put: 1 px
      ];
    build
```

evaluates to:

```
div
{
    crazy-margin: 1px;
    -moz-crazy-margin: 1px;
    -webkit-crazy-margin: 1px;
    -o-crazy-margin: 1px;
    -ms-crazy-margin: 1px;
}
```

> **Note** If you really want to use a vendor specific extension, It's better to create an extension method sending the vendorPropertyAt:put: message.

13.7 Font Face Rules

The @font-face rule allows for linking to fonts that are automatically fetched and activated when needed. This allows authors to select a font that closely matches the design goals for a given page rather than limiting the font choice to a set of fonts available on a given platform. A set of font descriptors define the location of a font resource, either locally or externally, along with the style characteristics of an individual face.

This support is implemented in the builder:

```
CascadingStyleSheetBuilder new
   declareFontFaceRuleWith: [ :style |
      style
         fontFamily: 'Gentium';
         src: 'http://example.com/fonts/gentium.woff' asZnUrl ];
   build
```

evaluates to:

```
@font-face
{
   font-family: Gentium;
   src: url("http://example.com/fonts/gentium.woff");
}
```

This kind of rule allows for multiple `src` definitions specifying the resources containing the data. This resources can be external (fonts fetched from a URL) or local (available in the user system). This kind of resources are supported using `CssLocalFontReference` and `CssExternalFontReference` abstractions:

```
CascadingStyleSheetBuilder new
   declareFontFaceRuleWith: [ :style |
      style
         fontFamily: 'MainText';
         src: (CssExternalFontReference
            locatedAt: 'gentium.eat' asZnUrl relativeToStyleSheet);
         src: (CssLocalFontReference toFontNamed: 'Gentium'),
            (CssExternalFontReference locatedAt: 'gentium.woff'
       asZnUrl relativeToStyleSheet withFormat: CssFontConstants woff);
         src: (CssExternalFontReference svgFontLocatedAt:
      'fonts.svg' asZnUrl relativeToStyleSheet withId: 'simple') ];
   build
```

```
@font-face
{
   font-family: MainText;
   src: url("gentium.eat");
   src: local(Gentium), url("gentium.woff") format("woff");
   src: url("fonts.svg#simple") format("svg");
}
```

13.8 Interaction with other Frameworks and Libraries

Units

The Units package (available using the ConfigurationBrowser in Pharo) includes some extensions colliding with RenoirSt. RenoirST can automatically load a compatibility package if it's loaded after the Units package. To test this integration there's a specific continuous integration job[4], that loads Units first and then RenoirSt.

Seaside

RenoirSt includes an optional group including some useful extensions. The Seaside[5] framework includes its own class modeling URLs: when this group is loaded the instances of WAUrl can be used in the properties requiring an URI:

```
CascadingStyleSheetBuilder new
    declareRuleSetFor: [:selector | selector div class: 'logo' ]
    with: [:style |
        style backgroundImage: 'images/logo.png' seasideUrl ];
    build
```

evaluates to:

```
div.logo
{
    background-image: url("/images/logo.png");
}
```

This optional group also loads extensions to CssDeclarationBlock so it can be used as a JSObject in plugins requiring some style parameter or as the argument in a component style: method.

To load these extensions in an image with Seaside already loaded, you need to load the group Deployment-Seaside-Extensions, or Development-Seaside-Extensions if you want the test cases (there is also a stable-pharo-40 branch if needed):

```
Metacello new
    baseline: 'RenoirSt';
    repository: 'github://gcotelli/RenoirSt:stable-pharo-50/source';
    load: 'Deployment-Seaside-Extensions'
```

---

[4] https://ci.inria.fr/pharo-contribution/job/RenoirSt-UnitsCompatibility
[5] http://www.seaside.st

CHAPTER **14**

Documenting and Presenting with Pillar

Damien Cassou and Cyril Ferlicot Delbecque

This chapter describes Pillar version 2. The original author of Pillar and current maintainer is Damien Cassou. Many people have also contributed: Ben Coman, Stéphane Ducasse, Guillermo Polito, Lukas Renggli (original author of Pier from which Pillar has been extracted), Benjamin van Ryseghem and Cyril Ferlicot-Delbecque. Pillar is sponsored by ESUG[1].

14.1 Introduction

Pillar[2] is a markup syntax and associated tools to write and generate documentation, books (such as this one) and slide-based presentations. The Pillar screenshot in Figure 14-1 shows the HTML version of chapter 11.

Pillar has many features, helpful tools, and documentation:

- simple markup syntax with references, tables, pictures, captions, syntax-highlighted code blocks;
- export documents to HTML, LaTeX, Markdown, AsciiDoc and Pillar itself, and presentations to Beamer and Deck.js;
- customization of the export through a dedicated STON configuration file (see chapter 9) and Mustache templates (see chapter 12).

---

[1] http://www.esug.org
[2] http://www.smalltalkhub.com/#!/~Pier/Pillar

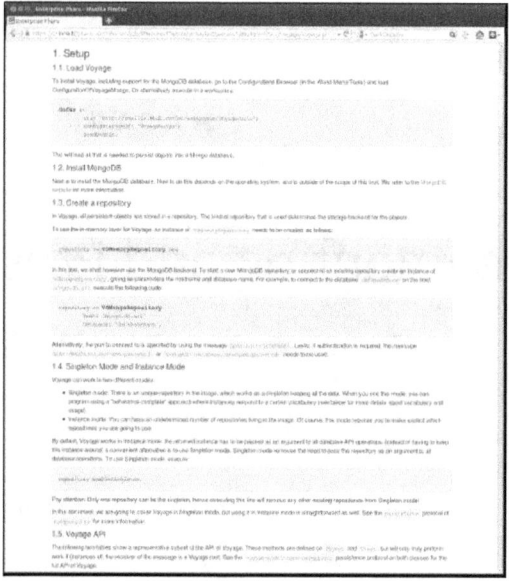

Figure 14-1 An example Pillar output

- many tests with good coverage (94% with more than a 2100 executed tests), which are regularly run by a continuous integration job[3]
- a command-line interface and dedicated plugins for several text editors: Emacs[4], Vim[5], TextMate[6], and Atom[7]
- a cheat sheet[8]

Pillar Users

This book was written in Pillar. If you want to see how Pillar is used, have a look at the book's source code available from its website[9], or check the following other real-world projects:

- the Updated Pharo by Example book[10]
- the Pharo MOOC[11] (Massive open online course)

---

[3] https://ci.inria.fr/pharo-contribution/job/Pillar
[4] https://github.com/pillar-markup/pillar-mode
[5] https://github.com/cdlm/vim-pillar
[6] https://github.com/Uko/Pillar.tmbundle
[7] https://github.com/Uko/language-pillar
[8] http://pillarhub.pharocloud.com/hub/pillarhub/pillarcheatsheet
[9] http://books.pharo.org/enterprise-pharo/
[10] https://github.com/SquareBracketAssociates/UpdatedPharoByExample
[11] https://github.com/SquareBracketAssociates/PharoMooc

- the PillarHub open-access shared blog[12]

14.2 5 Minutes Tutorial

In this section we give the basic steps to get you started with your first Pillar document and exports. You first need to create a *base directory* inside which we will put all your text, configuration files, and Pillar itself.

```
mkdir mydocument
cd mydocument
```

Installing and Exporting your First Document

You first need to get Pillar. For that, I recommend downloading and executing this script[13] in the base directory if you are on an Unix environment.

If you are on Windows you can get a new Pillar image by extracting an archive[14]. Then you need a Pharo Virtual Machine for Windows[15].

Then, you can check everything is working fine by creating a `first.pillar` file with this content:

```
!Hello World
```

And finally compiling it from a terminal (see Section 14.6 for more information about the command-line interface):

```
./pillar export --to=html first.pillar
```

Or in windows open a new shell (Windows key + r then type cmd) then run:

```
Pharo.exe Pillar.image pillar export --to=html first.pillar
```

This should generate an *output.html* file you can open in a web browser. The content of this file will be something like:

```
<!DOCTYPE html>
<html lang="en">
   <head>
      <title></title>
      [...]
   </head>
   <body>
      <div class="container"> [...]
         <h1>I. Hello World</h1>
      </div>
```

---

[12]http://pillarhub.pharocloud.com
[13]https://raw.githubusercontent.com/pillar-markup/book-skeleton/master/download.sh
[14]https://ci.inria.fr/pharo-contribution/job/Pillar/PHARO=40,VERSION=stable,VM=vm/lastSuccessfulBuild/artifact/Pillar.zip
[15]http://files.pharo.org/get-files/40/pharo-win-stable.zip

```
        [...]
    </body>
</html>
```

Configuring a Document

As you can see, there is no document title in the generated *output.html* file. This is because we did not specify any. To specify a title, we have to add it with a configuration at the beginning of the *first.pillar* file:

```
{
    "title": "My first document while reading the 5 minutes Pillar
        tutorial"
}

!Hello World
```

When you compile using the same command line,

```
./pillar export --to=html first.pillar
```

or

```
Pharo.exe Pillar.image pillar export --to=html first.pillar
```

you should now get a web page with a title:

```
<!DOCTYPE html>
<html lang="en">
    <head>
        <title>My first document while reading the 5 minutes Pillar
        tutorial</title>
    </head>
```

Another way to achieve the same is to use a dedicated configuration file. This configuration is typically named `pillar.conf` and is written in the STON format (see Section 14.4 for more information about the configuration file). Create your first `pillar.conf` file:

```
{
    "title" : "My first document from pillar.conf"
}
```

Meta-information specified in Pillar files take precedence over configuration in the `pillar.conf` file. To see the new title, you thus have to remove the one in `first.pillar`.

Output and Multi Files

You have the possibility to export all your files into a specific directory. To do that you have to add a parameter to `pillar.conf`:

5 Minutes Tutorial

```
{
    "title" : "My first document from pillar.conf",
    "outputDirectory" : "result"
}
```

If you export you will have a file *result/output.html*.

You have two ways to export files:

1. separate output files
2. as one output file

By default Pillar exports all the input files as one. If you create a file *second.pillar* that contains `I am a second file` you can add a parameter *inputFiles* to your configuration.

```
{
    "title" : "My first document from pillar.conf",
    "outputDirectory" : "result",
    "inputFiles" : [ "first.pillar", "second.pillar" ]
}
```

If you export this with the command:

```
./pillar export --to=html
```

You will get a file *result/output.html* that contains:

```
<h1>I. Hello World</h1>
<p>
I am a second file
</p>
```

If you want to change the name of the output file you can use the parameter *outputFile*.

If you want separate files you can add a parameter:

```
{
    "title" : "My first document from pillar.conf",
    "outputDirectory" : "result",
    "inputFiles" : [ "first.pillar", "second.pillar" ],
    "separateOutputFiles" : true
}
```

You will get a file *result/first.html* and a file *result/second.html*.

Exporting a Different Content Using a Template

If you want to tweak the content of the exported file, for example to reference your CSS or to add a footer, you need to create your own template (see Section 14.5 for more information about templating). You must write such template in its own file, e.g., `myhtml.template`:

```
<!DOCTYPE html>
<html lang="en">
    <head>
        <title>{{{title}}}</title>
    </head>
    <body>
        <div class="container">
            {{{content}}}
        </div>
        <footer>
            <p>{{author}}, {{year}}</p>
        </footer>
    </body>
</html>
```

Then, you need to reference this template from your configuration file. So, edit your `pillar.conf` configuration file:

```
{   [...]
    "year" : 2016,
    "configurations" : {
        "html": {
            "outputType" : #html,
            "template" : "myhtml.template"
        }
    }
}
```

Now, write your name in `first.pillar`:

```
{
    "author": "Damien Cassou"
}

!Hello World
```

Finally, compile `first.pillar` one last time

```
./pillar export --to=html first.pillar
```

to generate a file containing:

```
<!DOCTYPE html>
<html lang="en">
    <head>
        <title>My first document from pillar.conf</title>
    </head>
    <body>
        <div class="container"> [...]
            <h1>Hello World</h1>
        </div>
        <footer>
```

```
            <p>Damien Cassou, 2016</p>
        </footer>
    </body>
</html>
```

Look at how the HTML template (`myhtml.template`) references `title`, author and year. These variables are referenced by enclosing them in 3 curly braces. The templating engine that transforms your templates in documents is Mustache (see chapter 12. As you can see, I decided to put the author of the document in the `first.pillar` file whereas the year and title are specified in `pillar.conf`: this is arbitrary and you can do whatever suits you best: the differences being that the `pillar.conf` file applies to all Pillar files of the project and that file meta-information takes precedence.

This concludes our 5 minutes tutorial.

14.3 Writing Pillar Documents

In this section we show how to write Pillar documents by presenting the Pillar syntax. You might want to have a look at the cheat sheet[16] and even download and print it.

Meta-Information

Meta-information of a particular file is written at the start of the file between curly braces using the STON syntax (see chapter 9). A meta-information starts with a word between quotation marks acting as a key, is followed by a colon :, and finishes with a value. For example, the following Pillar file,

```
{
    "title": "My first document from pillar.conf",
    "author": "Damien Cassou"
}

!Hello World
```

represents a Pillar document with the title and author set. You can use whatever keys you like. Use them by referencing them in templates (see section 14.5 for more information about templating).

Chapters & Sections

A line starting with ! represents a heading. Use multiple ! to create sections and subsections. To refer to a section or chapter, put an anchor (equivalent to \label{chapterAndSections} in Latex) using the @chapterAndSections syntax on a *separate line*. Then, when you want to link to it (equivalent to

---

[16]http://pillarhub.pharocloud.com/hub/pillarhub/pillarcheatsheet

\ref{chapterAndSections} in Latex), use the *@chapterAndSections* syntax. Anchors are invisible and links will be rendered as: 14.3.

Paragraphs and Framed Paragraphs

An empty line starts a new paragraph.

An annotated paragraph starts with @@ followed by a keyword such as todo and note. For example,

```
@@note this is a note annotation.
```

generates

> **Note** this is a note annotation.

And,

```
@@todo this is a todo annotation
```

generates a todo annotation

> **To do** this is a todo annotation

The annotation (e.g., todo and note) can be any word that is meaningful to the author. In HTML, an annotated paragraph triggers the generation of a paragraph with the annotation as the paragraph class. In LaTeX, an environment with the annotation name is generated. In HTML, you can tweak the output to make it look nice, for example with such JavaScript code:

```
// Wraps paragraphs with class pClass inside a div and adds an H4
    element with pTitle.
function transformAnnotatedParagraphs(pClass, pTitle) {
   $("p." + pClass).wrap( "<div class='annotated-paragraph "
       + pClass + "' />" ).prepend("<h4>"+ pTitle +"</h4>");
}

transformAnnotatedParagraphs("note", "Note");
transformAnnotatedParagraphs("todo", "To do");
```

Above code will prepend the titles "Note" and "To do" to the @@note and @@todo paragraphs. You can make that looks nice using a little bit of CSS:

```
.annotated-paragraph {
   margin: 20px 0;
   padding: 15px 30px 15px 15px;
   border-left: 5px solid #eee;
}

.annotated-paragraph h4 {
   margin-top: 0;
```

14.3 Writing Pillar Documents

```
}

.annotated-paragraph p:last-child {
    margin-bottom: 0;
}

.note {
    background-color: #f0f7fd;
    border-color: #d0e3f0;
}

.note h4 {
    color: #3a87ad;
}

.todo {
    background-color: #dff0d8;
    border-color: #d6e9c6;
}

.todo h4 {
    color: #3c763d;
}
```

Lists

Unordered Lists

```
-A block of lines,
-where each line starts with ==-==
-is transformed to a bulleted list
```

generates

- A block of lines,
- where each line starts with -
- is transformed to a bulleted list

Ordered Lists

```
#A block of lines,
#where each line starts with ==#==
#is transformed to an ordered list
```

generates

1. A block of lines,
2. where each line starts with #
3. is transformed to an ordered list

Definition Lists

Definition lists (*aka.* description lists) are lists with labels:

```
;blue
:color of the sky
;red
:color of the fire
```

generates

blue color of the sky

red color of the fire

List Nesting

```
-Lists can also be nested.
-#Thus, a line starting with ==-#==
-#is an element of an unordered list that is part of an ordered list.
```

generates

- Lists can also be nested.
    1. Thus, a line starting with -#
    2. is an element of a bulleted list that is part of an ordered list.

Formatting

There is some syntax for text formatting:

- To make something **bold**, write `""bold""` (with 2 double quotes)
- To make something *italic*, write `''italic''` (with 2 single quotes)
- To make something monospaced, write `==monospaced==`
- To make something ~~strikethrough~~, write `--strikethrough--`
- To make something $_{subscript}$, write `@@subscript@@`
- To make something ^{superscript}, write `^^superscript^^`
- To make something underlined, write `__underlined__`

Tables

To create a table, start the lines with | and separate the elements with |. Each new line represents a new row of the table. Add a single ! to let the cell become a table heading.

14.3 Writing Pillar Documents

```
||!Language ||!Coolness
|Smalltalk | Hypra cool
|Java | baaad
```

Language	Coolness
Smalltalk	Hypra cool
Java	baaad

The contents of cells can be aligned left, centered or aligned right by using |{, || or |} respectively.

```
||centered|||!centered header||centered
|{ left |}·right || center
```

generates

centered	**centered header**	centered
left	right	center

Links

Internal Links and Anchors

To put an anchor (equivalent to \label in Latex), use the @anchorName syntax on a *separate line*. Then, when you want to link to it (equivalent to \ref in Latex), use the *@anchorName* syntax. Anchors are invisible and links will be rendered as: 14.3.

To create a link to an other pillar file, use the *Alias>path.pillar@anchorName*. The Alias and the anchor are optional but you will need them in some cases (for example if you have an inter-file link and you export in LaTeX, or if you have an inter-file link and you export all your file in the same html file).

External Links

To create links to external resources, use the *Pharo>http://pharo.org/* syntax which is rendered as Pharo[17]. The same syntax can also represent email addresses: write *damien@cassou.me* to get damien@cassou.me.

Pictures

To include a picture, use the syntax +caption>file://filename|parameters+:

```
+Caption of the
    picture>file://figures/pharo-logo.png|width=50|label=pharoLogo+
```

---

[17]http://pharo.org/

Figure 14-2 This is the caption of the picture

Listing 14-3 My script
```
self foo bar
```

generates Figure 14-2 (this reference has been generated using *@pharoLogo*).

Scripts

Use scripts when you want to add code blocks to your document.
```
[[[
foo bar
]]]
```

generates
```
foo bar
```

Script with a Label or Caption

If you want either a label (to reference the script later) or a caption (to give a nice title to the script), write the following:
```
[[[label=script1|caption=My script|language=smalltalk
self foo bar
]]]
```

which produces script 14-3 (this reference is produced with *@script1*).

Syntax Highlighting

To specify the syntax a script is written in, you need to use the `language` parameter. For example on 14-3 we used the `smalltalk` value for the `language` parameter.

> **Note** The currently supported languages are bash, css, html, http, json, javascript, pillar, sql, ston, shellcommands and smalltalk

If you don't want syntax highlighting for a particular script, specify no language as value to the `language` parameter.

14.3 Writing Pillar Documents

Script with Line Numbers

If you need to explain a long piece of code, you may want a script to have line numbers:

```
[[[lineNumber=true
self foo bar.
self bar foo.
]]]
```

produces

```
1 self foo bar.
2 self bar foo.
```

Script from an External File

If you want you can also include a script from a external file. For example if you have a file 'myProject.html' and you want to take the code from line 15 to line 45, instead of copy/pasting the code you can use:

```
[[[language=html|fromFile=myProject.html|firstLine=15|lastLine=45
]]]
```

The `firstLine` and `lastLine` parameters are optional.

Generate a Part of your Document with a Script

If you want you can also evaluate a script to generate a part of your document. For example if you write a project's documentation and want to give some metrics about its code, you can write something like this:

```
[[[eval=true
| packages classes |
packages := RPackageOrganizer default packages select: [ :each |
            each name includesSubstring: 'Pillar' ].
classes := packages flatCollect: [ :each | each classes ].
stream
   nextPutAll: 'The Pillar project contains:';
   lf;
   nextPutAll: '- ==';
   print: packages size;
   nextPutAll: ' packages==.';
   lf;
   nextPutAll: '- ==';
   print: classes size;
   nextPutAll: ' classes=='.
]]]
```

will generate:

The Pillar project contains:

- 27 packages.
- 309 classes.

For example section 14.4 of this chapter is generated.

Raw

If you want to include raw text into a page you must enclose it between {{{ and }}}, otherwise Pillar ensures that text appears as you type it which might require transformations.

A good practice is to always specify for which kind of export the raw text must be outputted by starting the block with {{{latex: or {{{html:. For example, the following shows a formula, either using LaTeX or plain text depending on the kind of export.

```
{{{latex:
\begin{equation}
   \label{eq:1}
   \frac{1+\sqrt{2}}{2}
\end{equation}
}}}
{{{html:
(1+sqrt(2)) / 2
}}}
```

Take care: avoid terminating the verbatim text with a } as this will confuse the parser. So, don't write {{{\begin{scriptsize}}}} but {{{\begin{scriptsize} }}} instead.

Annotations

Annotations are the Pillar way to have extensible syntax. An annotation has this syntax:

```
${tag:parameter=value|parameter2=value2}$
```

InputFile Annotation

You can include a file into another pillar file. The `inputFile` annotation takes as parameter the path of the file relative to `baseDirectory` (if you don't change the base directory, it is your working directory). In this example, 2 files are included:

```
${inputFile:test.pillar}$

${inputFile:chapter2/chapter2.pillar}$
```

Slide Annotation

This annotation is used to create slides structure for a beamer or a deck.js export. The parameter **title** is required. The **label** parameter can be used to reference this slide in another slide:

```
${slide:title=My slide|label=sld:mySlide}$
```

Columns

With Pillar you can put text and other contents in columns. To do that, you need to delimit an environment with the columns and endColumns annotations. Then you can create columns with the column annotation. The column annotation takes 1 required parameter: the width of the column. Here is an example:

```
${columns}$
    ${column:width=60}$
        bla
    ${column:40}$
        bla
${endColumns}$
```

> **Note** The column annotations currently works only for the beamer, HTML and Deck.js export.

Preformatted (less used)

To create a preformatted block, begin each line with =. A preformatted block uses equally spaced text so that spacing is preserved. In general you should prefer scripts over preformatted blocks.

```
= this is preformatted text
= this line as well
```

Commented Lines

Lines that start with a % are considered comments and will not be rendered in the resulting document.

Escaping Characters

Special characters (e.g., + and *) must be escaped with a backslash: to get a +, you actually have to write \+. The list of characters to escape is:

```
^, _, :, ;, =, @, {, |, !, ", #, $, %, ', *, +, [, -
```

14.4 Configuring your Output

In this section we show how to configure the export.

Configuration File

Pillar exporting mechanism can be configured using STON[18] (see chapter @ston), a lightweight, text-based, human-readable data interchange format (similar to the popular JSON[19]). Configuration is done either in `pillar.conf` or at the beginning of Pillar files.

Configuration Parameters

baseDirectory

Indicate where to look for files.

Default value: The current working directory

configurations

Each configuration can define several sub configurations, each of which inherits the properties of its parent.

Default value: A dictionary of default configurations from the exporters.

defaultExporters

Collection of exporters to use when none is explicitely specified. You can specify the exporter you want through the `--to=` command-line argument.

Default value: By default only the text exporter is enabled.

defaultScriptLanguage

Indicate the language in scripts when none is specified. This language is used for syntax highlighting. The currently supported languages are bash, css, html, http, json, javascript, pillar, sql, ston, shellcommands and smalltalk.

Default value: An unspecified language

disableTransformers

Collection of transformers that Pillar should ignore.

Transformers and keywords to disable them:

---

[18] http://smalltalkhub.com/#!/~SvenVanCaekenberghe/STON
[19] http://www.json.org

14.4 Configuring your Output

`capitalization` I visit a document and i capitalize all header following the rule in the configuration, `raw` by default

`columns` I replace each `columns` annotation with a structure of columns.

`fileInclusion` I replace each `inputFile` annotation with the content of the referenced file.

`numerator` I add numbers to all titles, scripts, figures, and internal links.

`pdf` I generate PDF files out of LaTeX ones.

`scriptEvaluator` I replace each script with `eval=true` with the result of its evaluation.

`scriptHide` I visit a document and I hide scripts with `hideable` parameter at `true`

`scriptInclusion` I replace each script with a `fromFile` parameter with the content of the referenced file.

`scriptLineNumber` I add line numbers to each script with `lineNumber=true`.

`section` For each header, I add a section structure. This is useful in export formats (such as HTML5 and Docbook) where sub-sections are embedded in their parent section.

`sectionAutoAnchor` I visit a document and I evaluate a header of a section if his `autoAnchor` parameter is `true`.

`slide` I replace each slide annotation with a slide structure.

For exemple, a value of `["scriptEvaluator", "section"]` will disable script evaluation (useful when security is important) and sectioning (useful when generating HTML 4).

Default value: By default the collection is empty, i.e., all transformers are active.

headingLevelOffset

Indicate how to convert from the level of a Pillar heading to the level of heading in your exported document. For example, a `headingLevelOffset` of 3 converts a 1st level Pillar heading to an `<h4>` in HTML.

Default value: `0`

inputFiles

List the Pillar files that must be exported. You can also specify input files by listing them at the end of the command-line interface.

Default value: `#()`

latexCommand

Indicate which LaTeX command to use to generate pdf files. Write `{fileName}` to reference the name of the file, `{fileNameWithoutExtension}` to get the file without `.tex`, `{filePath}` to get a relative path to the directory that contains the file from `outputDirectory`.

Default value: `'pdflatex {fileName}'`

level1

Configure how headers at level 1 will be rendered. Value must be a dictionnary. These keys are recognized:

`numbering` a boolean indicating if headers at this level must be numbered

`size` a positive number indicating how many parent levels should be visible in the number: e.g., if 2, the parent header's number and the current header's number will be shown (must be lower than or equal to 1)

`renderAs` a string indicating how the numbering is done (must be one of `"number"`, `"roman"`, `"letter"` or `"upperLetter"`)

Default value: All levels are numbered with digits and all parents are visible.

level2

Configure how headers at level 2 will be rendered. Value must be a dictionnary. These keys are recognized:

`numbering` a boolean indicating if headers at this level must be numbered

`size` a positive number indicating how many parent levels should be visible in the number: e.g., if 2, the parent header's number and the current header's number will be shown (must be lower than or equal to 2)

`renderAs` a string indicating how the numbering is done (must be one of `"number"`, `"roman"`, `"letter"` or `"upperLetter"`)

Default value: All levels are numbered with digits and all parents are visible.

level3

Configure how headers at level 3 will be rendered. Value must be a dictionnary. These keys are recognized:

`numbering` a boolean indicating if headers at this level must be numbered

`size` a positive number indicating how many parent levels should be visible in the number: e.g., if 2, the parent header's number and the current header's number will be shown (must be lower than or equal to 3) `renderAs` a string indicating how the numbering is done (must be one of `"number"`, `"roman"`, `"letter"` or `"upperLetter"`)

Default value: All levels are numbered with digits and all parents are visible.

level4

Configure how headers at level 4 will be rendered. Value must be a dictionnary. These keys are recognized:

`numbering` a boolean indicating if headers at this level must be numbered

`size` a positive number indicating how many parent levels should be visible in the number: e.g., if 2, the parent header's number and the current header's number will be shown (must be lower than or equal to 4)

`renderAs` a string indicating how the numbering is done (must be one of `"number"`, `"roman"`, `"letter"` or `"upperLetter"`)

Default value: All levels are numbered with digits and all parents are visible.

level5

Configure how headers at level 5 will be rendered. Value must be a dictionnary. These keys are recognized:

`numbering` a boolean indicating if headers at this level must be numbered

`size` a positive number indicating how many parent levels should be visible in the number: e.g., if 2, the parent header's number and the current header's number will be shown (must be lower than or equal to 5)

`renderAs` a string indicating how the numbering is done (must be one of `"number"`, `"roman"`, `"letter"` or `"upperLetter"`)

Default value: All levels are numbered with digits and all parents are visible.

newLine

The string that separates lines in the exported document. This is often either LF or CR+LF but any string is possible.

Default value: Depend on the operating system.

outputDirectory

Indicate where Pillar will create generated files.

Default value: The value of `baseDirectory`

outputFile

If `separateOutputFiles` is `false`, indicate the name of the output file. This can also be a write stream.

Default value: A file named 'output' with an extension depending on `outputType`.

outputType

Indicate the kind of output desired. Can be any of markdown, latex, html, pillar, text, mock, asciidoc, githubmarkdown, latex:sbabook, beamer and deckJS.

Default value: `nil`

renderStructureAsSlide

When `true` (the default), Pillar will create a dedicated slide for each Pillar header. This parameter is meaningless when generating a written document.

Default value: `true`

scrambledEmailAddresses

Indicate if email addresses should appear scrambled to defeat the stupidest spammers looking for them (the default). If `false`, email addresses will appear unscrambled.

Default value: `true`

separateOutputFiles

If `true`, each input file is exported to one output file. If `false` (the default), all input files are exported to `outputFile`.

Default value: `false`

slideInTemplateForDeckJS

Indicate the number of slides created by the DeckJS template. This is important to create anchors.

Default value: 1

support

A collection of files to copy inside the `outputDirectory` folder. Wildcard can be used like this: `*/figures`, `Chapter#/figures`, `**/figures` or `**/*.css`.

Default value: By default nothing is copied.

template

Indicate the overall structure of the exported documents. Exporters may override this setting to include their preamble.

Default value: "'{{{content}}}' (output the document as is, without any preamble or postamble)."

title

Indicate the main title of the document.

Default value: 'No title'

verbose

Indicate whether Pillar should write a verbose log when exporting.

Default value: false

14.5 Templating

Pillar comes with the Mustache templating engine (see chapter 12). This means you can specify a preamble and postamble for your document. Here is an example HTML template using Mustache:

```
<!DOCTYPE html>
<html lang="en">
   <head>
      <title>{{{title}}}</title>
   </head>
   <body>
      <div class="container">
         {{{content}}}
      </div>
   </body>
</html>
```

In this example, we can see the use of {{{title}}} and {{{content}}} to refer to the title of the document and its actual content (the one exported from Pillar). You have to put such a template in a dedicated file (named chapter.html.template for example) and reference this file from the template configuration parameter.

14.6 Command-Line Interface

In this section we show how to use the Pillar command-line interface.

One of the basic uses of the command line is:

```
$ ./pillar export --to=latex PharoSound.pier
# or in Windows
$ Pharo.exe Pillar.image pillar export --to=latex
```

You can select an export type with the parameter `--to`. The possible exports are: markdown, latex, html, pillar, text, mock, asciidoc, githubmarkdown, latex:sbabook, beamer and deckJS.

In the case of a LaTeX or Beamer export Pillar will generate a script named `pillarPostExport.sh` to generate PDF files from the TeX files. This script will create a symbolic link named `root` referencing the output directory into each directory containing TeX files. You can use this symbolic link to reference files in specified in the `support` collection. You can customize the LaTeX command with the `latexCommand` parameter of the configuration. For this book, we use:

```
"latexCommand" : "lualatex --file-line-error --interaction=batchmode
    {fileName} 2>&1 1>/dev/null
  ret=$?
  if [[ $ret -ne 0 ]]; then
      cat {fileNameWithoutExtension}.log
      echo \"Can't generate the PDF!\"
      exit 1
  fi"
```

Multiple Exports

Pillar can take care of several exports in parallel thanks to the `defaultExporters` parameter. For example, you can add this to your *pillar.conf*:

```
"defaultExporters" : [ "html", "latex", "text" ],
"inputFiles" : [ "doc.pillar" ]
```

and launch:

```
$ ./pillar export
```

to get three files: `doc.html`, `doc.tex` and `doc.txt` (and you will also get a `pillarPostExport.sh` script to generate a PDF).

14.7 Pillar from Pharo

Pillar has a document model (the root of which being `PRDocument`), a parser (`PRPillarParser`) and several export types (subclasses of `PRDocumentWriter`) implemented as visitors over the document model. Pillar also has transformers (subclasses of `PRTransformer`) that take a document model as input and produce a modified document model as output.

14.7 Pillar from Pharo

How to Create a Pillar Document

It is possible to create a Pillar document by parsing a string or by instantiating the document model.

Creating a document by parsing a String requires using the PRPillarParser:

```
| wiki |
wiki := '!My Document'.
PRPillarParser parse: wiki
```

Or from a file:

```
PRPillarParser parse: (FileSystem workingDirectory / 'foo.pillar')
    readStream
```

You can also instantiate the document model, one node after the other, starting with PRDocument and adding sub-instances of PRDocumentItem:

```
| document title figure|
document := PRDocument new.
title := PRHeader new
    level: 1;
    add: (PRText content: 'foo');
    yourself.
figure := PRFigure new
    add: (PRText content: 'Alias');
    reference: 'file://test.png';
    yourself.
document add: title; add: figure.
```

How to Export a Document

Once you have your document, you may want to export it. But exporting, there's an optional step: transforming your document. A transformer is an abstraction that visits a document and changes it. For instance, PRScriptEvaluator replaces a script with eval=true by the result of its evaluation. Exporting is done with a subclass of PRDocumentWriter, like this:

```
PRHTMLWriter write: document
```

To specify export parameters (see above for a comprehensive list), you may want to use a configuration.

```
| configuration |
configuration := PRPillarConfiguration new.
configuration outputType: PRHTMLWriter.
PRExportPhase executeOn: { document } with: configuration.
```

14.8 Conclusion

Pillar is still in active development because authors keep writing new documents. Because Pillar's source code is of great quality (mainly due to Lukas Renggli), features can be added easily by new developers. Pillar is different from competition thanks to its notion of project that allows managing multiple files coherently.

CHAPTER **15**

Generate PDF Documents with Artefact

Olivier Auverlot and Guillaume Larchevêque with Johan Fabry

The Adobe PDF format is probably one of the most widespread electronic document formats. Used daily, it is the basis for the production of exchangeable documents that contain both text and graphics. If you receive a bill, follow a purchase on a web site, download a report, a book or an administrative form, these files will most likely be PDF documents. For programmers that need to provide any such reporting functionality, supporting this format has become a must and the generation of PDF documents is part of their toolkit.

In Pharo, Artefact is an innovative framework that supports the design and generation of PDF documents and is developed by Olivier Auverlot and Guillaume Larcheveque.

15.1 Overview of Artefact

Artefact is a PDF framework whose design was guided by the goals of efficiency, productivity and scalability. To achieve this, each document is described by a tree of objects. A document is an object containing a collection of other objects, each corresponding to a page. On each page both visible and non-visible items are also objects. These objects then have the possibility to be reused in the same document but also across documents. Objects are elements that can be simple, e.g. a piece of text or an image, but also be complex elements with advanced behavior and a special appearance, e.g. that display data in a table or generate a barcode.

Artefact contains default elements such as paragraphs or tables that allow to quickly generate reports. The strength of these elements is that they are independent of each other. The order in which you position them in the document does not affect their appearance. This is in contrast to many PDF frameworks that exploit the notion of stream in the definition of styles (a piece of blue text will be followed by another piece of blue text in the absence of a directive to use a different style), Artefact considers that every element includes its own style. If an attribute is not defined in the element, Artefact then uses a style sheet that is set at the document level by default.

This autonomy of elements and style management is a strong feature of Artefact. It makes it easy to generate a document and quickly customize it for a particular operation.

Concepts, Key Aspects and Limits

After more than a year of development, the concepts used in Artefact are considered stable and it is already used in industry. In this section we list its current features and known limitations.

- Artefact has a simple architecture that facilitates scalability and new features.
- It supports the definition of a PDF document and its contents.
- It can specify meta information such as title or author.
- It manages display options when opening a document in a reader that is compatible with this feature.
- It supports compressed PDF document generation.

Each page of a PDF document can have its own particular format and orientation. By default, Artefact supports a set of common formats, e.g. A3, A4, or ebook. It can easily be extended to fit specific needs. Page location is determined not when the page is created but when it is added to a document. Hence each page is independent, which allows one to generate documents with variable architecture.

On each page, Artefact places simple or complex elements. A complex element is generally defined using simple elements or other complex elements. Each element is independent and is positioned relative to the upper left corner of a page.

Artefact provides greyscale management and colors defined by the RGB model (where each color component is represented by one byte). Character fonts are those imposed by the PDF but Artefact does not support true type fonts (TTF) specification. You can insert images into a PDF document but only the JPEG format is currently supported. Artefact does not support the definition of interactive input fields, integrating JavaScript or safety aspects of PDF such as certificates. Of course, these specifications are subject to change as and when the framework changes.

15.2 Getting Started in 10 Minutes

Say, you already program in Pharo and you want to generate PDF documents. This section will show you how to do so in less than 10 minutes.

First you should load the framework. The good news is that there is no need for native libraries as Artefact is written entirely in Pharo. Whatever your execution platform (Microsoft Windows, Mac OS X, Linux, Android, IOS, etc.), Artefact will be available and usable.

Installing Artefact

Artefact is hosted on SmalltalkHub[1]. To install Artefact, execute the following expressions:

```
Gofer new
    smalltalkhubUser: '' project: 'RMoD/Artefact';
    package: 'ConfigurationOfArtefact';
    load.

ConfigurationOfArtefact load
```

Loading the configuration automatically load projets such as the Unit framework (which supports the definition of different measurement units. By default the configuration loads the stable version that is production ready.

Once loaded, you can browse the main packages and classes.

- The Artefact-Examples package contains many usage examples.
- The Artefact-Core package contains the main elements such as documents, pages or style sheets but also electronic documentation that is accessible via the Help Browser.
- The PDF objects (text, geometric shapes, images, etc.) offered by the basic framework are in Artefact-Core-Elements-Basic and Artefact-Core-Elements-Composites.
- The fonts are defined in the package Artefact-Core-Fonts and document formats in the package Artefact-Core-Formats.

Executing the First Demo's

The best way to start with Artefact is to have a look at the Artefact-Examples-Demos package and to run each of PDFDemos class methods.

If you want to run all demos, just execute PDFDemos runAllDemos

---

[1] http://smalltalkhub.com/#!/~RMoD/Artefact

By default each generation result is written in the default Pharo directory but you can define your own by modifying the `demoPath` class method, e.g. as follows:

```
PDFDemos class>>demoPath
    ^ '/Users/pharo/pdf/'
```

Finally "Hello World!"

You will now create your first and simplest PDF document, which is a text on a page. To do this, you must define an instance of a PDF document that contains a page where you will position a text component.

```
PDFDocument new
    exportTo: 'helloworld.pdf' asFileReference writeStream
```

Once the instance of `PDFDocument` is created, it is exported using a stream to a file named `helloworld.pdf`. By default, the produced PDF document is placed in the directory of Pharo. If you open the file, it is empty. This is normal since you have not yet defined and added any content to the document.

Let us enrich the previous example and add a page to the document.

```
PDFDocument new
    add: PDFPage new;
    exportTo: 'helloworld.pdf' asFileReference writeStream
```

Now if you open the file the result is different since the document contains an empty page. Let us add a first text component to our page.

```
PDFDocument new add:
    (PDFPage new add:
        (PDFTextElement new text: 'Hello World!'; from: 10mm @ 10mm));
    exportTo: 'helloworld.pdf' asFileReference writeStream
```

To place the text on the page we create a component of type `PDFTextElement`. We add it to the page and define its position using the message `from:`. Note that we can specify dimensions using several units such as millimeters (mm), centineters (cm) or inches (inch). These coordinates are defined from the upper left corner of the page.

Artefact uses a set of defaults to get compact code when creating elements that are part of a document. More specifically, style parameters are set to what are considered the most common values. In this example the page format is set to A4, and its orientation to portrait. Also, text is by default written in black using the Helvetica font.

This first example introduced some basic concepts and shows how simple it is to produce a PDF document with Pharo. The following sections go deeper in Artefact and show how to define more complex documents.

15.3 Document Definition

Artefact represents PDF documents as objects that are instance of the class PDFDocument. They play the role of containers for receiving pages. A PDF-Document also supports advanced options such as the document size, management of compression, the opening in the PDF reader and the definition of meta information.

The order in which pages are added to the PDFDocument object define the organization of data within the document, **not** the order in which the pages are created. This mode of operation allows you to produce documents whose contents can be dynamically generated and organized at a later time.

Page Addition

To add pages to a document, the message add: is used. It appends a page after those already present in the document. When generating the PDF file, Artefact traverses the list of pages starting from the earliest added to the last. The following script defines a document with a single blank page.

```
PDFDocument new
    add: PDFPage new;
    exportTo: 'EmptyPage.pdf' asFileReference writeStream
```

Document Properties

A PDFDocument can be configured with a specific format, orientation, compression and display mode, as we show next.

Document Format and Orientation

By default, a document is generated in the A4 format but other formats are available. The Package Artefact-Core-Formats contains a list of predefined formats covering many needs. Examples are: A3 (PDFA3Format), letter size (PDFLetterFormat) and a format suitable for e-readers (PDFEbookFormat). If you need a particular format, you can define it. A format is simply defined by the value returned by the message defaultSize.

A PDFDocument accepts the message format: to specify the format of all pages of the document. For each page, this value will be the default if not redefined otherwise. Each page can specify a different format. The following example creates a document using the A3 format:

```
PDFDocument new
    format: PDFA3Format new;
    add: PDFPage new;
    exportTo: 'A3.pdf' asFileReference writeStream
```

The abstract superclass of all formats (PDFFormat) is responsible for defining the page orientation. There are two alternatives: portrait or landscape. Page orientation is set by sending one of the two messages to the format object: setPortrait and setLandscape.

The following example generates a document whose pages are in A3 format and landscape orientation.

```
PDFDocument new
    format: PDFA3Format new setLandscape;
    add: PDFPage new;
    exportTo: 'A3landscape.pdf' asFileReference writeStream
```

Note that setting the default landscape mode for a document does not exclude the possibility for a particular page to be oriented in portrait mode. Artefact fully supports pages of different sizes and different orientations within a single document.

Compression

The PDF format allows you to compress the data, which is a good thing as a PDF document can contain large amounts of data. To to minimize the weight of generated documents Artefact defaults to compressing the data. If you need to disable this option, you should send the uncompressed message to the document.

The following example generates an uncompressed PDF document:

```
PDFDocument new
    uncompressed;
    add: PDFPage new;
    exportTo: 'uncompressed.pdf' asFileReference writeStream
```

Another message, named compressed, sets the compression.

Controling Document Opening

Adobe Acrobat reader supports various display modes when opening a PDF document. The selected mode is defined directly into the PDF document. Note that if the PDF reader that is used to look at the document is not compatible with these options, they will be ignored.

Display mode properties are divided in two categories: those determining the size of the pages and those related to the page organization on the screen. The former are set using the messages fullPage, fullWidth, real and zoom:, and the latter using singlepage, twoPages and continuousPages. These messages should be sent to an PDFDocument instance.

With fullPage, each page of the document occupies the entire display space. With fullWidth, the display is optimized to the page width. With real, the display meets the dimensions specified in the PDF document.

15.3 Document Definition

The following example creates a document that will occupy all available display space:

```
pdfdoc := PDFDocument new fullPage.
```

With the message zoom:, you can define a zoming ratio, expressed in percentages. The following example defines that the document should be opened with zoom of 400 percent.

```
pdfdoc := PDFDocument new zoom: 400.
```

You can also choose to display a single page (singlePage), pages two by two (twoPages) or one after the other (continousPages) as in the following example:

```
pdfdoc := PDFDocument new continousPages.
```

Theses messages can be combined as shown in the following example:

```
pdfdoc := PDFDocument new zoom: 200; continuousPages.
```

Setting Meta Information

Each PDF document contains a set of information about its origins. These data are not to be overlooked, especially if your document is intended to contribute to an EDM (Electronic Document Management) system or is part of an editorial workflow. With this information it is possible to search among a set of PDF documents and select, for example, those written by a particular author or those for which certain keywords have been specified.

Artefact implements this information by using an instance of PDFMetaData. To each instance of PDFDocument, an instance of PDFMetaData is associated and is accessible using the message metaData. By default, the producer is set to 'Artefact'. You can specify the document title, subject or a short summary, the name of the author, a list of keywords and the document creator.

The following example generates a new document and its meta data information:

```
pdfdoc := PDFDocument new.

pdfdoc metaData
    title: 'Document title';
    subject: 'subject of the document';
    author: 'The Pasta Team';
    keywords: 'cool rock best';
    creator: 'Pharo'.
```

15.4 Pages, Formats and Models

Pages are the support for writing and drawing in your PDF documents. A page defines a page size, orientation and position within a PDF document. A page can be built from a model that provides an overlay on which the page contents are deposited.

Page Creation

A page is represented by an instance of the class `PDFPage`. Creating is a page is simply done by sending the message `new` to the class.

```
page := PDFPage new.
```

Sending the message `add:` to a document with a page as argument will append the page to the document.

```
pdfdoc := PDFDocument new.
page := PDFPage new.
pdfdoc add: page.
```

By default, a page takes the dimensions and orientation of its document. If your PDF document is A4 landscape, all added pages will use these settings. However, Artefact can assign specific dimensions and orientation to each page, allowing one document to have a mix of pages with different characteristics. To allow this, each instance of `PDFPage` understands the message `format:`, which takes an instance of `PDFFormat` as argument.

The following example creates a two-page document. The first uses the default format of the document, the second is in A4 landscape.

```
pdfdoc := PDFDocument new.
page1 := PDFPage new.
page2 := PDFPage new format: (PDFA3Format new setLandscape).
pdfdoc add: page1; add: page2.
```

Templates

A template is an instance of class `PDFTemplate`, which inherits from the class `PDFPage`. It is a page with predefined contents that will act as the background page on which you will draw or add your components. For example, it can be composed of a header for a letter, a header and a footer for a report, or a delimited surface.

The package `Artefact-Examples-Demos-Templates` offers two example of template to create CD or DVD sleeve pages. The following code snippet produces a A4 page on which the outlines of a CD sleeve are drawn.

```
pdfdoc := PDFDocument new.
cover := PDFCompactDiscTemplate new.
```

A template is defined using the message drawTemplate which adds the Artefact elements to the page. This builds the page background. For example, the code of the CD template is below. (As it is relatively straightforward we do not explain the code here.)

```
PDFCompactDiscTemplate>>drawTemplate
    self add: ((PDFRectElement
        from: 10 mm @ 10 mm
        dimension: 240 mm @ 120 mm)
        dotted: self dotted
    ).
    self add: ((PDFLineElement
        from: 130mm @ 10mm
        to: 130mm @ 130mm)
        dotted: self dotted
    ).
```

15.5 Elements

The contents of pages is defined using reusable components called elements. Artefact has basic elements that perform simple operations such as drawing a line, but also complex elements that can, for example, display data in a table or generate a barcode. Of course, it is possible to identify and define new components.

More specifically, a PDFElement is a reusable component that represents a text, an image, a geometric shape or even a complex graph or table. There are two kinds of PDFElement:

- Simple elements inherit from PDFBasic (a primitive operation in the pdf specification).
- Composite elements inherit from PDFComposite (a wrapper around multiple PDFElements whether they are basic or composite).

Simple elements are as follows, and their hierarchy is shown in Figure 15-1:

- PDFBezierCurveElement
- PDFCircleElement
- PDFLineElement
- PDFPolygonElement
- PDFRectElement
- PDFJpegElement
- PDFTextElement

Composite elements are as follows, and their hierarchy is shown in Figure 15-2:

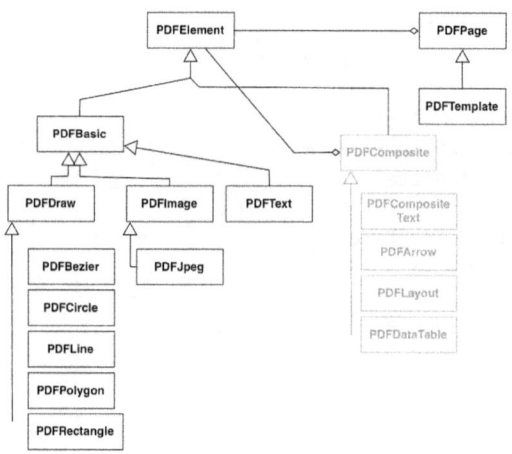

Figure 15-1 Page and Document Elements

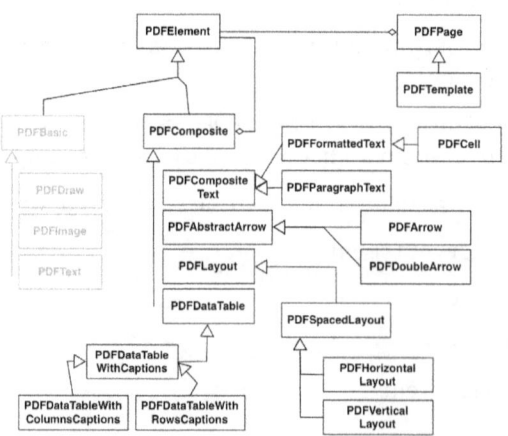

Figure 15-2 Composite Elements

15.5 Elements

- PDFFormattedTextElement
- PDFParagraphElement
- PDFArrowElement
- PDFDoubleArrowElement
- PDFCellElement
- PDFDataTableElement
- PDFDataTableWithColumnsCaptionElement
- PDFDataTableWithRowsCaptionElement

Each PDFElement has a set of properties that define its appearance (text color, font, dots, etc). These properties are grouped in a stylesheet owned by each element. Every element controls its own appearance and doesn't affect other elements. This is in contrast to many PDF frameworks that use a flow logic. This behavior allows you to move an element around or even use the same element in multiple pages or documents.

Composing and Placement

Artefact's elements have a generic behavior that manages their location on a page as well as their dimensions. The Artefact coordinate system is used to place components. Values can be expressed in several units such as mm, cm or inch. The origin of the coordinate system is the top left of a page.

Element Positioning

Sending the message from: to the class of an element instantiates it and sets its position. The following example creates a PDFTextElement and places it at 15 mm from the left border and 30 mm from the top

```
PDFTextElement from: 15 mm @ 30 mm
```

In addition, Artefact offers other constructors that fix the position and size of the element, and we present them next.

Element Size

Artefact offers two ways to set the size of an element: either through the from:to: message or through from:dimension:.

The message from:to: takes as arguments the start and the end position. For example, the following code draws a rectangle whose origin is 15mm from the left and 30mm from the top and its end is at 90 mm from the left border and 80mm from the top of the page:

```
[    PDFRectElement from: 15 mm @ 30 mm to: 90 mm @ 80 mm
```

The message from:dimension:, takes as arguments the start position and the size of the component. For example, the following code sets the size of the component to be 50 by 40 millimeters.

```
[    PDFRectElement from: 15mm @ 30 mm dimension: 50mm @ 40mm
```

The messages width and height return the width and height of the component.

Simple Elements

The package Artefact-Core-Elements-Basic contains elementary components. There are grouped in three categories: text, images, and geometric forms.

Text and Images

To write text on a page, use instances of PDFTextElement. The method text: sets the text to be displayed. The class method from:text: supports positioning and text definition.

```
[    PDFTextElement from: 15mm @ 30mm text: 'hello!'
```

Using the PDFJpegElement class, images in JPEG format can also be inserted in a document, using the fromStream: and from:dimension:fromStream: class messages. The messages width: and height: set the size of the image while respecting its original aspect ratio.

The following example generates a PDF document with one page. This page contains one image placed at two different locations. In the first case, the image is 80mm in width and 30mm in height. In the second case, the width is 80mm and the height is automatically computed keeping the original image ratio.

```
| pdf page |
pdf := PDFDocument new.
page := PDFPage new.
page add: (
    PDFJpegElement
        from: 10 mm @ 10 mm
        dimension: 80 mm @ 30 mm
        fromStream: (FileStream fileNamed:
    '/home/enterprise/image.jpg')).
page add: ((
    PDFJpegElement
        fromStream: (FileStream fileNamed:
    '/home/enterprise/image.jpg'))
        from: 10 mm @ 50 mm; width: 80 mm).
pdf add: page;
```

15.5 Elements

```
pdf exportTo: (FileStream forceNewFileNamed:
    '/home/enterprise/image.pdf')
```

Geometric Shapes

Artefact has the following components for geometric shapes:

The class `PDFLineElement` draws a line using `from:to:`.

```
PDFLineElement from: 15mm @ 30mm to: 90mm@170mm
```

The class message `from:angle:length:` draws a line with the given start position, angle and length.

```
PDFLineElement from: 10mm @ 20mm angle: 70 length: 50mm
```

The class `PDFRectElement` represents a rectangle. Two messages are relevant: `from: dimension:` and `from: to:` . The two following examples are equivalent:

```
PDFRectElement from: 10 mm@10mm dimension: 100 mm @ 30 mm.

    PDFRectElement from: 10mm@10mm to: 110mm@40mm
```

The class `PDFPolygonElement` draws polygons. To define a polygon, we set the start point and a series of points using the message `from:points:`.

```
PDFPolygonElement
    from: 10mm@10mm
    points: { 30mm@30mm . 15mm@40mm . 5mm@20mm }
```

Circles are defined with the class `PDFCircleElement` and using the message `center:radius:`.

```
PDFCircleElement center: 100mm@100mm radius: 50mm
```

Bezier curves are represented by the class `PDFBezierCurveElement` and defined using the message `from:points`.

```
PDFBezierCurveElement
    from: 10mm@50mm
    points: { 0mm@0mm. 100mm@20mm. 150mm@0mm. 50mm@50mm }
```

Composite Elements

Artefact comes with a rich set of high-level components, grouped in the package `Artefact-Core-Elements-Composites`. These components are the result of the assembly of single components and other high-level components. They are used to create layouts and complex contents with minimal coding and a high degree of reuse. These components can be used in several different applications and materials. They are divided in three areas: management of text, drawing arrows and reporting.

Advanced Text

So far you have used the class PDFTextElement to place text on a page. This component is limited in terms of functionality since it only handles the position on the page. In addition to this, Artefact offers three high-level components that support advanced features: PDFFormatedTextElement, PDFCellElement and PDFParagrapElement.

The component PDFFormatedTextElement is similar to PDFTextElement but includes managing the alignment (left, center, right). A PDFCellElement is a PDFFormatedTextElement with a border. Finally, a PDFParagraphElement allows the insertion of a paragraph of text and automatically manages the breaks at the end of lines.

Drawing Arrows

Arrows are very useful for generating sketches and diagrams. The component PDFArrowElement draws an arrow with a tip at its end. The component PDFDoubleArrowElement draws a tip at both extremities.

```
PDFArrowElement from: 10mm@10mm to: 100mm@30mm

PDFDoubleArrowElement from: 10mm@80mm to: 100mm@150mm
```

Report Creation

Components inheriting from PDFDatatable are the perfect illustration of the power and comfort provided by the composite elements of Artefact. With these data tables, you can quickly generate reports and customize them to your needs.

With the class PDFDataTableElement you define a report with specific dimensions on the page and showing a given data set. The data is organized in a tabular manner: a report contains a number of rows, each representing a line of the report.

```
PDFDataTableElement new
   data: #(
      #('Smith' 'Peter' 43)
      #('Jones' 'Mickael' 25)
      #('washington' 'robert' 30) );
   from: 10mm @ 20mm;
   dimension: 150mm @ 60mm
```

The subclass PDFDataTableWithColumnsCaptionElement extends the table behavior to support captions. The message captions: takes an array as argument, which contains the title of each column of your report. It is important to note that the number of column headings should be the same as the number of columns and each line must have the same number of columns.

15.5 Elements

```
PDFDataTableWithColumnsCaptionElement new
    captions: #('Name' 'Surname' 'Age');
    data: #(
        #('Smith' 'Peter' 43)
        #('Jones' 'Mickael' 25)
        #('washington' 'robert' 30)
    );
    from: 10 mm @ 20 mm;
    dimension: 150 mm @ 60 mm
```

Finally Artefact also provides a `PDFDataTableWithRowsCaptionElement` subclass, which is a variant of `PDFDataTableWithColumnsCaptionElement`. Its behavior is different since the caption is used to give a title to each line. In this case, the table given as argument to the `caption:` message must have a number of elements equal to the number of rows.

Lastly, `PDFDataTableElement` offers a callback mechanism defined by the message `customizationBlock:`. The associated block is activated for the drawing of each cell. It takes four parameters that are the cell being drawn, the vertical and horizontal position of the cell in the table and the data presented in the cell. Using a block of code, it is then possible to change the appearance of the table or to trigger special treatment.

The following example shows a use of the `customizationBlock:` message. The block replaces the age of a person by the text `'Older than 30'` if the person is older than thirty. Note that the block only considers the third cell of each line and excludes the title of each column.

```
(PDFDataTableWithColumnsCaptionElement new
    captions: #('Name' 'Surname' 'Age');
    data: #(
        #('Smith' 'Peter' 43)
        #('Jones' 'Mickael' 25)
        #('washington' 'robert' 30)
    );
    from: 10 mm @ 20 mm;
    dimension: 150 mm @ 60 mm;
    customizationBlock: [ :cell :x :y :data |
        (x = 3 and: [ y > 1 ]) ifTrue: [
            (data > 30) ifTrue: [ cell text: 'Older than 30' ]
        ]
    ])
```

Composite elements bring a lot of flexibility to PDF document creation. Obviously, the default ones do not cover all needs and you will most likely need to create your own components. We suggest to study the existing ones to see how to proceed.

15.6 Stylesheets for Newbies

A `PDFStyleSheet` is a dictionary that contains rendering properties, e.g. the color or the font for pieces of text. Following the same logic for pages and elements, a stylesheet can be reused across different elements or documents. When documents are created, they are automatically given a default stylesheet that then applies to their elements. Consequently, you don't have to specify every rendering property for the elements of a document.

Following the hierarchy logic, a stylesheet defined at a lower level of a document will override properties set at a higher level. For example, if you define a textColor in the document stylesheet, every piece of text will be written in that color except for elements where textColor is defined in their own stylesheet.

Artefact also includes a dictionary of styles that allows every `PDFElement` to be given a specific, named style. For example the code below is given the #title style.

```
PDFText from: 10mm@15mm text: 'My title' style: #title
```

At any upper level (document, page, etc), you can define the named style using the message >, e.g. as follows:

```
myDocument stylesheet > #title
    at: #font
    put: PDFCourierFont size: 32 pt
```

The message > gives access to the style attribute of `PDFStyleSheet`. Here we specify the #title attribute of the document.

Stylesheet Elements

Defining a stylesheet allows one to specify specific presentation attributes for a set of elements. These attributes can also be set directly for an element. We show here the different attributes and how to set them for an element.

Fonts

Artefact supports integrated PDF fonts through different subclasses of PDF-Font: `PDFCourierFont`, `PDFHelveticaFont`, `PDFSymbolFont`, `PDFTimesFont` and `PDFZapfdingbatsFont`. These fonts are available in any PDF viewer. A `PDFFont` instance supports the basic styles `bold` and `italic`.

As said above, fonts can be set directly for a piece of text, which is shown below:

```
PDFText
    from: 10mm@15mm
    text: 'My title'
    font: ((PDFTimesFont size: 24 pt) bold).
```

15.6 Stylesheets for Newbies

The class PDFFont offers two extremely useful messages when creating a document: getStringWidth: and getIdealFontSizeForTheString:width:.

With the message getStringWidth: you get the width of a string calculated based on the attributes of the font used. For example, the following example returns the width of the string 'hello' in Courier measuring 20 points:

```
(PDFCourierFont size: 20 pt) getStringWidth: 'hello'
```

The message getIdealFontSizeForTheString:width: returns the optimal size for the used font based on the desired width. The following example determines the required size for a Courier font to display the 'Hello' text if the width should be 15 cm:

```
(PDFCourierFont new)
    getIdealFontSizeForTheString: 'hello' width: 15 cm
```

Dots

All geometric shapes can use a dotted style. It is defined by a PDFDotted object that specifies the length of each line segment and the space between them, as shown below:

```
((PDFArrowElement from: 125 mm @ 40 mm to:   100 mm @ 80 mm)
    dotted: (PDFDotted new length: 2 mm; space: 3 mm)).
```

Colors and Shades of Gray

Colors and shades of gray are represented by the class PDFColor. To define a color, Artefact uses the traditional RGB schema where the ratio of each color is expressed using a value from 0 to 255. A deep black corresponds to the triple (0,0,0), the color red to (255,0,0), the color green to (0,255,0), blue to (0,0,255) and white to (255,255,255). Grayscales are expressed with a single value ranging from 0 to 255. A value of 0 corresponds to white, while the value of 255 is equivalent to black.

To specify the color or grayscale used, the messages drawColor:, fill-Color:, and textColor: are used. They respectively manage the drawing color, fill color and text color.

For example, the following code draws a rectangle whose border will be blue and will have a red fill:

```
PDFRectElement new
    from: 10 mm @ 10 mm;
    dimension: 100 mm @ 30 mm;
    fillColor: (PDFColor r: 255 g: 0 b: 0);
    drawColor: (PDFColor r: 0 g: 0 b: 255).
```

The code below produces a gray piece of text:

```
PDFTextElement new
    textColor: (PDFColor greyLevel: 128);
    from: 10 mm @ 50 mm;
    text: 'A text in blue';
```

Drawing Thickness

The thickness of a line, a segment, or a border, is controlled by the message `thickness:`, as shown below:

```
(PDFRectElement from: 10 mm @ 10 mm dimension: 50 mm @ 50 mm)
    thickness: 2 mm
```

Alignment

Text alignment is managed using the `PDFAlignment` class. Text can be aligned left, center or right. Messages are `left`, `center` and `right`. The following example creates a right-aligned text:

```
(PDFFormattedTextElement from: 0 mm @ 0 mm dimension: 100 mm @ 10 mm)
    alignment: (PDFAlignment right);
    text: 'At right!'
```

Abstracting a Style

A document is associated to a default stylesheet whose properties are applied to any element that does not specify its own properties. For example, if you create a `PDFTextElement` without setting a font and text color, the color of text and the fonts set in the document will be used.

The default stylesheet is always filled up by Artefact with sensible defaults. That's why you did not have to specify values of style in the previous examples. You can access the stylesheet using the message `styleSheet`. To change the values of the default style, you simply change the properties of the stylesheet, for example as follows:

```
myDocument := PDFDocument new.
myDocument styleSheet
    textColor: (PDFColor r: 0 g: 100 b: 200);
    font: (PDFHelveticaFont size: 32pt) italic.
```

Artefact styles form a tree. Each sub style points to its parent and the root of styles is the default style attached to the document. This way properties can be customized and default behavior can be reused when needed.

Stylesheet Application

Often you want to apply a style to a set of elements but not to all the elements of a document. As said above, Artefact allows you to define a named

15.6 Stylesheets for Newbies

style and apply it to the elements that should follow this custom style.

For example, that you want to use a certain font and style for some text element or quotes, you can define a style named #quote as follows:

```
myDocument := PDFDocument new.
myDocument styleSheet > #quote
    textColor: (PDFColor r: 0 g: 50 b: 200);
    font: (PDFCourierFont size: 8pt) italic.
```

This style is defined here as the sub-document style and it will be applied to all elements of that use the #quote style. In the following example we assign the #quote style to a piece of text using the message style:.

```
(PDFTextElement from: 5cm @ 5cm)
    text: 'my Quote with the quote style'; style: #quote
```

In the above example, we only have one level of styles. However, Artefact supports an infinite levels of styles. This behavior is essential for composite elements where the nesting of the elements implies the nesting of their styles.

For example, below we create a data table with a title for each column.

```
(PDFDataTableWithColumnsCaptionElement
    from: 10 mm @ 20 mm dimension: 190 mm @ 60 mm)
        captions: #('Name' 'Surname' 'email');
        data: #(
            #('Smith' 'Peter' 'peter.smith@mail.org')
            #('Jones' 'Mickael' 'mickael.jones@epr.com')
            #('washington' 'robert' 'robert.washington@blif.com'));
        style: #dataTableWithColoredCaption;
        yourself).
```

PDFDataTableWithColumnsCaptionElement is a composite element. This element uses as styles of its sub-elements #cell and #caption, respectively for captions and cells. By using the specialisation based on style nesting, it is then possible a to use a style uniquely for this table, in this case it will be #dataTableWithColoredCaption

To define this style, the second expression below = access the caption style of the dataTableWithColoredCaption style, and then customizes it.

```
pdfdoc := PDFDocument new.
pdfdoc styleSheet > #dataTableWithColoredCaption > #caption
    fillColor: (PDFColor r: 158 g: 158 b: 79);
    drawColor: (PDFColor r: 158 g: 158 b: 79).
pdfdoc styleSheet > #dataTableWithColoredCaption margin: 4 pt.
pdfdoc styleSheet > #dataTableWithColoredCaption > #cell
        alignment: PDFAlignment right.
```

Here we see that we can change a nested element attribute: we change the alignment of a cell in the table using a sequence of > messages. Style management brings a lot of flexibility for the production of a document. It separates the presentation appearance from the component definition. This distinction between structure and presentation allows users to easily create their own components just as customizable as those provided with Artefact.

15.7 Create your own PDF Composite Elements

The spirit of Artefact is to reduce the complexity of pdf generation. When you have to create a document, a good idea is to avoid wasting time reinventing the wheel. When you create a composite element, if your component is based around a string, inherit from PDFCompositeText. Otherwise, your component should be a subclass of PDFComposite.

In this tutorial we will create a clock, which is basically a circle and two arrows. These elements will be drawn depending on the provided time and properties (size, colors, thickness).

Clock Creation

First create the class of your element and generate accessors for its variable time that will contain the time to display.

```
PDFComposite subclass: #PDFClockElement
    instanceVariableNames: 'time'
    classVariableNames: ''
    category: 'Artefact-Tutorial'
```

The two relevant methods for Artefact are defaultStyle and getSubElementsWith:styleSheet:. The first one must return a collection of PDFElements (basic or composites). The second one must return a symbol that associates the elements with a style definition. However it's not necessary to define this style in your document, Artefact will use the default style instead.

Define the default style:

```
PDFClockElement>>defaultStyle
    ^ #clock
```

Then define the method that will draw the clock. As a first approximation, this method just returns a circle:

```
PDFClockElement>>getSubElementsWith: aGenerator styleSheet:
    aStyleSheet
    ^ { PDFCircleElement from: self from to: self to }
```

The circle will be drawn depending on this composite position and size. We are using from: to: for the circle instead of center:radius: because it's easier for us to create a clock using the boundary box of the circle.

15.7 Create your own PDF Composite Elements

To complete the clock, we add the hands using two `PDFArrowElements` and a filled little circle in the middle:

```
PDFClockElement>>getSubElementsWith: aGenerator styleSheet:
    aStyleSheet
    | hourAngle minuteAngle |
    hourAngle := Float pi / 2 - (time hour12 * 2 * Float pi / 12).
    minuteAngle := Float pi / 2 - (time minute * 2 * Float pi / 60).
    ^ {
      (PDFCircleElement from: self from to: self to).
      (PDFCircleElement
            center: self center radius: self dimension x * 0.05).
      (PDFArrowElement
            from: self center angle: hourAngle length: dimension x
    * 0.25).
      (PDFArrowElement
            from: self center angle: minuteAngle length: dimension
    x * 0.45)
    }
```

Don't be afraid about the two angle calculus, it's just to convert hours and minutes to radian angles.

At this time, your `PDFClockElement` is already usable and fully integrated into Artefact. We can insert it into a PDF document and export it:

```
PDFDocument new
    add: (PDFPage new add: ((
      PDFClockElement
          from: 2 cm @ 2 cm
          to: 10 cm @ 10 cm) time: Time current));
    exportTo: 'clockTutorialStep1.pdf' asFileReference writeStream
```

Make the Clock Personalizable

Your clock is already personnalizable independently of other elements because you previously defined its style as `#clock`. This is shown below:

```
| doc |
doc := PDFDocument new.
doc add: (PDFPage new add:
    ((PDFClockElement from: 2 cm @ 2 cm to: 10 cm @ 10 cm)
        time: Time current)).
doc styleSheet > #clock
    drawColor: (PDFColor r:180 g: 24 b:24);
    fillColor: (PDFColor r:230 g: 230 b:10).
doc exportTo: 'clockTutorialStep2.pdf' asFileReference writeStream
```

At this time, you don't have defined specific styles for sub elements of your clock. Consequently, you will not be able to personalize each element with different styles (so you cannot have hands of differents colors for example).

To increase personalization possibilities, you should define specific styles for sub elements you reuse, as follows:

```
PDFClockElement>>getSubElementsWith: aGenerator styleSheet:
    aStyleSheet
    | hourAngle minuteAngle |
    hourAngle := Float pi / 2 - (time hour12 * 2 * Float pi / 12).
    minuteAngle := Float pi / 2 - (time minute * 2 * Float pi / 60).
    ^ {
       (PDFCircleElement from: self from to: self to).
       (PDFCircleElement
          center: self center radius: self dimension min * 0.05).
       ((PDFArrowElement
          from: self center angle: hourAngle
          length: dimension min * 0.25) style: #hourHand).
       ((PDFArrowElement
          from: self center angle: minuteAngle
          length: dimension min * 0.45) style: #minuteHand)
    }
```

As you can see, we just send the message `style:` to each subelement that we want to define a specific style.

Now, we can personalize each hand as follows:

```
| doc |
doc := PDFDocument new.
doc add: (PDFPage new add: ((PDFClockElement
    from: 2 cm @ 2 cm to: 10 cm @ 10 cm) time: Time current)).
doc styleSheet > #clock
    drawColor: (PDFColor r:180 g: 24 b:24);
    fillColor: (PDFColor r:230 g: 230 b:10).
doc styleSheet > #clock > #hourHand
    drawColor: (PDFColor r:0 g: 45 b:200).
doc styleSheet > #clock > #minuteHand
    drawColor: (PDFColor r:0 g: 200 b:45).
doc exportTo: 'clockTutorialStep4.pdf' asFileReference writeStream
```

This gives the clock hands have different colors. Moreover, like for any element in Artefact, you can specify a style for a given instance of a PDFClockElement, allowing you to reuse and adapt each clock:

```
| doc |
doc := PDFDocument new.
doc add: (
    PDFPage new
       add: (
          (PDFClockElement from: 2 cm @ 2 cm to: 10 cm @ 10 cm)
             time: Time current);
       add: (
          (PDFClockElement from: 12 cm @ 2 cm to: 20 cm @ 10 cm)
```

```
                time: Time current;
                style: #apocalypseClock)).
doc styleSheet > #clock
    drawColor: (PDFColor r: 180 g: 24 b: 24);
    fillColor: (PDFColor r: 230 g: 230 b: 10).
doc styleSheet > #clock > #hourHand
    drawColor: (PDFColor r: 0 g: 45 b: 200).
doc styleSheet > #clock > #minuteHand
    drawColor: (PDFColor r: 0 g: 200 b: 45).
doc styleSheet > #apocalypseClock
    fillColor: (PDFColor r: 244 g: 221 b: 25);
    thickness: 2 mm;
    roundCap: true.
doc styleSheet > #apocalypseClock > #minuteHand
    drawColor: (PDFColor r: 240 g: 6 b: 7);
    thickness: 1 mm.
doc exportTo: 'clockTutorialStep5.pdf' asFileReference writeStream
```

15.8 Conclusion

We presented the key aspects of Artefact, a powerful framework to generate PDF documents. It is based on innovative design aspects: it features an object-oriented design where each element defines its own attributes. This supports much stronger possibilities for reuse than traditional stream-based approaches. With Artefact you can freely compose, customize and reuse your PDF elements.

Part V

Deployment

CHAPTER **16**

Deploying a Pharo Web Application in Production

Christophe Demarey with Johan Fabry

In the previous chapters we discussed several frameworks and libraries for facilitating the development of web applications. In this chapter, we focus on deploying such a web application. While doing so, we will try to answer some questions such as: which operating system should I use, how do I run my application, how do I ensure my application will be restarted after a reboot or a crash, and how do I log data.

16.1 Where to Host your Application?

The easiest and fastest way to host your application is to host it in the cloud.

PharoCloud[1], for example, proposes pre-packaged solutions (including Seaside, Pier and database support) as well as the possibility to use your own Pharo image. You could start very quickly from there but you do not have full control of your Pharo stack. It is however enough in most cases as PharoCloud manages the defaults for you.

There are many other cloud providers including Amazon AWS[2], Openshift[3], OVH[4] and Microsoft Azure[5]. Many Pharo users use DigitalOcean[6] as it is both simple and cheap. Choose your cloud provider according to your needs.

---

[1] http://pharocloud.com
[2] https://aws.amazon.com/
[3] https://www.openshift.com/
[4] https://www.ovh.com/
[5] http://azure.microsoft.com
[6] https://www.digitalocean.com/

In the rest of this chapter, we detail how to setup a server to host a Pharo web application.

16.2 Which Operating System?

Many Pharo developers use Mac OS X to develop their applications but it is not a popular solution for a production deployment due to a lack of dedicated Apple server hardware. A popular deployment OS is GNU/Linux. Deploying on Windows is a bit more complex and less supported by cloud providers.

There are many Linux distributions to choose from. If you restrict your choice to well-known free open-source distributions, competitors are Centos[7], Debian[8] and Ubuntu[9]. Most distributions will do the job, choose the most appropriate for you. A long-term support (*aka.*, LTS) version is a good option if you do not want to update your operating system too often. The Pharo Virtual Machine (VM) comes pre-packaged for some distributions. For other distributions, you will have to compile the VM sources yourself. Pay attention that the Pharo VM is still 32bits as of early 2016 and you will have to install 32-bit libraries on your 64-bit Operating System.

16.3 Build your Image

The best option to obtain a clean image to deploy is to start from a fresh stable pharo image[10] and to install the required packages through your application's Metacello configuration (read more in the *Deep into Pharo* book) and the command line handler. The configuration has to explicitely describe all dependencies used in your application.

First, create a copy of the clean image with your application name:

```
$ ./pharo Pharo.image save myapp
```

Then, install your dependencies:

```
$ ./pharo myapp.image config \
    http://www.smalltalkhub.com/mc/Me/MyApp/main \
    ConfigurationOfMyApp --install=stable
===========================================================
Notice: Installing ConfigurationOfMyApp stable
===========================================================
[...]
```

After loading all necessary code, the `config` option will also save the image so that the image now permanently includes your code.

---

[7] http://www.centos.org
[8] http://www.debian.org
[9] http://www.ubuntu.com
[10] http://files.pharo.org/image/stable/latest.zip

To make sure that your deployment image is reproducible, the best approach is to create a Continuous Integration job that automatically produces clean deployment-ready images of your application.

16.4 Run your Application

When you have a Pharo image with your application inside, the next step is to start the application. To make this process reproducible, it is recommended to create a dedicated file (*e.g.*, named `myapp.st`) with the instructions needed to start your application. Here is an example of a script used to start a web application using Zinc.

```
ZnServer defaultOn: 8080.
ZnServer default logToStandardOutput.
ZnServer default delegate
   map: 'image'
     to: MyFirstWebApp new;
   map: 'redirect-to-image'
     to: [ :request | ZnResponse redirect: 'image' ];
   map: '/'
     to: 'redirect-to-image'.
ZnServer default start
```

This script starts an instance of the Zinc Web Server on `localhost` on the port 8080 and stores it as the default instance. It configures the Zinc instance to log on the standard output and changes the default root (/) handler to redirect to your new /image web app. The `MyFirstWebApp` class is from chapter Small Web Application, it handles HTTP requests by implementing the `#handleRequest:` message.

You can test the startup script like this:

```
$ ./pharo myapp.image myapp.st
2013-07-10 11:46:58 660707 I Starting ZnManagingMultiThreadedServer
    HTTP port 8080
2013-07-10 11:46:58 670019 D Initializing server socket
2013-07-10 11:47:12 909356 D Executing request/response loop
2013-07-10 11:47:12 909356 I Read a ZnRequest(GET /)
2013-07-10 11:47:12 909356 T GET / 302 16B 0ms
2013-07-10 11:47:12 909356 I Wrote a ZnResponse(302 Found
    text/plain;charset=utf-8 16B)
2013-07-10 11:47:12 909356 I Read a ZnRequest(GET /image)
2013-07-10 11:47:12 909356 T GET /image 200 282B 0ms
2013-07-10 11:47:12 909356 I Wrote a ZnResponse(200 OK
    text/html;charset=utf-8 282B)
2013-07-10 11:47:12 909356 I Read a ZnRequest(GET /image?raw=true)
2013-07-10 11:47:12 909356 T GET /image?raw=true 200 18778B 82ms
2013-07-10 11:47:12 909356 I Wrote a ZnResponse(200 OK image/png
    18778B)
```

Type `Ctrl-c` to kill the server.

In Unix systems, init scripts are used to automatically start services when the server reboots and to monitor the status of these services. These scripts typically have a `start` command, a `stop` command and a `status` command (some init scripts have more than these 3 commands). Your application's init script should be configured to be automatically executed when the server restarts. This init script is typically placed in the */etc/init.d* directory.

You can find a template for such an init script in the GitHub pharo deployment scripts repository[11], named `pharo-service-script.sh`. Give this script the name of your application. This script is derived from the template provided by the Ubuntu distribution in `/etc/init.d/skeleton`.

In the same repository, the `pharo-run-script.sh` is another useful script. It runs a Pharo image with a pre-defined Smalltalk script file to evaluate (i.e. the `myapp.st` you wrote above). You may need to edit this file to configure the Pharo VM path and options. To use this script, create a folder with your application name *myapp*, then copy the `pharo-run-script.sh` script into this folder with name *myapp* as well. Give the script execution permissions: `chmod a+x ./myapp`.

You should end with a file hierarchy like this one:

- /etc/init.d/myapp (init script)
- /opt/myapp
    - myapp (generic pharo run script)
    - myapp.st (image startup script)
    - myapp.image
    - myapp.changes
- /usr/bin/pharo-vm

When the file hierarchy is ready, you can start your application by executing the `./myapp` script or by using the init script at the command line by executing `service myapp start`.

16.5 Dealing with Crashes

When the Pharo image crashes (which *will* happen), there must be a way to automatically recover from this crash. For this to work, the application data must be backed up, there must be a way to know when the application has crashed, and there must be a way to automatically restart the application.

---

[11] https://github.com/pharo-project/pharo-deployment-scripts

16.5 Dealing with Crashes

To avoid data loss, the simplest solution is to make your image stateless: if your image crashes, no data should be lost because no data is in the image. If your application requires persistent data (*e.g.*, user accounts), the best is to use a database (*e.g.*, PostgreSQL, MongoDB). You must then make sure that your database is backed up properly.

To automatically restart your application when it crashes, there must be a way to detect that it has crashed. With a standard operating system's init script such as the one described above, you can use the `status` command to detect if Pharo is running or not. We will later discuss how to handle a frozen Pharo.

A simple solution to both monitor your application and take appropriate actions (*e.g.*, restart) is to use the monit utility[12]. In the remainder of this section we will show how to configure monit.

Monit Dashboard

You can first activate the embedded HTTP dashboard of monit. This monit configuration, only allows local connections with a dedicated username and password pair.

```
set httpd port 2812 and
    use address localhost   # only accept connection from localhost
    allow localhost         # allow localhost to connect to the server
    allow admin:monit       # require user 'admin' with pass 'monit'
```

Apply the new configuration:

```
$ sudo monit reload
```

To connect from a different place than localhost, use an SSH tunnel. For example, if the server running both your application and monit is named myserver.com, execute the following to connect to your server and open a local port:

```
$ ssh -L 2812:localhost:2812 myserver.com
```

Keep the SSH connection open, and browse http://localhost:2812 to display the monit dashboard.

Email Settings

If you want notifications from monit, you need to configure email settings so that monit can send emails. Edit the monit configuration file again and add a line to set the mail server:

```
set mailserver <smtp.domain>
```

For more monit configuration options, refer to the monit documentation.

---

[12] https://mmonit.com/monit

Monitor System Services

Configuration files related to an application (or a service) should be put into the /etc/monit/monitrc.d directory (which is more modular than putting everything in the core configuration file). To enable a configuration just symlink it to conf.d. We will first enable a pre-defined configuration for SSH.

```
$ sudo ln -s /etc/monit/monitrc.d/openssh-server
    /etc/monit/conf.d/openssh-server
$ sudo monit reload
```

Warning: default configurations for well-known services are provided by monit but may require some adaptations (e.g., wrong path to the PID file).

To check for errors, you may need to run monit in verbose mode:

```
$ sudo monit -v
```

and check the monit error log, by default in /var/log/monit.log.

Monit Configuration to Control a Pharo Application

Application-specific configuration files must be added to the /etc/monit/monitrc.d directory. Create a new myapp file in this directory:

```
alert me@domain.com

check process myapp with pidfile /var/run/myapp.pid
    start program = "/etc/init.d/myapp start"
    stop program  = "/etc/init.d/myapp stop"
    if 5 restarts within 5 cycles
        then timeout
```

With this in place, when a problem occurs, the *alert* instruction makes sure me@domain.com is notified by email. The kind of monitoring is described with the check command. We ask monit to check a given PID file. If there is no PID or no process associated to the PID, monit will start the program with the given instruction. The last instruction prevents infinite loops if there is a problem with the script. The following then activates the monitoring of myapp:

```
$ sudo ln -s /etc/monit/monitrc.d/myapp /etc/monit/conf.d/myapp
$ sudo monit reload
```

At this point, you have ensured you have a running Pharo image at any time.

Monit Configuration for a Pharo Web Application

A Pharo image may be running, i.e. the process is alive, but not responding to HTTP requests. In such cases, your application is unusable. This unresponsive state can be verified by sending a simple HTTP request and checking for the response. We can ask monit to monitor your web server by doing regular checks to a predifined URL and validating the HTTP response content:

```
alert me@domain.com

check process myapp with pidfile /var/run/myapp.pid
    start program = "/etc/init.d/myapp start"
    stop program  = "/etc/init.d/myapp stop"
    if failed (url http://localhost:8080/ping
        and content == "pong"
        and timeout 10 seconds)
        then restart
    if 5 restarts within 5 cycles
        then timeout
```

This configuration will try to connect to the /ping URL on localhost. If monit can not connect, or no answer arrives before 10 seconds, or the content is not exactly pong, monit will restart the application.

You may also want to monitor Apache if there is an Apache server in front of your application. You can do that by adapting the already existing apache2 monit configuration file:

```
if failed host localhost port 80 with protocol http with timeout 25
    seconds for 4 times within 5 cycles then restart
```

Activate the Apache monitoring and reload the monit configuration:

```
$ sudo ln -s /etc/monit/monitrc.d/apache2 /etc/monit/conf.d/apache2
$ sudo monit reload
```

You are done! Your Pharo aplication is now monitored.

16.6 Put an HTTP server in front of your web application

It is a good idea to put a web server like Apache or Nginx in front of a Pharo web application. Mature web servers fully implement standards and commoditized functionalities, e.g. virtual host handling (multiple domains on the same IP address), URL rewriting, etc. They are also more stable, have built-in mechanisms for binding to privileged ports below 1024 as root and then executing as a non-privileged user, and are more robust to attacks. They can also be used to serve static content and to display a maintenance page.

Apache

Here is a simple Apache configuration that can be used to redirect the incoming internet traffic on the default HTTP port (80) to your Pharo web application running on the local interface on the port 8080.

```
<VirtualHost *:80>
   ServerName mydomain.com
   #ServerAlias anothercooldomain.org

   ProxyPreserveHost On
   ProxyRequests Off
   <Proxy *>
      Order allow,deny
      Allow from all
   </Proxy>
   ProxyPass / http://127.0.0.1:8080/
   ProxyPassReverse / http://127.0.0.1:8080/

   ErrorLog /var/log/apache2/myapp-error.log
   CustomLog /var/log/apache2/myapp-access.log combined
</VirtualHost>
```

The first section declares the full server name (including the domain), the second one activates the proxy to forward the traffic to your Pharo web application, and the last one creates dedicated log files.

Nginx

The following configuration also redirects the incoming traffic to the default HTTP port (80) of your Pharo web application running on the local interface on the port 8080.

```
server {
   listen 80;
   server_name mydomain.com;

   access_log  /var/log/nginx/myapp-access.log;
   error_log   /var/log/nginx/myapp-error.log;

   location / {
      proxy_set_header  Host $host;
      proxy_pass http://127.0.0.1:8080;
   }
}
```

With this simple configuration, you will get a more secure and flexible configuration of your web application.

16.7 Conclusion

In this chapter we have seen how to deploy a Pharo web application. We presented places where to deploy and gave insights as to which operating system to use. We then talked about how to deploy and run a Pharo web appli-

16.7 Conclusion

cation. Lastly we discussed how to monitor Pharo with monit and putting a HTTP server in front of the web application.

This chapter ends the Enterprise Pharo book. We hope you enjoyed learning about this set of libraries and frameworks, and that they prove useful for you. We wish you success!

www.ingramcontent.com/pod-product-compliance
Lightning Source LLC
Chambersburg PA
CBHW060826170526
45158CB00001B/97